Winter 2002 Edition

# Ty®
# Beanie Babies®

12TH EDITION

Collector Handbook and Price Guide

# Ty® Beanie Babies®



ISBN 1-58598-226-1

306 Industrial Park Road
Middletown, CT 06457
www.checkerbee.com

# Table Of Contents

Table Of Contents

# Introducing The Collector's Value Guide™

Going "Batty" trying to find out how much your *Beanie Babies*® are worth? Are you all "Ears" for the newest information on *Beanie Buddies*®? Do you share hobbies and interests with a *Beanie Bopper*™? You'll find the answers to these questions and so much more in the Winter 2002 Collector's Value Guide™ to Ty® *Beanie Babies*®, now in its 12th edition!

With the Value Guide, you'll be able to document your collection of *Beanie Babies*, *Beanie Buddies*, *Beanie Boppers*™, *Beanie Kids*™, *Jingle Beanies*™ and *Teenie Beanie Babies*™. You'll find issue and retirement dates and current market values for all tag generations. If you collect Ty's cuddly critters or just love them, the Collector's Value Guide™ is where to look and find:

A spotlight on all the newest pieces, including special patriotic pieces for charity

Full-color photos of the stylin' Beanie Boppers

The story of how Ty Warner's creations have taken the collectibles world by storm

And so much more!

# The Beanie Babies® Story

Can you believe that there once was a world without *Beanie Babies*? Those pellet-filled plush animals have become a big part of people's lives. But the best-loved collectible in America didn't just happen overnight.

## The Man Behind The Mania

The *Beanie Babies* story begins with H. Ty Warner, a very private man. As a sales representative for Dakin Inc. in the 1970s, Warner's quirky style came to the fore, often dressing in a fur coat and top hat to meet potential clients and then took them for drives in a Rolls Royce.

Warner left Dakin in the early 1980s and spent several years traveling abroad. Upon his return, Warner had the idea to design his own line of plush toys. In 1986, he launched his own company, Ty Inc., based in Oakbrook, Illinois.

## A Beanie Is Born

By now, most *Beanie Babies* collectors know that Ty Warner never expected his line of palm-sized, pellet-filled animals to be so popular. He was simply designing a line of toys with children in mind.

The "Original Nine" *Beanie Babies* made their first public appearance at a trade show near Chicago late in 1993. Early in 1994, these "Original Nine" began appearing in small gift and specialty shops that also sold Ty's other plush. By June, Ty had introduced 25 more *Beanie Babies*, and people noticed.

But *Beanie* fever didn't set in until Ty Inc. began retiring *Beanie Babies* in 1995. Now, collectors who had enjoyed the pick of the litter had to scramble for hard-to-find designs and rare color variations to complete their collections and by the end of 1996, the craze was well underway.

Ty launched the official *Beanie Babies* website (*www.ty.com*) in 1996.

The *Beanie Babies* phenomenon took another big leap forward with the 1998 launch of the *Beanie Babies* Official Club™.

## A Plethora Of Plush

In 1998, Ty introduced *Beanie Buddies*, a line of oversized, super-soft versions of popular *Beanie Babies*. Then, on January 8, 2000, Ty introduced a new line of *Beanie Kids*. On August 19, Ty released its *Zodiac Collection*, each representing a year of the Chinese

Zodiac. Then in July 2001, Ty got even hipper with the introduction of *Beanie Boppers*. But the introductions don't stop there. In September, 2001, Ty introduced a line of *Jingle Beanies* – Beanie ornaments that are just the right size for your tree!

And Ty has proved that its heart is just not on its tag. The charity bear "Ariel" has raised over $3 million for the Elizabeth Glaser Pediatric AIDS Foundation. And 100% of the proceeds from the "America" *Beanie* is being donated to the American Red Cross.

## Is That A Beanie In Your Happy Meal?

Today, *Beanie Babies* seem to be everywhere – even at the ballpark. The Chicago Cubs were the first team to have a *Beanie Babies* promotion, as 10,000 "Cubbies" were given away to fans at a game on May 18th. That year also saw the first McDonald's *Teenie Beanie Babies* promotion. Promotions later branched out to include Four Seasons Hotels and even MasterCard.

Times may change, but one thing is sure: with more and more new *Beanie* products available every year, their popularity is sure to continue!

# Club News

In a moment that *Beanie Babies* collectors have been eagerly awaiting, Ty announced details about brand new Beanie Babies Official Club pieces in September 2001.

## Clubby-ing It

Since the club began, members have been able to add exclusive *Beanies* and *Buddies* to their collections. First came "Clubby" in 1998. Now, in 2001, members can line up for "Clubby IV" the *Beanie Baby*, which is available for purchase at authorized Ty dealers.

## More Surprises Await

Once you're a registered club member, there are several exclusive piece you are eligible to purchase. For 2001, those pieces are "Clubby IV" the *Beanie Buddy*, "Cuddly Crystal" the *Beanie Bopper* and the "Clubby Edition" set of four *Jingle Beanie* ornaments.

## Next Up . . .

Check the club website (*www.beaniebabyofficial-club.com*) for the latest on upcoming offers and news!

# What's New - Beanie Babies®

Among the many recent *Beanie Babies* releases, holiday themes and patriotic pieces abound.

## 2001 Holiday Teddy™

This festive green teddy with sparkling fur is the fifth Holiday Teddy to be released since 1997.

## America™

Dedicated to those who lost their lives in the September 11 disaster, the tag on this patriotic bear concludes with "God Bless America."

## Beani™

This fluffy new cat is reminiscent of early Ty plush designs before the days of *Beanie Babies*.

## Billionaire 4™

For the fourth year in a row, Ty employees have been given an exclusive "Billionaire" bear as a gesture of appreciation.

## Clubby IV™

The Beanie Babies Official Club (BBOC) is back, and "Clubby IV" is available through retailers for a limited time.

## Creepers™

"Creepers" the skeleton is a scary sight to behold. It's a good thing he only likes to come out around Halloween!

## Fraidy™

If you catch "Fraidy" cat crossing your path this year, you can consider yourself a lucky one.

## Haunt™

"Haunt" the black bear proudly wears a pumpkin on his chest.

## Jinglepup™

"Jinglepup" gets so excited about the holidays that he's vowed to wear his festive hat all year long!

## Kirby™

"Kirby" might be the cutest dog you've ever seen, but he's even more dashing when he's dressed up with his holiday ribbon.

## Mistletoe™

The lovable charm of "Mistletoe" will bring you holiday cheer throughout the year – and he may even surprise you with a kiss!

## November™

Ty welcomes a new bear for the month of November – a time for remembering veterans, celebrating Thanksgiving and holiday shopping!

## October™

The "October" bear loves the crisp air and colorful foliage of his month and looks forward to trick-or-treating before the month is through!

## Scary™

This witch is scary – and it's not just because of her name. One look at her and you can just imagine her cackling over her hot cauldron.

## Ty® Beanie Babies® Help Comfort During Difficult Times



The *Beanie Babies* collection has always been a patriotic bunch – with classic designs like "Glory," "Patriot," "USA" and many, many other pieces commemorating the United States. So it comes as no surprise that Ty introduced several special Beanie Babies to help a nation in mourning over the tragic events of September 11, 2001.

On September 13, Ty announced the introduction of **"America,"** a blue Beanie Baby with an American flag stitched to its chest. All of Ty's profits from this special bear (which is available through Ty retailers) will be donated to the American Red Cross.

Then, on October 12, Ty introduced two more special Beanie Babies that are currently available only online. **"Courage"** is a German shepherd that symbolizes the courageous police officers and **"Rescue"** is a dalmatian that symbolizes the heroic firefighters who rushed to the scene of the tragedy. Proceeds from these two pieces will be donated to The New York Police & Fire Widows' and Children's Benefit Fund.

# Beanie Buddies®

Among the highlights of the latest round of *Beanie Buddies* releases are the quartet of Holiday Teddies and an intriguing new bear named "Tangerine."

## 1997 Holiday Teddy™

Now *Beanie Buddies* collectors can also enjoy the first Holiday Teddy design from 1997.

## 2001 Holiday Teddy™

This sparkling, green teddy bear is the 2001 version of the popular Holiday Teddies.

## Clubby IV™

This exclusive *Beanie Buddy* is only available to members of the Beanie Babies Official Club – one of many perks to joining!

## Extra Large 1997 Holiday Teddy™

This teddy is so big, he might be able to help you put the tree topper on the top of your holiday tree!

## Large 1997 Holiday Teddy™

A large version of the "1997 Holiday Teddy," this bear is big enough for a satisfying bear hug!

## Loosy™

"Loosy" the goose is the latest flying, feathered friend to join the *Beanie Buddies* collection.

## Radar™

Another flying creature, "Radar" the bat, is poised to swoop down for a Halloween celebration.

## Snowball™

A classic snowman, "Snowball" joins his other frosty pal, "Snowboy," in the *Beanie Buddies* collection.

## Spooky™

"Spooky" sometimes gets frustrated. His permanent grin means that no one ever gets scared when he pops out to say, "BOO!"

### Tangerine™

"Tangerine," a rare *Buddy* without a *Beanie Baby* counterpart (at least not yet), has been spotted in two different fabrics.

### Unity™

"Unity" the Beanie Buddy commemorates the beginning of the European Union (EU) and is exclusively sold in Europe.

## Beanie Boppers™

The *Beanie Boppers*, which debuted in the summer of 2001, are taking the Ty world by storm with oodles of fun designs and exclusive pieces.

### Bubbly Betty™

Betty is a happy-go-lucky gal who loves pizza and movies.

### Cuddly Crystal™

Available only to members of the Beanie Babies Official Club, this *Bopper* will only be available for a limited time.

## Dazzlin' Destiny™

Destiny is fashionable girl from the state of Washington who enjoys spending lots of time on the Internet!

## Holiday Heidi™

A Michigan native, Heidi is a jokester who loves the holidays!

## Ivy Leaguer™

Named for the ivy-covered walls of Wrigley Field, "Ivy Leaguer" was available exclusively at a 2001 Chicago Cubs game.

## Jazzy Jessie™

Jessie is a smart and friendly New Yorker who has a heart of gold – she wants to be a nurse someday.

## Jolly Janie™

Even though Janie claims to be a little bit shy right now, she dreams of becoming a television news anchor in the future.

### Sweet Sally™

Sally is a native of Georgia. She loves to baby-sit and has a pet canary called Tweeter.

## Beanie Kids™

One new *Beanie Kid* was introduced with Ty's 2001 holiday releases.

### Noelle™

"Noelle" loves her holiday outfit so much, she wishes she could wear it all year long!

## Ty Gear™

Great for dressing up the Beanie Kids, Ty continues to introduce new Ty Gear apparel.

### Skeleton & The Count

If you dare, let your *Beanie Kids* try on these scary, new costumes!

# Jingle Beanies™

Great for decorating your tree, your backpack – or just about anywhere, Ty has introduced *Jingle Beanie* ornaments in September 2001. The first ornaments feature many classic *Beanie Babies* designs.

## 1997 Holiday Teddy™

This brown bear with a red hat and red scarf was the first Holiday Teddy design.

## 1998 Holiday Teddy™

The second bear is white with red and white holiday decorations.

## 1999 Holiday Teddy™

The 1999 piece is the first Holiday Teddy not wearing a hat.

## Clubby Edition™ (set/4)

A set of ornaments featuring all four "Clubby" designs is available through the club.

## Halo™

This angelic bear adds a nice touch to your holiday decorating.

## Loosy™

Here's wishing you a loosy-goosy holiday season!

## Peace™

Decorate your tree with this popular, "ty"-dye teddy bear.

## Quackers™

Friendly "Quackers" the duck reappears as a *Jingle Beanie*.

## Rover™

With his shiny red coat, Rover is a perfect decoration for the season.

## Twigs™

Most giraffes would be too tall for your tree, but this one is just the right size!

# Plenty Of Plush

Before there were *Beanies*, Ty Inc. made its way into the plush universe in 1986 with *Ty Plush,* later renamed *Ty Classic* in 2000. It all started with a bunch of traditional pets, but it wasn't long before more exotic critters were introduced to the family.

Another type of classic is the *Attic Treasures* collection, which began in 1993. These critters' distinctive old-time faces, jointed limbs and outfits give them each a personality all their own.

Then when Ty introduced the pastel (and later vibrantly-colored), infant-friendly *Pillow Pals* in 1995, he reached out to a whole new audience. Although all 44 critters that make up this family have been retired, they remain a favorite toy in cribs and playpens everywhere!

Yet Ty knew that the young, as well as the young at heart, love soft, huggable critters. With that in mind, the year 2000 brought the introduction of the *Baby Ty* collection, with each piece featuring a rattle inside.

# Recent Retirements

Pieces seem to retire faster than ever, so it's hard to keep up. Here's a list of recent *Beanie Baby* and *Buddy* retirements.

## BEANIE BABIES®

### Retired June 2001

**6/17:** Dearest™ (bear, #4350)
**6/18:** Frills™ (hornbill bird, #4367)
**6/18:** Huggy™ (bear, #4306)
**6/18:** Oats™ (horse, #4305)
**6/18:** Purr™ (kitten, #4346)
**6/18:** Tricks™ (dog, #4311)
**6/20:** Pellet™ (hamster, #4313)
**6/20:** Prince™ (frog, #4312)
**6/20:** Patriot™ (bear, #4035)
**6/20:** Bananas™ (orangutan, #4316)
**6/21:** Addison™ (bear, #4362)

### Retired July 2001

**7/12:** Kooky™ (cat, #4357)
**7/12:** Propeller™ (flying fish, #4366)
**7/25:** Dart™ (blue dart frog, #4352)
**7/25:** Cassie™ (collie, #4340)
**7/25:** Poseidon™ (whale shark, #4356)

### Retired August 2001

**8/8:** Dizzy™ (dalmatian, #4365)
**8/8:** Hornsly™ (triceratops, #4345)
**8/30:** July™ (bear, #4370)
**8/31:** Cheery™ (bear, #4359)

### Retired September 2001

**9/7:** Classy™ (bear, #4373)
**9/10:** Darling™ (dog, #4368)
**9/14:** August™ (bear, #4371)

### Retired October 2001

**10/8:** Regal™ (dog, #4358)
**10/11:** Celebrate™ (bear, #4385)

## BEANIE BUDDIES®

### Retired June 2001

**6/14:** Bananas™ (orangutan, #9402)
**6/14:** Spunky™ (cocker spaniel, #9400)
**6/22:** Glory™ (bear, #9410)

### Retired July 2001

**7/17:** Cassie™ (collie, #9405)
**7/26:** Sakura™ (bear, #9608)

### Retired August 2001

**8/6:** Pugsly™ (pug dog, #9413)
**8/6:** Trumpet™ (elephant, #9403)

### Retired September 2001

**9/13:** Mooch™ (monkey, #9416)
**9/13:** Rufus™ (dog, #9393)
**9/20:** Neon™ (seahorse, #9417)
**9/20:** Pinchers™ (lobster, #9424)
**9/21:** Lips™ (fish, #9355)
**9/21:** Prince™ (frog, #9401)

### Retired October 2001

**10/11:** Celebrate™ (bear, #9423)
**10/16:** Almond™ (bear, #9425)

Keep checking **www.ty.com** for more retirement announcements

# Beanie Babies® Top Five

Make sure to check if that old *Beanie Baby* in your collection matches one on our list! If so, your special *Beanie* is even more valuable than you even imagined!

**#1 Bear™**
Bear, Ty Sales Rep Gift
Market Value: Special Tag $7,000

**Peanut™**
Elephant, dark blue
Market Value: ③ $3,400

**Nana™**
Monkey
Market Value: ③ $2,700

**Teddy™ (violet)**
Bear, Ty Employee Gift
Market Value: No Tag $2,600

**Brownie™**
Bear
Market Value: ① $2,350

# Beanie Buddies® Top Five

Is your big *Buddy* also worth big bucks? Some of the early designs and exclusive pieces are very valuable.

1

**Quackers™**
Duck, Without Wings
Market Value: 1 $250

**Twigs™**
Giraffe
Market Value: 1 $150

2

3

**Britannia™**
Bear
Market Value: 1 $135

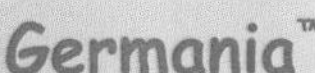

**Germania™**
Bear
Market Value: 2 $100

4

5

**Maple™**
Bear
Market Value: 1 $90

*Note: Oversized Beanie Buddies were excluded from this list.*

# Teenie Beanie Babies™ Top Five

Who would have imagined that these tiny "extras" in McDonald's Happy Meals would become so coveted?

**Pinky™**
Flamingo
Market Value: 1 $30

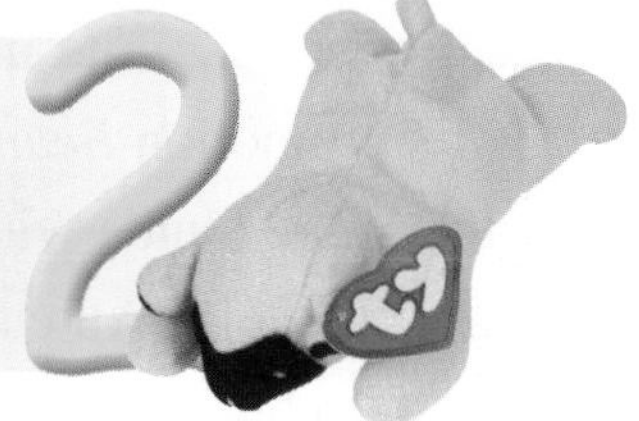

**Chops™**
Lamb
Market Value: 1 $22

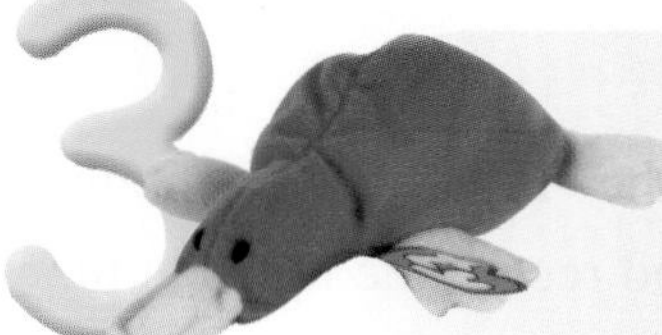

**Patti™**
Platypus
Market Value: 1 $21

**Glory™**
Bear, McDonald's Employee Gift
Market Value: 1 $20

**Chocolate™**
Moose
Market Value: 1 $15

# How To Use Your Value Guide

**1. Record** the price you paid for the piece in the "Price Paid" column, then circle the tag generation of your piece.

**2. Find** the market value of each piece next to the swing tag generation icon in the "Market Value" column. For current pieces, write in the retail value. Sports promotion *Beanies* are identified in the Value Guide with the appropriate sports symbols. All current *Beanies* are rated as to how easy or difficult they are to find at retail price in stores.

**Beanie Babies® Swing Tag Key**

7 – 7th Generation
6 – 6th Generation
5 – 5th Generation
4 – 4th Generation
3 – 3rd Generation
2 – 2nd Generation
1 – 1st Generation
Z – Zodiac Collection

**Beanie Buddies® Swing Tag Key**

2 – 2nd Generation
1 – 1st Generation

**3. Add** up the "Price Paid" columns on each page and record the totals in the "Page Totals" section at the bottom. Do the same for the "Market Value." Copy the page totals onto the worksheets on pages 214-216, then add them together to get the "Grand Total" of your collection!

**Sports Promotion Beanie Babies® Key**

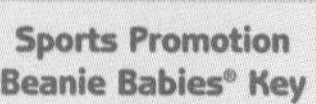

Canadian Special Olympics

Major League Baseball

National Basketball Association

National Football League

National Hockey League

Women's National Basketball Association

**Degree Of Difficulty Ratings**

- Just Released
- Easy To Find
- Moderate To Find
- Hard To Find
- Very Hard To Find
- Impossible To Find

# Beanie Babies®

The world of Ty's *Beanie Babies* collection is as exciting and fast-paced as ever, with a seemingly endless stream of new releases, exclusive pieces and sudden retirements. The collection, which began with a mere 9 pieces, now totals over 350 in all! How many do you have?

## #1 Bear™ 1

**(exclusive Ty sales representative gift)**

Bear • N/A
Issued: December 12, 1998
Not Available In Retail Stores

Birthdate: N/A

Dedication Appearing On Special Tag
In appreciation of selling over several Billion dollars in 1998 and achieving the industry ranking of #1 in Gift sales, #1 in Collectible sales, #1 in Cash register area sales, #1 in Markup %, I present to you This Signed and Numbered bear!

| Version | Dates Produced | Price Paid | Market Value |
|---|---|---|---|
| Original | Dec. 1998 | | Special Tag $7,000 |

## 1997 Teddy™ 2

Bear • #4200
Issued: October 1, 1997
Retired: December 31, 1997

Birthdate: December 25, 1996

Beanie Babies are special no doubt
All filled with love - inside and out
Wishes for fun times filled with joy
Ty's holiday teddy is a magical toy!

| Version | Dates Produced | Price Paid | Market Value |
|---|---|---|---|
| Original | Oct. 1997-Dec. 1997 | | ④ $33 |

| Page Totals | Price Paid | Market Value |
|---|---|---|
| | | |

3

## 1998 Holiday Teddy™

Bear · #4204
Issued: September 30, 1998
Retired: December 31, 1998

Birthdate: December 25, 1998

Dressed in his PJ's, and ready for bed
Hugs given, good nights said
This little Beanie will stay close at night
Ready for a hug at first morning light!

| Version | Issue Dates | Price Paid | Market Value |
|---|---|---|---|
| Original | Sept. 1998-Dec. 1998 | | 5 $36 |

4

## 1999 Holiday Teddy™

Bear · #4257
Issued: August 31, 1999
Retired: December 23, 1999

Birthdate: December 25, 1999

Peace on Earth as the holidays grow near
The season is all about giving good cheer
With love and joy in your hearts
Lets all be friends as the century starts!

| Version | Issue Dates | Price Paid | Market Value |
|---|---|---|---|
| Original | Aug. 1999-Dec. 1999 | | 5 $22 |

5

## 1999 Signature Bear™

Bear · #4228
Issued: January 1, 1999
Retired: October 25, 1999

Birthdate: N/A

No Poem

| Version | Issue Dates | Price Paid | Market Value |
|---|---|---|---|
| Original | Jan. 1999-Oct. 1999 | | 5 $15 |

| Page Totals | Price Paid | Market Value |
|---|---|---|
| | | |

Beanie Babies®

## 2000 Holiday Teddy™ 6

Bear • #4332
Issued: September 28, 2000
Retired: December 12, 2000

Birthdate: December 24, 2000

When you're tucked in bed tonight
Hug Holiday Teddy really tight
He'll bring you much joy and cheer
And lots of love throughout the year!

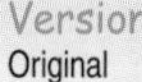
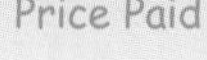

| Version | Issue Dates | Price Paid | Market Value |
|---|---|---|---|
| Original | Sept. 2000-Dec. 2000 | | 6 $20 |

## 2000 Signature Bear™ 7

Bear • #4266
Issued: February 13, 2000
Retired: May 16, 2000

Birthdate: N/A

No Poem

| Version | Issue Dates | Price Paid | Market Value |
|---|---|---|---|
| Original | Feb. 2000-May 2000 | | 6 $20 |

## 2001 Holiday Teddy™ 8

New!

Bear • #4395
Issued: October 1, 2001
Current - Just Released

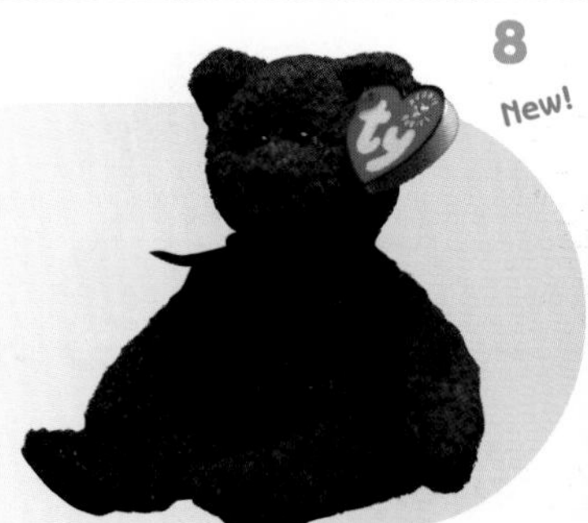

Birthdate: December 24, 2000

This year has flown by very fast
It's hard to believe 2001 has passed
Time to look forward to a brand new year
We hope it brings you joy and cheer!

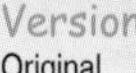

| Version | Issue Dates | Price Paid | Market Value |
|---|---|---|---|
| Original | Oct. 2001-Current | | 7 $________ |

| Page Totals | Price Paid | Market Value |
|---|---|---|
| | | |

9

## 2001 Signature Bear™

Bear • #4375
Issued: July 31, 2001
Current - Very Hard To Find

Birthdate: N/A

No poem

| Version | Issue Dates | Price Paid | Market Value |
|---|---|---|---|
| Original | July 2001-Current | | 7 $________ |

10

## Addison™

Bear • #4362
Issued: May 20, 2001
Retired: June 21, 2001

Birthdate: May 20, 2001

In the bleachers we see all
Hope we'll catch a long fly ball
When the day is finally done
Hopefully, our team has won!

| Version | Issue Dates | Price Paid | Market Value |
|---|---|---|---|
| Original | May 2001-June 2001 | | 7 $20 |

11

## Ally™

Alligator • #4032
Issued: June 25, 1994
Retired: October 1, 1997

Birthdate: March 14, 1994

When Ally gets out of classes
He wears a hat and dark glasses
He plays bass in a street band
He's the coolest gator in the land!

| Version | Issue Dates | Price Paid | Market Value |
|---|---|---|---|
| Original | June 1994-Oct. 1997 | | 4 $40 3 $85 2 $200 1 $320 |

| Page Totals | Price Paid | Market Value |
|---|---|---|
| | | |

## Almond™ 12

Bear • #4246
Issued: April 19, 1999
Retired: December 23, 1999

Birthdate: April 14, 1999

Leaving her den in early spring
So very hungry, she'll eat anything
Nuts, fruit, berries and fish
Mixed together make a great dish!

| Version | Issue Dates | Price Paid | Market Value |
|---|---|---|---|
| Original | April 1999-Dec. 1999 | | 5 $9 |

## Amber™ 13

Cat • #4243
Issued: April 20, 1999
Retired: December 23, 1999

Birthdate: February 21, 1999

Sleeping all day and up all night
Waiting to pounce and give you a fright
She means no harm, just playing a game
She's very lovable and quite tame!

| Version | Issue Dates | Price Paid | Market Value |
|---|---|---|---|
| Original | April 1999-Dec. 1999 | | 5 $10 |

## America™ 14

Bear • #4506
Issued: September 13, 2001
Current - Just Released

New!

Birthdate: N/A

In memory of those who lost their
lives in the national catastrophe that
took place on September 11, 2001.
We mourn for them and express our
deepest sympathy to their families.
God Bless America

| Version | Issue Dates | Price Paid | Market Value |
|---|---|---|---|
| Original | Sept. 2001-Current | | 7 $________ |

| | Price Paid | Market Value |
|---|---|---|
| Page Totals | | |

15

## Ants™

Anteater · #4195
Issued: May 30, 1998
Retired: December 31, 1998

Birthdate: November 7, 1997

Most anteaters love to eat bugs
But this little fellow gives big hugs
He'd rather dine on apple pie
Than eat an ant or harm a fly!

| Version | Issue Dates | Price Paid | Market Value |
|---|---|---|---|
| Original | May 1998-Dec. 1998 | | 5 $9 |

16

## Ariel™

Bear · #4288
Issued: June 1, 2000
Current – Moderate To Find

Birthdate: N/A

Tribute Appearing On Special Tag
In Memory 1981-1988
May little children everywhere
Remember that we'll always care
And Ariel's dreams will all come true
Because she'll share them all with you!

| Version | Issue Dates | Price Paid | Market Value |
|---|---|---|---|
| Original | June 2000-Current | | Special Tag $________ |

17

## Aruba™

Angelfish · #4314
Issued: July 8, 2000
Retired: April 11, 2001

Birthdate: April 8, 2000

If you wander by the sea
And want to take a look at me
I'm swimming in the water blue
And want to throw a kiss to you!

| Version | Issue Dates | Price Paid | Market Value |
|---|---|---|---|
| Original | July 2000-April 2001 | | 6 $9 |

| Page Totals | Price Paid | Market Value |
|---|---|---|
| | | |

## August™ 18

**(Birthday Beanies Collection™)**

Bear • #4371
Issued: July 3, 2001
Retired: September 14, 2001

Birthdate: N/A

My nose is the color of my birthstone.
Peridot
It brings romance,
loyalty and laughter.

| Version | Issue Dates | Price Paid | Market Value |
|---|---|---|---|
| Original | July 2001-Sept. 2001 | | ❼ $11 |

## Aurora™ 19

Polar Bear • #4271
Issued: February 13, 2000
Retired: May 21, 2001

Birthdate: February 3, 2000

The midnight sun puts on a show
For all the polar bears below
Under ribbons of shining light
Aurora hugs you and says goodnight!

| Version | Issue Dates | Price Paid | Market Value |
|---|---|---|---|
| Original | Feb. 2000-May 2001 | | ❻ $11 |

## B.B. Bear™ 20

Bear • #4253
Issued: Summer 1999
Retired: December 23, 1999

Birthdate: N/A

This birthday Beanie was made for you
Hope your wishes and dreams come true
Be happy today and tomorrow too
Let's all celebrate the whole year through!

| Version | Issue Dates | Price Paid | Market Value |
|---|---|---|---|
| Original | Summer 1999-Dec. 1999 | | ❺ $19 |

| Page Totals | Price Paid | Market Value |
|---|---|---|
| | | |

## 21

# Baldy™

Eagle · #4074
Issued: May 11, 1997
Retired: May 1, 1998

Birthdate: February 17, 1996

Hair on his head is quite scant
We suggest Baldy get a transplant
Watching over the land of the free
Hair in his eyes would make it hard to see!

| Version | Issue Dates | Price Paid | Market Value |
|---|---|---|---|
| Original | May 1997-May 1998 | | (5) $13 (4) $13 |

## 22

# Bananas™

Orangutan · #4316
Issued: July 8, 2000
Retired: June 20, 2001

Birthdate: June 30, 2000

If you'll come and play with me
We will swing from tree to tree
Then we'll go and have some lunch
We'll eat bananas by the bunch!

| Version | Issue Dates | Price Paid | Market Value |
|---|---|---|---|
| Original | July 2000-June 2001 | | (6) $9 |

## 23

# Batty™

Bat · #4035
Issued: October 1, 1997
Retired: March 31, 1999

Birthdate: October 29, 1996

Bats may make some people jitter
Please don't be scared of this critter
If you're lonely or have nothing to do
This Beanie Baby would love to hug you!

| Version | Issue Dates | Price Paid | Market Value |
|---|---|---|---|
| A. Ty-dye | Jan. 1999-March 1999 | | (5) $15 |
| B. Brown | Est Oct. 1997-Jan. 1999 | | (5) $12 (4) $13 |

| Page Totals | Price Paid | Market Value |
|---|---|---|
| | | |

## Beak™ 24

Kiwi • #4211
Issued: September 30, 1998
Retired: December 23, 1999

Birthdate: February 3, 1998

Isn't this just the funniest bird?
When we saw her, we said "how absurd"
Looks aren't everything, this we know
Her love for you, she's sure to show!

| Version | Issue Dates | Price Paid | Market Value |
|---|---|---|---|
| Original | Sept. 1998-Dec. 1999 | | ⑤ $8 |

## Beani™ 25

New!

Cat • #4397
Issued: October 1, 2001
Current - Just Released

Birthdate: July 26, 2000

Why is my name Beani the cat?
It's funny you should ask me that
My owner loves her Beanies so
She wanted the whole world to know!

| Version | Issue Dates | Price Paid | Market Value |
|---|---|---|---|
| Original | Oct. 2001-Current | | ⑦ $________ |

## Bernie™ 26

St. Bernard • #4109
Issued: January 1, 1997
Retired: September 22, 1998

Birthdate: October 3, 1996

This little dog can't wait to grow
To rescue people lost in the snow
Don't let him out - keep him on your shelf
He doesn't know how to rescue himself!

| Version | Issue Dates | Price Paid | Market Value |
|---|---|---|---|
| Original | Jan. 1997-Sept. 1998 | | ⑤ $10 ④ $12 |

| Page Totals | Price Paid | Market Value |
|---|---|---|
| | | |

27

## Bessie™

Cow • #4009
Issued: June 3, 1995
Retired: October 1, 1997

Birthdate: June 27, 1995

Bessie the cow likes to dance and sing
Because music is her favorite thing
Every night when you are counting sheep
She'll sing you a song to help you sleep!

| Version | Issue Dates | Price Paid | Market Value |
|---|---|---|---|
| Original | June 1995-Oct. 1997 | | ④ $46 ③ $85 |

28

## Billionaire bear™

**(exclusive Ty employee gift)**

Bear • N/A
Issued: September 26, 1998
Not Available In Retail Stores

Birthdate: N/A

Dedication Appearing On Special Tag

In recognition of value and
contributions in shipping over
a billion dollars since Jan '98,
I present to you this exclusive signed bear!

| Version | Issue Dates | Price Paid | Market Value |
|---|---|---|---|
| Original | Sept. 1998 | | Special Tag $2,000 |

29

## Billionaire 2™

**(exclusive Ty employee gift)**

Bear • N/A
Issued: September 12, 1999
Not Available In Retail Stores

Birthdate: N/A

Dedication Appearing On Special Tag

Ty is the company that can't be beat
Mattel and Hasbro can take a back seat
We did it again and it was fun
In the toy biz, we're #1!

| Version | Issue Dates | Price Paid | Market Value |
|---|---|---|---|
| Original | Sept. 1999 | | Special Tag $2,100 |

| Page Totals | Price Paid | Market Value |
|---|---|---|
| | | |

## Billionaire 3™ 30

**(exclusive Ty employee gift)**

Bear • N/A
Issued: September 23, 2000
Not Available In Retail Stores

Birthdate: N/A

Dedication Appearing On Special Tag
With openings of Ty Singapore
Ty Malaysia, Ty India and Ty Trade,
our brand is #1 in global sales, profits
and awareness. Thank you for your
support and hard work!

| Version | Issue Dates | Price Paid | Market Value |
|---|---|---|---|
| Original | Sept. 2000 | | Special Tag $2,300 |

## Billionaire 4™ 31

New!

**(exclusive Ty employee gift)**

Bear • N/A
Issued: September 8, 2001
Not Available In Retail Stores

Birthdate: N/A

Dedication Appearing On Special Tag
A special gift from Ty to you
This worldwide bear makes his debut
A billion plus in sales we've done
So again this year, we're #1!

| Version | Issue Dates | Price Paid | Market Value |
|---|---|---|---|
| Original | Sept. 2001 | | Special Tag $2,000 |

## Blackie™ 32

Bear • #4011
Issued: June 25, 1994
Retired: September 15, 1998

Birthdate: July 15, 1994

Living in a national park
He only played after dark
Then he met his friend Cubbie
Now they play when it's sunny!

| Version | Issue Dates | Price Paid | Market Value |
|---|---|---|---|
| Original | June 1994-Sept. 1998 | | ❺ $11 ❹ $13<br>❸ $50 ❷ $200<br>❶ $290 |

| Page Totals | Price Paid | Market Value |
|---|---|---|
| | | |

Beanie Babies®

33

## Blizzard™

Tiger · #4163
Issued: May 11, 1997
Retired: May 1, 1998

Birthdate: December 12, 1996

In the mountains, where it's snowy and cold
Lives a beautiful tiger, I've been told
Black and white, she's hard to compare
Of all the tigers, she is most rare!

| Version | Issue Dates | Price Paid | Market Value |
|---|---|---|---|
| Original | May 1997-May 1998 | | 5 $16 4 $19 |

34

## Bones™

Dog · #4001
Issued: June 25, 1994
Retired: May 1, 1998

Birthdate: January 18, 1994

Bones is a dog that loves to chew
Chairs and tables and a smelly old shoe
"You're so destructive" all would shout
But that all stopped, when his teeth
Fell out!

| Version | Issue Dates | Price Paid | Market Value |
|---|---|---|---|
| Original | June 1994-May 1998 | | 5 $14 4 $16 3 $63 2 $210 1 $335 |

35

A B

## Bongo™

**(name changed from "Nana™")**

Monkey · #4067
Issued: June 3, 1995
Retired: December 31, 1998

Birthdate: August 17, 1995

Bongo the monkey lives in a tree
The happiest monkey you'll ever see
In his spare time he plays the guitar
One of these days he will be a big star!

| Version | Issue Dates | Price Paid | Market Value |
|---|---|---|---|
| A. Tan Tail | June 1995-Dec. 1998 | | 5 $11 4 $11 3 $95 |
| B. Brown Tail | Feb. 1996-June 1996 | | 4 $46 3 $100 |

| Page Totals | Price Paid | Market Value |
|---|---|---|
| | | |

## Brigitte™

**36**

Dog • #4374
Issued: July 3, 2001
Current – Moderate To Find

Birthdate: April 20, 2000

A girl must always look her best
You can tell by how she's dressed
Pretty bows, pink poofy hair
Brigitte is full of charm and flair!

| Version | Issue Dates | Price Paid | Market Value |
|---|---|---|---|
| Original | July 2001-Current | | (7) $________ |

## Britannia™

**37**

**(exclusive to the United Kingdom)**

Bear • #4601
Issued: December 31, 1997
Retired: July 26, 1999

Birthdate: December 15, 1997

Britannia the bear will sail the sea
So she can be with you and me
She's always sure to catch the tide
And wear the Union Flag with pride

| Version | Issue Dates | Price Paid | Market Value (in U.S. market) |
|---|---|---|---|
| Original | Dec. 1997-July 1999 | | (5) $80 |

## Bronty™

**38**

Brontosaurus • #4085
Issued: June 3, 1995
Retired: June 15, 1996

Birthdate: N/A

No Poem

| Version | Issue Dates | Price Paid | Market Value |
|---|---|---|---|
| Original | June 1995-June 1996 | | (3) $550 |

39

## Brownie™

**(name changed to "Cubbie™")**

Bear • #4010
Issued: January 8, 1994
Retired: 1994

Birthdate: N/A

No Poem

| Version | Issue Dates | Price Paid | Market Value |
|---|---|---|---|
| Original | Jan. 1994-1994 | | 1 $2,350 |

40

## Bruno™

Dog • #4183
Issued: December 31, 1997
Retired: September 18, 1998

Birthdate: September 9, 1997

Bruno the dog thinks he's a brute
But all the other Beanies think he's cute
He growls at his tail and runs in a ring
And everyone says, "Oh, how darling!"

| Version | Issue Dates | Price Paid | Market Value |
|---|---|---|---|
| Original | Dec. 1997-Sept. 1998 | | 5 $8 |

41

## Bubbles™

Fish • #4078
Issued: June 3, 1995
Retired: May 11, 1997

Birthdate: July 2, 1995

All day long Bubbles likes to swim
She never gets tired of flapping her fins
Bubbles lived in a sea of blue
Now she is ready to come home with you!

| Version | Issue Dates | Price Paid | Market Value |
|---|---|---|---|
| Original | June 1995-May 1997 | | 4 $60 3 $95 |

| Page Totals | Price Paid | Market Value |
|---|---|---|
| | | |

## Buckingham™ 42

**(exclusive to the United Kingdom)**

Bear · #4603
Issued: September 3, 2000
Retired: January 31, 2001

Birthdate: October 16, 2000

Buckingham the bear has a little secret
He wants to tell you and hopes you'll keep it
He's taking his friend Britannia to see
Someone special for crumpets and tea!

| Version | Issue Dates | Price Paid | Market Value (in U.S. market) |
|---|---|---|---|
| Original | Sept. 2000-Jan. 2001 | | 6 $100 |

## Bucky™ 43

Beaver · #4016
Issued: January 7, 1996
Retired: December 31, 1997

Birthdate: June 8, 1995

Bucky's teeth are as shiny as can be
Often used for cutting trees
He hides in his dam night and day
Maybe for you he will come out and play!

| Version | Issue Dates | Price Paid | Market Value |
|---|---|---|---|
| Original | Jan. 1996-Dec. 1997 | | 4 $21   3 $62 |

## Bumble™ 44

Bee · #4045
Issued: June 3, 1995
Retired: June 15, 1996

Birthdate: October 16, 1995

Bumble the bee will not sting you
It is only love that this bee will bring you
So don't be afraid to give this bee a hug
Because Bumble the bee is a love-bug.

| Version | Issue Dates | Price Paid | Market Value |
|---|---|---|---|
| Original | June 1995-June 1996 | | 4 $350   3 $340 |

| Page Totals | Price Paid | Market Value |
|---|---|---|
| | | |

45

## Bushy™

Lion • #4285
Issued: February 13, 2000
Retired: June 11, 2001

Birthdate: January 27, 2000

I won't roar - I'll purr instead
So always pat me on the head
A cuddly kitten I promise to be
If you'll come over and play with me!

| Version | Issue Dates | Price Paid | Market Value |
|---|---|---|---|
| Original | Feb. 2000-June 2001 | | 6 $9 |

46

## Butch™

Bull Terrier • #4227
Issued: January 1, 1999
Retired: December 23, 1999

Birthdate: October 2, 1998

Going to the pet shop to buy dog food
I ran into Butch in a good mood
"Come to the pet shop down the street"
"Be a good dog, I'll buy you a treat!"

| Version | Issue Dates | Price Paid | Market Value |
|---|---|---|---|
| Original | Jan. 1999-Dec. 1999 | | 5 $9 |

47

## Buzzie™

Bee • #4354
Issued: April 1, 2001
Current - Easy To Find

Birthdate: October 20, 2000

Buzzing through the pretty flowers
She could frolic there for hours
The nectar that smells so sweet
Is her favorite tasty treat!

| Version | Issue Dates | Price Paid | Market Value |
|---|---|---|---|
| Original | April 2001-Current | | 7 $______ |

| Page Totals | Price Paid | Market Value |
|---|---|---|
| | | |

## Buzzy™ 48

Buzzard · #4308
Issued: July 8, 2000
Retired: March 23, 2001

Birthdate: July 6, 2000

Up in the sky is where I fly
I love to soar way up high
When I swoop down, don't run away
'cause all I want to do is play!

| Version | Issue Dates | Price Paid | Market Value |
|---|---|---|---|
| Original | July 2000-March 2001 | | 6 $9 |

## Canyon™ 49

Cougar · #4212
Issued: September 30, 1998
Retired: August 16, 1999

Birthdate: May 29, 1998

I climb rocks and really run fast
Try to catch me, it's a blast
Through the mountains, I used to roam
Now in your room, I'll call it home!

| Version | Issue Dates | Price Paid | Market Value |
|---|---|---|---|
| Original | Sept. 1998-Aug. 1999 | | 5 $9 |

## Cashew™ 50

Bear · #4292
Issued: June 24, 2000
Retired: June 2, 2001

Birthdate: April 22, 2000

I like to swim and climb trees
I like to visit with the bees
But what I really want to do
Is be your friend and play with you!

| Version | Issue Dates | Price Paid | Market Value |
|---|---|---|---|
| Original | June 2000-June 2001 | | 6 $10 |

51

## Cassie™

Collie • #4340
Issued: April 1, 2001
Retired: July 25, 2001

Birthdate: July 12, 2000

This loyal Collie will stay by your side
When you're last, she'll be your guide
If you need her, wherever she roams
Just call out, "Cassie, Come Home!"

| Version | Issue Dates | Price Paid | Market Value |
|---|---|---|---|
| Original | April 2001-July 2001 | | 7 $15 |

52

## Caw™

Crow • #4071
Issued: June 3, 1995
Retired: June 15, 1996

Birthdate: N/A

No Poem

| Version | Issue Dates | Price Paid | Market Value |
|---|---|---|---|
| Original | June 1995-June 1996 | | 3 $370 |

53

## Celebrate™

Bear • #4385
Issued: June 23, 2001
Retired: October 11, 2001

Birthdate: March 13, 2001

I'm the 15th birthday bear
With a wish I'd like to share
Many more years full of fun
Let's keep Ty #1!

| Version | Issue Dates | Price Paid | Market Value |
|---|---|---|---|
| Original | June 2001-Oct. 2001 | | 7 $20 |

| Page Totals | Price Paid | Market Value |
|---|---|---|
| | | |

## Cheeks™ 54

Baboon · #4250
Issued: April 17, 1999
Retired: December 23, 1999

Birthdate: May 18, 1999

Don't confuse me with an ape
I have a most unusual shape
My cheeks are round and ty-dyed red
On my behind as well as my head!

| Version | Issue Dates | Price Paid | Market Value |
|---|---|---|---|
| Original | April 1999-Dec. 1999 | | ❺ $10 |

## Cheery™ 55

Sunshine Bear · #4359
Issued: May 1, 2001
Retired: August 31, 2001

Birthdate: August 18, 2001

If you're feeling sad and blue
Cheery wants to be with you
Hug him and he'll make you smile
You'll feel better in a while!

| Version | Issue Dates | Price Paid | Market Value |
|---|---|---|---|
| Original | May 2001-Aug. 2001 | | ❼ $16 |

## Cheezer™ 56

Mouse · #4301
Issued: June 24, 2000
Retired: June 12, 2001

Birthdate: May 9, 2000

I hide in holes throughout the day
But when night falls I want to play
I sneak around and look for cheese
So be my friend and help me please!

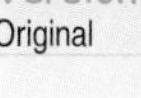

| Version | Issue Dates | Price Paid | Market Value |
|---|---|---|---|
| Original | June 2000-June 2001 | | ❻ $10 |

57

## Chilly™

Polar Bear • #4012
Issued: June 25, 1994
Retired: January 7, 1996

Birthdate: N/A

No Poem

| Version | Issue Dates | Price Paid | Market Value |
|---|---|---|---|
| Original | June 1994-Jan. 1996 | | ❸ $950<br>❷ $1,100<br>❶ $1,300 |

58

## China™

Panda • #4315
Issued: July 8, 2000
Retired: April 19, 2001

Birthdate: September 4, 2000

In the mountains you'll find me
Sitting near a bamboo tree
You'll laugh at such a funny sight
I only dress in black and white!

| Version | Issue Dates | Price Paid | Market Value |
|---|---|---|---|
| Original | July 2000-April 2001 | | ❻ $11 |

59

## Chinook™

**(exclusive to Canada)**

Bear • #4604
Issued: August 13, 2000
Retired: February 15, 2001

Birthdate: May 24, 2000

From this great land I'll never roam
Beloved Canada is my home
Her maple leaf I proudly wear
To show the world how much I care!

| Version | Issue Dates | Price Paid | Market Value (in U.S. market) |
|---|---|---|---|
| Original | Aug. 2000-Feb. 2001 | | ❻ $70 |

| Page Totals | Price Paid | Market Value |
|---|---|---|
| | | |

# Chip™

60

Cat • #4121
Issued: May 11, 1997
Retired: March 31, 1999

Birthdate: January 26, 1996

Black and gold, brown and white
The shades of her coat are quite a sight
At mixing her colors she was a master
On anyone else it would be a disaster!

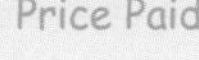

| Version | Issue Dates | Price Paid | Market Value |
|---|---|---|---|
| Original | May 1997-March 1999 | | (5) $9 (4) $10 |

# Chipper™

61

Chipmunk • #4259
Issued: August 31, 1999
Retired: December 23, 1999

Birthdate: April 21, 1999

I'm quick, I'm fast, I don't make a peep
But I love to snuggle when I sleep
Take me along when you go play
And I'll make sure you have a nice day!

| Version | Issue Dates | Price Paid | Market Value |
|---|---|---|---|
| Original | Aug. 1999-Dec. 1999 | | (5) $10 |

# Chocolate™

62

Moose • #4015
Issued: January 8, 1994
Retired: December 31, 1998

Birthdate: April 27, 1993

Licorice, gum and peppermint candy
This moose always has these handy
There is one more thing he likes to eat
Can you guess his favorite sweet?

| Version | Issue Dates | Price Paid | Market Value |
|---|---|---|---|
| Original | Jan. 1994-Dec. 1998 | | (5) $11 (4) $11 (3) $72 (2) $250 (1) $360 |

| Page Totals | Price Paid | Market Value |
|---|---|---|
| | | |

63

## Chops™

Lamb • #4019
Issued: January 7, 1996
Retired: January 1, 1997

Birthdate: May 3, 1996

Chops is a little lamb
This lamb you'll surely know
Because every path that you may take
This lamb is sure to go!

| Version | Issue Dates | Price Paid | Market Value |
|---|---|---|---|
| Original | Jan. 1996-Jan. 1997 | | ④ $82 ③ $115 |

64

## Cinders™

Bear • #4295
Issued: June 24, 2000
Retired: May 9, 2001

Birthdate: April 30, 2000

I sleep in caves and in the snow
A mountain life is all I know
In the Spring I wake again
And look around for my best friend!

| Version | Issue Dates | Price Paid | Market Value |
|---|---|---|---|
| Original | June 2000-May 2001 | | ⑥ $10 |

65

## Classy™

Bear • #4373
Issued: July 25, 2001
Retired: September 7, 2001

Birthdate: April 30, 2001

I'm proud to be the Beanie you chose
I know for sure my happiness shows
Thanks so much for creating me
It's great to be the People's Beanie!

| Version | Issue Dates | Price Paid | Market Value |
|---|---|---|---|
| Original | July 2001-Sept. 2001 | | ⑦ $12 |

| Page Totals | Price Paid | Market Value |
|---|---|---|
| | | |

## Claude™ 66

Crab • #4083
Issued: May 11, 1997
Retired: December 31, 1998

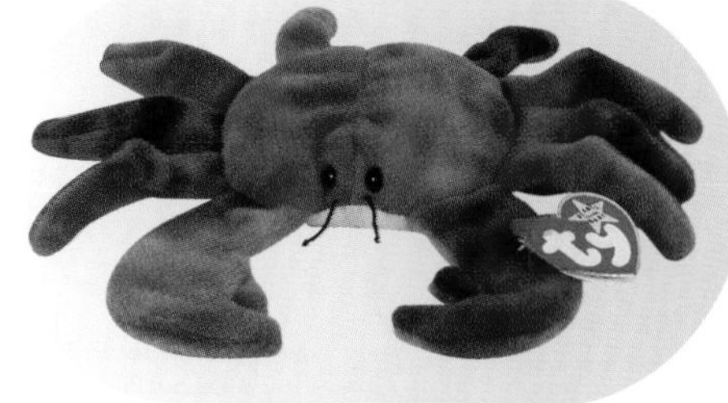

Birthdate: September 3, 1996

Claude the crab paints by the sea
A famous artist he hopes to be
But the tide came in and his paints fell
Now his art is on his shell!

| Version | Issue Dates | Price Paid | Market Value |
|---|---|---|---|
| Original | May 1997-Dec. 1998 | | 5 $9 4 $9 |

## Clubby® 67

**(Club exclusive)**

Bear • N/A
Issued: May 1, 1998
Retired: March 15, 1999

Birthdate: July 7, 1998

Wearing his club pin for all to see
He's a proud member like you and me
Made especially with you in mind
Clubby the bear is one of a kind!

| Version | Issue Dates | Price Paid | Market Value |
|---|---|---|---|
| Original | May 1998-March 1999 | | 5 $28 |

## Clubby II™ 68

**(Club exclusive)**

Bear • N/A
Issued: March 31, 1999
Retired: N/A

Birthdate: March 9, 1999

A proud club member, named Clubby II
My color is special, a purplish hue
Take me along to your favorite place
Carry me in my platinum case!

| Version | Issue Dates | Price Paid | Market Value |
|---|---|---|---|
| Original | March 1999-N/A | | 5 $19 |

| Page Totals | Price Paid | Market Value |
|---|---|---|

69

Set includes Beanie Baby® & Beanie Buddy®

## Clubby III™

**(set/2, Club exclusive)**

Bear • #4993
Issued: September 18, 2000
Retired: December 10, 2000

Birthdate: June 30, 2000

I'm as happy as can be
Because I joined BBOC
We'll play games, have lots of fun
Because this club is number 1!

| Version | Issue Dates | Price Paid | Market Value |
|---|---|---|---|
| Original | Sept. 2000-Dec. 2000 | | 6 $40 (set) |

70

New!

## Clubby IV™

**(Club exclusive)**

Bear • #4996
Issued: September 24, 2001
Current – Just Released

Birthdate: August 4, 2001

Which button do you think you'll get
A gold, a silver, or the whole set
Clubby IV has a surprise for you
Ty Warner autographed a few!

| Version | Issue Dates | Price Paid | Market Value |
|---|---|---|---|
| Original | Sept. 2001-Current | | 7 $_______ |

71

## Congo™

Gorilla • #4160
Issued: June 15, 1996
Retired: December 31, 1998

Birthdate: November 9, 1996

Black as the night and fierce is he
On the ground or in a tree
Strong and mighty as the Congo
He's related to our Bongo!

| Version | Issue Dates | Price Paid | Market Value |
|---|---|---|---|
| Original | June 1996-Dec. 1998 | | 5 $10 4 $11 |

| Page Totals | Price Paid | Market Value |
|---|---|---|
| | | |

## Coral™

**72**

Fish • #4079
Issued: June 3, 1995
Retired: January 1, 1997

Birthdate: March 2, 1995

Coral is beautiful, as you know
Made of colors in the rainbow
Whether it's pink, yellow or blue
These colors were chosen just for you!

| Version | Issue Dates | Price Paid | Market Value |
|---|---|---|---|
| Original | June 1995-Jan. 1997 | | ❹ $88 ❸ $110 |

## Creepers™

**73**

New!

Skeleton • #4376
Issued: September 3, 2001
Current - Just Released

Birthdate: October 18, 2000

In your closet I will hide
Until the door is opened wide
You may think that I'll shout "BOO!"
But I just want to play with you!

| Version | Issue Dates | Price Paid | Market Value |
|---|---|---|---|
| Original | Sept. 2001-Current | | ❼ $________ |

## Crunch™

**74**

Shark • #4130
Issued: January 1, 1997
Retired: September 24, 1998

Birthdate: January 13, 1996

What's for breakfast? What's for lunch?
Yum! Delicious! Munch, munch, munch!
He's eating everything by the bunch
That's the reason we named him Crunch!

| Version | Issue Dates | Price Paid | Market Value |
|---|---|---|---|
| Original | Jan. 1997-Sept. 1998 | | ❺ $9 ❹ $10 |

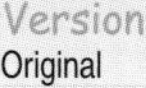

| Page Totals | Price Paid | Market Value |
|---|---|---|
| | | |

75

## Cubbie™

**(name changed from "Brownie™")**

Bear • #4010

Issued: January 8, 1994

Retired: December 31, 1997

Birthdate: November 14, 1993

Cubbie used to eat crackers and honey
And what happened to him was funny
He was stung by fourteen bees
Now Cubbie eats broccoli and cheese!

| Version | Issue Dates | Price Paid | Market Value |
|---|---|---|---|
| Original | Jan. 1994-Dec. 1997 | | 5 $16 4 $27 3 $90 2 $240 1 $400 |

76

## Curly™

Bear • #4052

Issued: June 15, 1996

Retired: December 31, 1998

Birthdate: April 12, 1996

A bear so cute with hair that's Curly
You will love and want him surely
To this bear always be true
He will be a friend to you!

| Version | Issue Dates | Price Paid | Market Value |
|---|---|---|---|
| Original | June 1996-Dec. 1998 | | 5 $15 4 $15 |

77

## Daisy™

Cow • #4006

Issued: June 25, 1994

Retired: September 15, 1998

Birthdate: May 10, 1994

Daisy drinks milk each night
So her coat is shiny and bright
Milk is good for your hair and skin
What a way for your day to begin!

| Version | Issue Dates | Price Paid | Market Value |
|---|---|---|---|
| Original | June 1994-Sept. 1998 | | 5 $12 4 $12 3 $70 2 $200 1 $320 |

| Page Totals | Price Paid | Market Value |
|---|---|---|
| | | |

# Darling™

78

Dog · #4368
Issued: July 3, 2001
Retired: September 10, 2001

Birthdate: August 22, 2001

How cute can a puppy be?
Pick me up and you will see
I'm soft and cuddly, this is true
Won't you take me home with you?

| Version | Issue Dates | Price Paid | Market Value |
|---|---|---|---|
| Original | July 2001-Sept. 2001 | | 7 $13 |

# Dart™

79

Blue Dart Frog · #4352
Issued: April 1, 2001
Retired: July 25, 2001

Birthdate: November 22, 2000

In the rainforest you will find
A special frog that's one of a kind
His bright blue color warns a stranger
That his poison could be danger!

| Version | Issue Dates | Price Paid | Market Value |
|---|---|---|---|
| Original | April 2001-July 2001 | | 7 $9 |

# Dearest™

80

Bear · #4350
Issued: April 1, 2001
Retired: June 17, 2001

Birthdate: May 8, 2000

You cheer me up when I am blue
You make sure I know what to do
Your gentle words and your sweet touch
Are why I love you very much!

| Version | Issue Dates | Price Paid | Market Value |
|---|---|---|---|
| Original | April 2001-June 2001 | | 7 $15 |

| Page Totals | Price Paid | Market Value |
|---|---|---|
| | | |

81

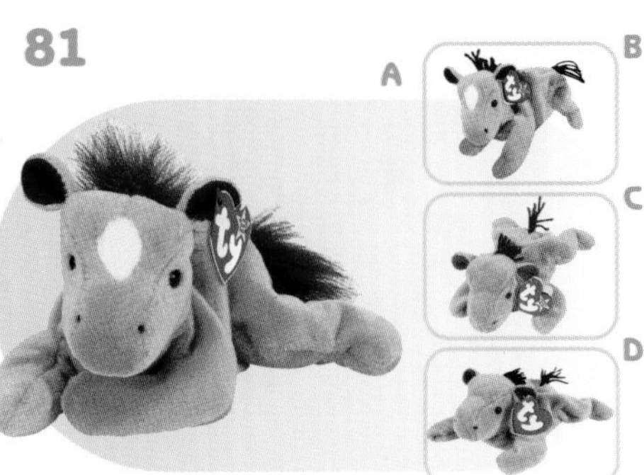

A B C D

## Derby™

Horse • #4008
Issued: June 3, 1995
Retired: May 26, 1999

Birthdate: September 16, 1995

All the other horses used to tattle
Because Derby never wore his saddle
He left the stables, and the horses too
Just so Derby can be with you!

| Version | Issue Dates | Price Paid | Market Value |
|---|---|---|---|
| A. Star/Fluffy Mane | Jan. 1999-May 1999 | | 5 $10 |
| B. Star/Coarse Mane | Dec. 1997-Dec. 1998 | | 5 $10 |
| C. No Star/Coarse Mane | Est. Late 1995-Dec. 1997 | | 4 $15 3 $210 |
| D. No Star/Fine Mane | Est. June 1995-Est. Late 1995 | | 3 $1,500 |

82

## Diddley™

Fantasy Dog • #4383
Issued: July 31, 2001
Current – Moderate To Find

Birthdate: July 25, 2000

Whenever I go anywhere
People always stop and stare
They're not trying to be mean
They've never seen a dog that's green!

| Version | Issue Dates | Price Paid | Market Value |
|---|---|---|---|
| Original | July 2001-Current | | 7 $________ |

83

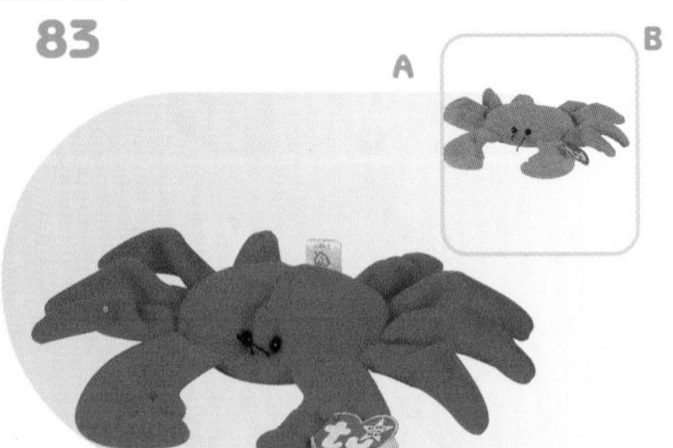

A B

## Digger™

Crab • #4027
Issued: June 25, 1994
Retired: May 11, 1997

Birthdate: August 23, 1995

Digging in the sand and walking sideways
That's how Digger spends her days
Hard on the outside but sweet deep inside
Basking in the sun and riding the tide!

| Version | Issue Dates | Price Paid | Market Value |
|---|---|---|---|
| A. Red | June 1995-May 1997 | | 4 $65 3 $90 |
| B. Orange | June 1994-June 1995 | | 3 $400 2 $450 1 $600 |

| Page Totals | Price Paid | Market Value |
|---|---|---|
| | | |

## Dinky™

84

Dodo Bird • #4341
Issued: January 1, 2001
Current - Moderate To Find

Birthdate: September 25, 2000

Alright I know, I'm a little small
But what's so great about being tall?
Soon I'll grow up and you will see
Just how beautiful I will be!

| Version | Issue Dates | Price Paid | Market Value |
|---|---|---|---|
| Original | Jan. 2001-Current | | (7) $________ |

## Dizzy™

85

Dalmatian • #4365
Issued: June 1, 2001
Retired: August 8, 2001

Birthdate: October 7, 2000

Black and white is just a bore
I can't stand it anymore
Purple, green or maybe blue
Think I'll see what I can do!

| Version | Issue Dates | Price Paid | Market Value |
|---|---|---|---|
| A. Pink & Blue Spots, One Pink & One Blue Ear | June 2001-Aug. 2001 | | (7) $20 |
| B. Pink & Blue Spots, Black Ears | June 2001-Aug. 2001 | | (7) $20 |
| C. Black Spots | June 2001-Aug. 2001 | | (7) $15 |

## Doby™

86

Doberman • #4110
Issued: January 1, 1997
Retired: December 31, 1998

Birthdate: October 9, 1996

This dog is little but he has might
Keep him close when you sleep at night
He lays around with nothing to do
Until he sees it's time to protect you!

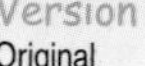

| Version | Issue Dates | Price Paid | Market Value |
|---|---|---|---|
| Original | Jan. 1997-Dec. 1998 | | (5) $11 (4) $11 |

87

## Dog

**(Zodiac Collection™)**

Dog • #4326
Issued: August 19, 2000
Retired: June 8, 2001

Years Of The Dog: 1946, 1958, 1970, 1982, 1994, 2006

You work well with people
Often loyal and very honest
Can be stubborn and selfish
Marry a horse or tiger
Beware of dragons!

| Version | Issue Dates | Price Paid | Market Value |
|---|---|---|---|
| Original | Aug. 2000-June 2001 | | ② $9 |

88

## Doodle™

**(name changed to "Strut™")**

Rooster • #4171
Issued: May 11, 1997
Retired: 1997

Birthdate: March 8, 1996

Listen closely to "cock-a-doodle-doo"
What's the rooster saying to you?
Hurry, wake up sleepy head
We have lots to do, get out of bed!

| Version | Issue Dates | Price Paid | Market Value |
|---|---|---|---|
| Original | May 1997-1997 | | ④ $18 |

89

## Dotty™

Dalmatian • #4100
Issued: May 11, 1997
Retired: December 31, 1998

Birthdate: October 17, 1996

The Beanies all thought it was a big joke
While writing her tag, their ink pen broke
She got in the way, and got all spotty
So now the Beanies call her Dotty!

| Version | Issue Dates | Price Paid | Market Value |
|---|---|---|---|
| Original | May 1997-Dec. 1998 | | ⑤ $12 ④ $12 |

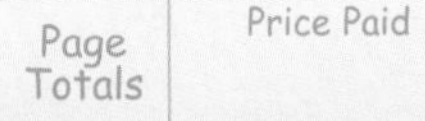

| Page Totals | Price Paid | Market Value |
|---|---|---|
| | | |

## Dragon
**(Zodiac Collection™)**

90

Dragon · #4322
Issued: August 19, 2000
Retired: June 8, 2001

Years Of The Dragon: 1940, 1952, 1964, 1976, 1988, 2000

You are eccentric and passionate
Have good health but complex life
Marry a monkey or rat late in life
Avoid the dog!

| Version | Issue Dates | Price Paid | Market Value |
|---|---|---|---|
| Original | Aug. 2000-June 2001 | | (2) $10 |

## Early™

91

Robin · #4190
Issued: May 30, 1998
Retired: December 23, 1999

Birthdate: March 20, 1997

Early is a red breasted robin
For a worm he'll soon be bobbin'
Always known as a sign of spring
This happy robin loves to sing!

| Version | Issue Dates | Price Paid | Market Value |
|---|---|---|---|
| Original | May 1998-Dec. 1999 | | (5) $8 |

## Ears™

92

Rabbit · #4018
Issued: January 7, 1996
Retired: May 1, 1998

Birthdate: April 18, 1995

He's been eating carrots so long
Didn't understand what was wrong
Couldn't see the board during classes
Until the doctor gave him glasses!

| Version | Issue Dates | Price Paid | Market Value |
|---|---|---|---|
| Original | Jan. 1996-May 1998 | | (5) $15 (4) $16 (3) $55 |

| Page Totals | Price Paid | Market Value |
|---|---|---|
| | | |

93

## Echo™

Dolphin · #4180
Issued: May 11, 1997
Retired: May 1, 1998

Birthdate: December 21, 1996

Echo the dolphin lives in the sea
Playing with her friends, like you and me
Through the waves she echoes the sound
"I'm so glad to have you around!"

| Version | Issue Dates | Price Paid | Market Value |
| --- | --- | --- | --- |
| Original | May 1997-May 1998 | | 5 $13 4 $15 |

94

## Eggbert™

Chick · #4232
Issued: January 1, 1999
Retired: July 28, 1999

Birthdate: April 10, 1998

Cracking her shell taking a peek
Look, she's playing hide and seek
Ready or not, here I come
Take me home and have some fun!

| Version | Issue Dates | Price Paid | Market Value |
| --- | --- | --- | --- |
| Original | Jan. 1999-July 1999 | | 5 $11 |

95

## Eggs™

Bear · #4337
Issued: January 1, 2001
Retired: March 23, 2001

Birthdate: April 23, 2000

Decorating eggs is fun to do
Coloring them with pink and blue
Hiding them is lots of fun
Make sure you find every one!

| Version | Issue Dates | Price Paid | Market Value |
| --- | --- | --- | --- |
| Original | Jan. 2001-March 2001 | | 7 $20 |

| Page Totals | Price Paid | Market Value |
| --- | --- | --- |
| | | |

## Erin™

96

Bear · #4186
Issued: January 31, 1998
Retired: May 21, 1999

Birthdate: March 17, 1997

Named after the beautiful Emerald Isle
This Beanie Baby will make you smile,
A bit of luck, a pot of gold,
Light up the faces, both young and old!

| Version | Issue Dates | Price Paid | Market Value |
|---|---|---|---|
| Original | Jan. 1998-May 1999 | | ⑤ $15 |

## Eucalyptus™

97

Koala · #4240
Issued: April 8, 1999
Retired: October 27, 1999

Birthdate: April 28, 1999

Koalas climb with grace and ease
To the top branches of the trees
Sleeping by day under a gentle breeze
Feeding at night on two pounds of leaves!

| Version | Issue Dates | Price Paid | Market Value |
|---|---|---|---|
| Original | Apr. 1999-Oct. 1999 | | ⑤ $12 |

## Ewey™

98

Lamb · #4219
Issued: January 1, 1999
Retired: July 19, 1999

Birthdate: March 1, 1998

Needles and yarn, Ewey loves to knit
Making sweaters with perfect fit
Happy to make one for you and me
Showing off hers, for all to see!

| Version | Issue Dates | Price Paid | Market Value |
|---|---|---|---|
| Original | Jan. 1999-July 1999 | | ⑤ $11 |

| Page Totals | Price Paid | Market Value |
|---|---|---|
| | | |

99

## Fetch™

Golden Retriever • #4189
Issued: May 30, 1998
Retired: December 31, 1998

Birthdate: February 4, 1997

Fetch is alert at the crack of dawn
Walking through dew drops on the lawn
Always golden, loyal and true
This little puppy is the one for you!

| Version | Issue Dates | Price Paid | Market Value |
|---|---|---|---|
| Original | May 1998-Dec. 1998 | | (5) $13 |

100

## Fetcher™

Dog • #4298
Issued: June 24, 2000
Retired: June 12, 2001

Birthdate: April 27, 2000

Through the house I love to dash
Then I'm back in a flash
Please don't fret, I won't go far
I'm only happy where you are!

| Version | Issue Dates | Price Paid | Market Value |
|---|---|---|---|
| Original | June 2000-June 2001 | | (6) $10 |

101

## Flash™

Dolphin • #4021
Issued: January 8, 1994
Retired: May 11, 1997

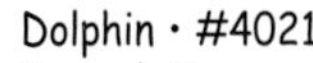

Birthdate: May 13, 1993

You know dolphins are a smart breed
Our friend Flash knows how to read
Splash the whale is the one who taught her
Although reading is difficult under the water!

| Version | Issue Dates | Price Paid | Market Value |
|---|---|---|---|
| Original | Jan. 1994-May 1997 | | (4) $70 (3) $95<br>(2) $280 (1) $400 |

| Page Totals | Price Paid | Market Value |
|---|---|---|
| | | |

## Flashy™ 102

Peacock · #4339
Issued: January 1, 2001
Retired: March 27, 2001

Birthdate: December 30, 2000

More colorful than the rest of the crowd
It's easy to see why he's so proud
He struts his stuff for all to see
It's like he's saying "Look At Me!"

| Version | Issue Dates | Price Paid | Market Value |
|---|---|---|---|
| Original | Jan. 2001-March 2001 | | (7) $12 |

## Fleece™ 103

Lamb · #4125
Issued: January 1, 1997
Retired: December 31, 1998

Birthdate: March 21, 1996

Fleece would like to sing a lullaby
But please be patient, she's rather shy
When you sleep, keep her by your ear
Her song will leave you nothing to fear.

| Version | Issue Dates | Price Paid | Market Value |
|---|---|---|---|
| Original | Jan. 1997-Dec. 1998 | | (5) $11 (4) $11 |

## Fleecie™ 104

Lamb · #4279
Issued: February 13, 2000
Retired: July 14, 2000

Birthdate: January 26, 2000

Fleecie is cuddly and soft as can be
Give her a hug and then you will see
When you hold her close to your ear
You'll hear her whisper "I love you, dear!"

| Version | Issue Dates | Price Paid | Market Value |
|---|---|---|---|
| Original | Feb. 2000-July 2000 | | (6) $11 |

## 105

### Flip™

Cat • #4012
Issued: January 7, 1996
Retired: October 1, 1997

Birthdate: February 28, 1995

Flip the cat is an acrobat
She loves playing on her mat
This cat flips with such grace and flair
She can somersault in mid air!

| Version | Issue Dates | Price Paid | Market Value |
|---|---|---|---|
| Original | Jan. 1996-Oct. 1997 | | 4 $26 3 $58 |

## 106

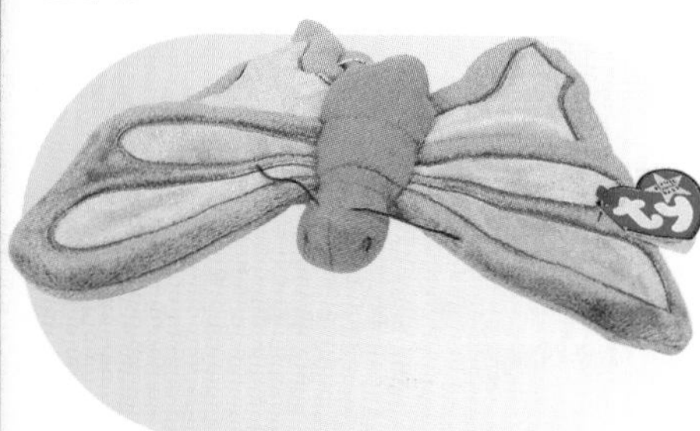

### Flitter™

Butterfly • #4255
Issued: Summer 1999
Retired: December 23, 1999

Birthdate: June 2, 1999

I did not know what I was to be
Covered in fuzz, it was hard to see
Now a butterfly, what a beautiful sight
On silken wings I take to flight!

| Version | Issue Dates | Price Paid | Market Value |
|---|---|---|---|
| Original | Summer 1999-Dec. 1999 | | 5 $12 |

## 107

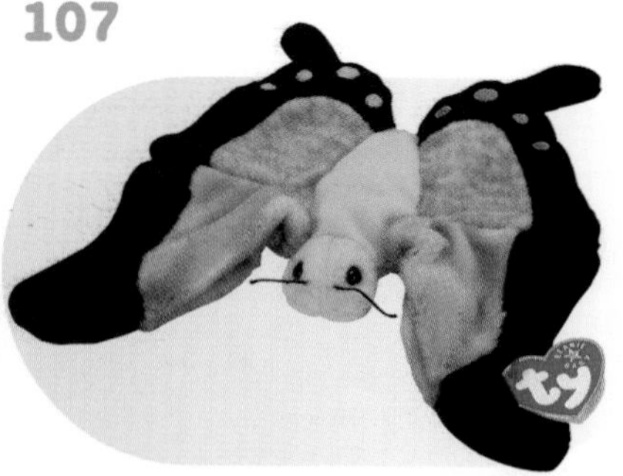

### Float™

Butterfly • #4343
Issued: March 1, 2001
Retired: April 11, 2001

Birthdate: November 12, 2001

She flitters and flies and floats around
Graceful and lovely, not making a sound
Although she flies both near and far
She'll always return to where you are!

| Version | Issue Dates | Price Paid | Market Value |
|---|---|---|---|
| Original | March 2001-April 2001 | | 7 $16 |

| Page Totals | Price Paid | Market Value |
|---|---|---|
| | | |

## Floppity™ 108

Bunny • #4118
Issued: January 1, 1997
Retired: May 1, 1998

Birthdate: May 28, 1996

Floppity hops from here to there
Searching for eggs without a care
Lavender coat from head to toe
All dressed up and nowhere to go!

| Version | Issue Dates | Price Paid | Market Value |
|---|---|---|---|
| Original | Jan. 1997-May 1998 | | (5) $14 (4) $15 |

## Flutter™ 109

Butterfly • #4043
Issued: June 3, 1995
Retired: June 15, 1996

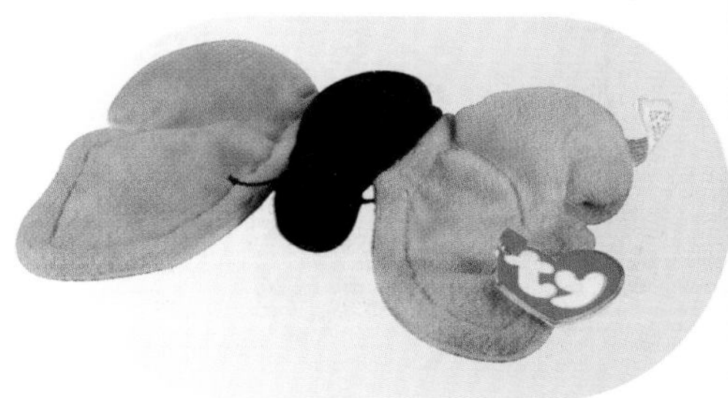

Birthdate: N/A

No Poem

| Version | Issue Dates | Price Paid | Market Value |
|---|---|---|---|
| Original | June 1995-June 1996 | | (3) $525 |

## Fortune™ 110

Panda • #4196
Issued: May 30, 1998
Retired: August 24, 1999

Birthdate: December 6, 1997

Nibbling on a bamboo tree
This little panda is hard to see
You're so lucky with this one you found
Only a few are still around!

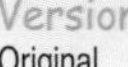

| Version | Issue Dates | Price Paid | Market Value |
|---|---|---|---|
| Original | May 1998-Aug. 1999 | | (5) $11 |

111

New!

## Fraidy™

Cat · #4379
Issued: September 3, 2001
Current - Just Released

Birthdate: October 13, 2000

Superstitious people fear
I'll bring bad luck if I am near
But I'm not into all of that
I'm really just a happy cat!

| Version | Issue Dates | Price Paid | Market Value |
|---|---|---|---|
| Original | Sept. 2001-Current | | (7) $________ |

112

## Freckles™

Leopard · #4066
Issued: June 15, 1996
Retired: December 31, 1998

Birthdate: June 3, 1996
or July 28, 1996

From the trees he hunts prey
In the night and in the day
He's the king of camouflage
Look real close, he's no mirage!

| Version | Issue Dates | Price Paid | Market Value |
|---|---|---|---|
| Original | June 1996-Dec. 1998 | | (5) $12 (4) $12 |

113

## Frigid™

Penguin · #4270
Issued: February 13, 2000
Retired: December 15, 2000

Birthdate: January 23, 2000

Waddling on the slippery ice
Frigid thinks the cold is nice
He jumps into the water below
Then does it again, he loves it so!

| Version | Issue Dates | Price Paid | Market Value |
|---|---|---|---|
| Original | Feb. 2000-Dec. 2000 | | (6) $9 |

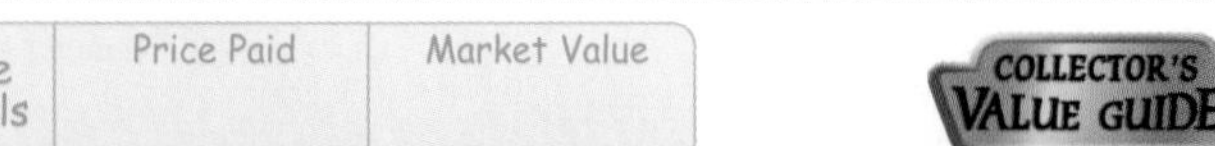

## Frills™ 114

Hornbill Bird · #4367
Issued: June 1, 2001
Retired: June 18, 2001

Birthdate: March 5, 2001

I wear a frill upon my head
Soft and fuzzy, it's very red
Don't know what it's there to do
No one seems to know, do you?

| Version | Issue Dates | Price Paid | Market Value |
|---|---|---|---|
| Original | June 2001-June 2001 | | (7) $13 |

## Fuzz™ 115

Bear · #4237
Issued: January 1, 1999
Retired: December 23, 1999

Birthdate: July 23, 1998

Look closely at this handsome bear
His texture is really quite rare.
With golden highlights in his hair
He has class, style and flair!

| Version | Issue Dates | Price Paid | Market Value |
|---|---|---|---|
| Original | Jan. 1999-Dec. 1999 | | (5) $13 |

## Garcia™ 116

Bear · #4051
Issued: January 7, 1996
Retired: May 11, 1997

Birthdate: August 1, 1995

The Beanies use to follow him around
Because Garcia traveled from town to town
He's pretty popular as you can see
Some even say he's legendary!

| Version | Issue Dates | Price Paid | Market Value |
|---|---|---|---|
| Original | Jan. 1996-May 1997 | | (4) $100 (3) $165 |

| Page Totals | Price Paid | Market Value |
|---|---|---|
| | | |

Beanie Babies®

117

## Germania™

**(exclusive to Germany)**

Bear · #4236
Issued: January 1, 1999
Retired: December 23, 1999

| Poem Translation | Geburtstag: Oktober 3, 1990 |
|---|---|
| Unity and Justice and Freedom<br>Is the song of German unity.<br>All good little girls and boys<br>Should love this little German bear. | Einigkeit und Recht und Freiheit<br>ist der Deutschen Einheistlied.<br>Allen Kindern brav und fein<br>soll dieser Bär das Liebste sein. |

| Version | Issue Dates | Price Paid | Market Value (in U.S. market) |
|---|---|---|---|
| Original | Jan. 1999-Dec. 1999 | | 5 $60 |

118

## Giganto™

Wooly Mammoth · #4384
Issued: July 31, 2001
Current - Hard To Find

Birthdate: December 17, 2000

When you see me, be prepared
I'm really big, so don't be scared
All that matters in the end
Is that I want to be your friend.

| Version | Issue Dates | Price Paid | Market Value |
|---|---|---|---|
| Original | July 2001-Current | | 7 $________ |

119

## GiGi™

Poodle · #4191
Issued: May 30, 1998
Retired: December 23, 1999

Birthdate: April 7, 1997

Prancing and dancing all down the street
Thinking her hairdo is oh so neat
Always so careful in the wind and rain
She's a dog that is anything but plain!

| Version | Issue Dates | Price Paid | Market Value |
|---|---|---|---|
| Original | May 1998-Dec. 1999 | | 5 $9 |



| Page Totals | Price Paid | Market Value |
|---|---|---|
| | | |

## Glory™ 120

Bear · #4188
Issued: May 30, 1998
Retired: December 31, 1998

Birthdate: July 4, 1997

Wearing the flag for all to see
Symbol of freedom for you and me
Red white and blue - Independence Day
Happy Birthday USA!

| Version | Issue Dates | Price Paid | Market Value |
|---|---|---|---|
| Original | May 1998-Dec. 1998 | | (5) $24 |

## Glow™ 121

Lightning Bug · #4283
Issued: February 13, 2000
Retired: March 27, 2001

Birthdate: January 4, 2000

To find me when you want to play
Look for my light to guide the way
I'll be the brightest in the park
I'm the Beanie that glows in the dark!

| Version | Issue Dates | Price Paid | Market Value |
|---|---|---|---|
| Original | Feb. 2000-March 2001 | | (6) $9 |

## Goat 122

**(Zodiac Collection™)**

Goat · #4329
Issued: August 19, 2000
Retired: May 17, 2001
Years Of The Goat: 1943, 1955, 1967, 1979, 1991, 2003

You are timid and prefer anonymity
Often elegant and creative
Compatible with pigs and rabbits
Beware of the ox!

| Version | Issue Dates | Price Paid | Market Value |
|---|---|---|---|
| Original | Aug. 2000-May 2001 | | (2) $9 |

| Page Totals | Price Paid | Market Value |
|---|---|---|
| | | |

123

## Goatee™

Mountain Goat · #4235
Issued: January 1, 1999
Retired: December 23, 1999

Birthdate: November 4, 1998

Though she's hungry, she's in a good mood
Searching through garbage, tin cans for food
For Goatee the goat, it's not a big deal
Anything at all makes a fine meal!

| Version | Issue Dates | Price Paid | Market Value |
|---|---|---|---|
| Original | Jan. 1999-Dec. 1999 | | ⑤ $8 |

124

## Gobbles™

Turkey · #4034
Issued: October 1, 1997
Retired: March 31, 1999

Birthdate: November 27, 1996

Gobbles the turkey loves to eat
Once a year she has a feast
I have a secret I'd like to divulge
If she eats too much her tummy will bulge!

| Version | Issue Dates | Price Paid | Market Value |
|---|---|---|---|
| Original | Oct. 1997-March 1999 | | ⑤ $9 ④ $9 |

125

## Goldie®

Goldfish · #4023
Issued: June 25, 1994
Retired: December 31, 1997

Birthdate: November 14, 1994

She's got rhythm, she's got soul
What more to like in a fish bowl?
Through sound waves Goldie swam
Because this goldfish likes to jam!

| Version | Issue Dates | Price Paid | Market Value |
|---|---|---|---|
| Original | June 1994-Dec. 1997 | | ⑤ $24 ④ $24 ③ $80 ② $235 ① $390 |

| Page Totals | Price Paid | Market Value |
|---|---|---|
| | | |

## Goochy™

126

Jellyfish · #4230
Issued: January 1, 1999
Retired: December 23, 1999

Birthdate: November 18, 1998

Swirl, swish, squirm and wiggle
Listen closely, hear him giggle
The most ticklish jellyfish you'll ever meet
Even though he has no feet!

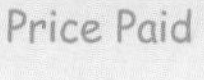

| Version | Issue Dates | Price Paid | Market Value |
|---|---|---|---|
| Original | Jan. 1999-Dec. 1999 | | ⑤ $8 |

## Grace™

127

Bunny · #4274
Issued: February 13, 2000
Retired: June 11, 2001

Birthdate: February 10, 2000

Please watch over me night and day
When I sleep and when I pray
Keep me safe from up above
With special blessings of your love!

| Version | Issue Dates | Price Paid | Market Value |
|---|---|---|---|
| Original | Feb. 2000-June 2001 | | ⑥ $9 |

## Gracie™

128

Swan · #4126
Issued: January 1, 1997
Retired: May 1, 1998

Birthdate: June 17, 1996

As a duckling, she was confused,
Birds on the lake were quite amused.
Poking fun until she would cry,
Now the most beautiful swan at Ty!

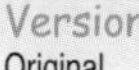
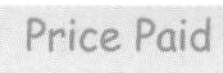

| Version | Issue Dates | Price Paid | Market Value |
|---|---|---|---|
| Original | Jan. 1997-May 1998 | | ⑤ $12 ④ $14 |

129

## Groovy™

Bear · #4256
Issued: August 31, 1999
Retired: December 23, 1999

Birthdate: January 10, 1999

Wearing colors of the rainbow
Making good friends wherever I go
Take me with you, don't let me stay
I need your love all night and day!

| Version | Issue Dates | Price Paid | Market Value |
|---|---|---|---|
| Original | Aug. 1999-Dec. 1999 | | 5 $17 |

130

## Grunt™

Razorback · #4092
Issued: January 7, 1996
Retired: May 11, 1997

Birthdate: July 19, 1995

Some Beanies think Grunt is tough
No surprise, he's scary enough
But if you take him home you'll see
Grunt is the sweetest Beanie Baby!

| Version | Issue Dates | Price Paid | Market Value |
|---|---|---|---|
| Original | Jan. 1996-May 1997 | | 4 $88 3 $105 |

131

## Hairy™

Spider · #4336
Issued: January 1, 2001
Retired: January 26, 2001

Birthdate: October 6, 2000

Hairy the spider hangs from a thread
Looking at you from overhead
Hanging around is his favorite way
Of spending each and every day!

| Version | Issue Dates | Price Paid | Market Value |
|---|---|---|---|
| Original | Jan. 2001-Jan. 2001 | | 7 $18 |

| Page Totals | Price Paid | Market Value |
|---|---|---|
| | | |

## Halo™ 132

Angel Bear • #4208
Issued: September 30, 1998
Retired: November 19, 1999

Birthdate: August 31, 1998

When you sleep, I'm always here
Don't be afraid, I am near
Watching over you with lots of love
Your guardian angel from up above!

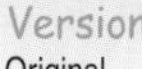

| Version | Issue Dates | Price Paid | Market Value |
|---|---|---|---|
| Original | Sept. 1998-Nov. 1999 | | ❺$17 |

## Halo II™ 133

Angel Bear • #4269
Issued: February 13, 2000
Retired: April 6, 2001

Birthdate: January 14, 2000

Little angel up above
Guard me with your special love
Make sure that you will always be
By my side and close to me!

| Version | Issue Dates | Price Paid | Market Value |
|---|---|---|---|
| Original | Feb. 2000-April 2001 | | ❻$12 |

## Happy™ 134

Hippo • #4061
Issued: June 25, 1994
Retired: May 1, 1998

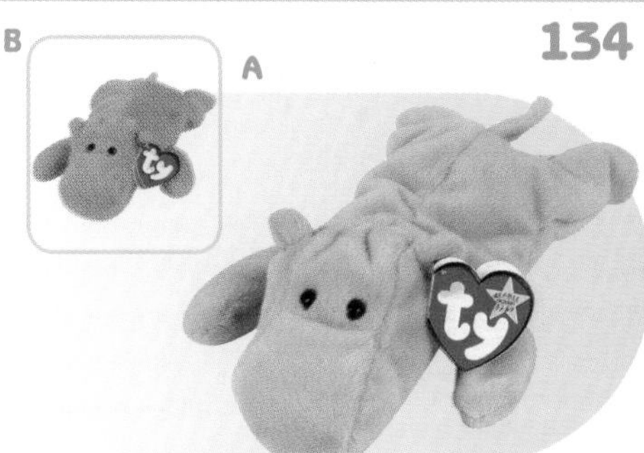


Birthdate: February 25, 1994

Happy the Hippo loves to wade
In the river and in the shade
When Happy shoots water out of his snout
You know he's happy without a doubt!

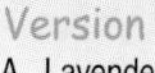

| Version | Issue Dates | Price Paid | Market Value |
|---|---|---|---|
| A. Lavender | June 1995-May 1998 | | ❺$18 ❹$18 ❸$100 |
| B. Gray | June 1994-June 1995 | | ❸$400 ❷$480 ❶$560 |

| Page Totals | Price Paid | Market Value |
|---|---|---|
| | | |

135

New!

## Haunt™

Bear • #4377
Issued: September 3, 2001
Current - Just Released

Birthdate: October 27, 2000

My favorite time is Halloween
When ghosts and goblins can be seen
It's so much fun to trick-or-treat
I hope you'll give me something sweet!

| Version | Issue Dates | Price Paid | Market Value |
|---|---|---|---|
| Original | Sept. 2001-Current | | 7 $________ |

136

## Hero™

Bear • #4351
Issued: April 1, 2001
Retired: May 9, 2001

Birthdate: June 18, 2001

You give me hugs when I am sad
You love me if I'm good or bad
Thank you for all you do
I can always count on you!

| Version | Issue Dates | Price Paid | Market Value |
|---|---|---|---|
| Original | April 2001-May 2001 | | 7 $15 |

137

## Hippie™

Bunny • #4218
Issued: January 1, 1999
Retired: July 12, 1999

Birthdate: May 4, 1998

Hippie fell into the dye, they say
While coloring eggs, one spring day
From the tips of his ears, down to his toes
Colors of springtime, he proudly shows!

| Version | Issue Dates | Price Paid | Market Value |
|---|---|---|---|
| Original | Jan. 1999-July 1999 | | 5 $13 |

| Page Totals | Price Paid | Market Value |
|---|---|---|
| | | |

## Hippity™ 138

Bunny • #4119
Issued: January 1, 1997
Retired: May 1, 1998

Birthdate: June 1, 1996

Hippity is a cute little bunny
Dressed in green, he looks quite funny
Twitching his nose in the air
Sniffing a flower here and there!

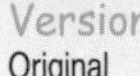

| Version | Issue Dates | Price Paid | Market Value |
| --- | --- | --- | --- |
| Original | Jan. 1997-May 1998 | | 5 $17 4 $17 |

## Hissy™ 139

Snake • #4185
Issued: December 31, 1997
Retired: March 31, 1999

Birthdate: April 4, 1997

Curled and coiled and ready to play
He waits for you patiently every day
He'll keep his best friend, but not his skin
And stay with you through thick and thin.

| Version | Issue Dates | Price Paid | Market Value |
| --- | --- | --- | --- |
| Original | Dec. 1997-Mar. 1999 | | 5 $9 |

## Honks™ 140

Goose • #4258
Issued: August 31, 1999
Retired: December 23, 1999

Birthdate: March 11, 1999

Honks the goose likes to fly away
South for Winter he will stay
When Spring comes back, North he will fly
And swim in ponds and lakes nearby!

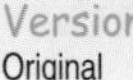

| Version | Issue Dates | Price Paid | Market Value |
| --- | --- | --- | --- |
| Original | Aug. 1999-Dec. 1999 | | 5 $9 |

| Page Totals | Price Paid | Market Value |
| --- | --- | --- |
| | | |

141

## Hoot™

Owl • #4073
Issued: January 7, 1996
Retired: October 1, 1997

Birthdate: August 9, 1995

Late to bed, late to rise
Nevertheless, Hoot's quite wise
Studies by candlelight, nothing new
Like a president, do you know Whooo?

| Version | Issue Dates | Price Paid | Market Value |
|---|---|---|---|
| Original | Jan. 1996-Oct. 1997 | | 4 $25 3 $65 |

142

## Hope™

Bear • #4213
Issued: January 1, 1999
Retired: December 23, 1999

Birthdate: March 23, 1998

Every night when it's time for bed
Fold your hands and bow your head
An angelic face, a heart that's true
You have a friend to pray with you!

| Version | Issue Dates | Price Paid | Market Value |
|---|---|---|---|
| Original | Jan. 1999-Dec. 1999 | | 5 $11 |

143

## Hopper™

Bunny • #4342
Issued: January 1, 2001
Retired: April 4, 2001

Birthdate: August 7, 2000

He hops around from place to place
To put a smile upon your face
Bringing baskets and good cheer
It's his favorite time of year!

| Version | Issue Dates | Price Paid | Market Value |
|---|---|---|---|
| Original | Jan. 2001-April 2001 | | 7 $10 |

| Page Totals | Price Paid | Market Value |
|---|---|---|
| | | |

## Hoppity™

**144**

Bunny · #4117
Issued: January 1, 1997
Retired: May 1, 1998

Birthdate: April 3, 1996

Hopscotch is what she likes to play
If you don't join in, she'll hop away
So play a game if you have the time,
She likes to play, rain or shine!

| Version | Issue Dates | Price Paid | Market Value |
|---|---|---|---|
| Original | Jan. 1997-May 1998 | | 5 $14  4 $14 |

## Hornsly™

**145**

Triceratops · #4345
Issued: March 1, 2001
Retired: August 8, 2001

Birthdate: August 24, 2000

I have horns, I'm quite a sight
Some people run away in fright
But I don't want to scare you away
All I want to do is play!

| Version | Issue Dates | Price Paid | Market Value |
|---|---|---|---|
| Original | March 2001-Aug. 2001 | | 7 $13 |

## Horse

**146**

**(Zodiac Collection™)**

Horse · #4324
Issued: August 19, 2000
Retired: May 29, 2001

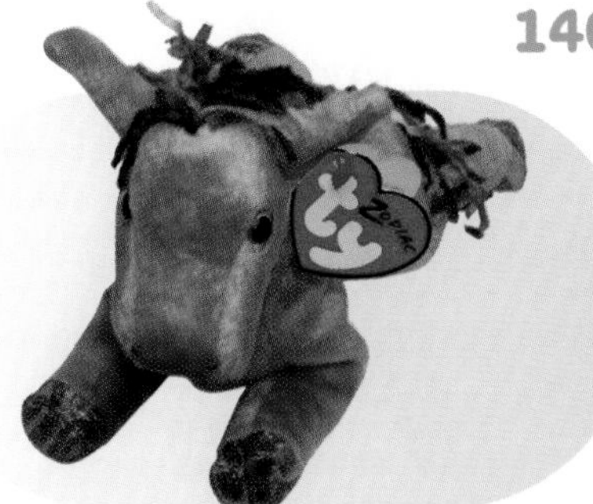

Years Of The Horse: 1942, 1954, 1966, 1978, 1990, 2002

Popular and very attractive to others
Often impatient and ostentatious
Marry a tiger early
The rat is your enemy!

| Version | Issue Dates | Price Paid | Market Value |
|---|---|---|---|
| Original | Aug. 2000-May 2001 | | 2 $10 |

| Page Totals | Price Paid | Market Value |
|---|---|---|
| | | |

147

## Howl™

Wolf · #4310
Issued: July 8, 2000
Retired: April 24, 2001

Birthdate: May 23, 2000

When the moon is round and bright
I howl and howl all through the night
But don't be scared and run away
I'm calling out, "Who wants to play?"

| Version | Issue Dates | Price Paid | Market Value |
|---|---|---|---|
| Original | July 2000-April 2001 | | (6) $10 |

148

## Huggy™

Bear · #4306
Issued: July 8, 2000
Retired: June 18, 2001

Birthdate: August 20, 2000

I'd love to be your special friend
I'll stick right by you to the end
So hold me close next to your heart
And from your side I'll never part!

| Version | Issue Dates | Price Paid | Market Value |
|---|---|---|---|
| Original | July 2000-June 2001 | | (6) $10 |

149

## Humphrey™

Camel · #4060
Issued: June 25, 1994
Retired: June 15, 1995

Birthdate: N/A

No Poem

| Version | Issue Dates | Price Paid | Market Value |
|---|---|---|---|
| Original | June 1994-June 1995 | | (3) $1,000 (2) $1,350 (1) $1,550 |

| Page Totals | Price Paid | Market Value |
|---|---|---|
| | | |

# Iggy™

150

Iguana • #4038
Issued: December 31, 1997
Retired: March 31, 1999

B A C

Birthdate: August 12, 1997

Sitting on a rock, basking in the sun
Is this iguana's idea of fun
Towel and glasses, book and beach chair
His life is so perfect without a care!

| Version | Issue Dates | Price Paid | Market Value |
|---|---|---|---|
| A. Blue/No Tongue | Mid 1998-March 1999 | | 5 $10 |
| B. Ty-dye/With Tongue | June 1998-Mid 1998 | | 5 $10 |
| C. Ty-dye/No Tongue | Dec. 1997-June 1998 | | 5 $10 |

# Inch™

151

Inchworm • #4044
Issued: June 3, 1995
Retired: May 1, 1998

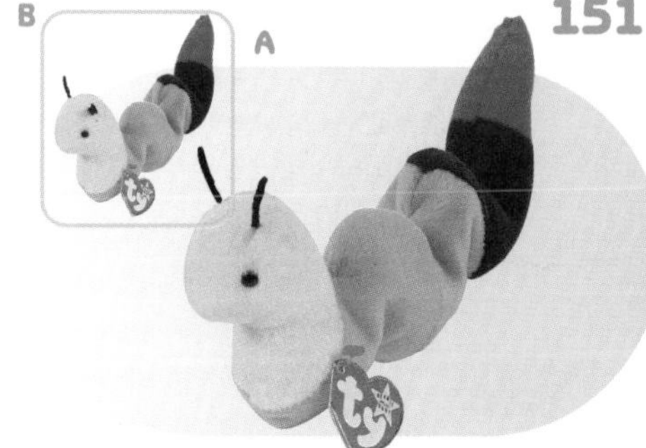

B A

Birthdate: September 3, 1995

Inch the worm is a friend of mine
He goes so slow all the time
Inching around from here to there
Traveling the world without a care!

| Version | Issue Dates | Price Paid | Market Value |
|---|---|---|---|
| A. Yarn Antennas | Oct. 1997-May 1998 | | 5 $18 4 $20 |
| B. Felt Antennas | June 1995-Oct. 1997 | | 4 $100 3 $115 |

# India™

152

Tiger • #4291
Issued: June 24, 2000
Retired: June 12, 2001

Birthdate: May 26, 2000

Through jungle shadows I will prowl
Don't be afraid, sometimes I growl
I'm not fierce, don't run away
We'll be best friends and play all day!

| Version | Issue Dates | Price Paid | Market Value |
|---|---|---|---|
| Original | June 2000-June 2001 | | 6 $9 |

153

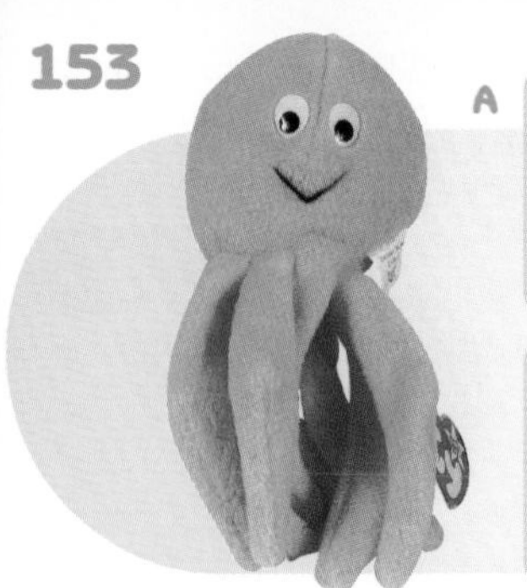

A

B

C

## Inky™

Octopus · #4028
Issued: June 25, 1994
Retired: May 1, 1998

Birthdate: November 29, 1994

Inky's head is big and round
As he swims he makes no sound
If you need a hand, don't hesitate
Inky can help because he has eight!

| Version | Issue Dates | Price Paid | Market Value |
|---|---|---|---|
| A. Pink | June 1995-May 1998 | | ❺ $20 ❹ $22 ❸ $150 |
| B. Tan With Mouth | Sept. 1994-June 1995 | | ❸ $570 ❷ $610 |
| C. Tan Without Mouth | June 1994-Sept. 1994 | | ❷ $675 ❶ $880 |

154

## Issy™

Bear · #4404
Issued: December 30, 2000
Current – Hard To Find

Birthdate: N/A

Tribute Appearing On Special Tag
In Memory of Christopher Sharp 1960-1978
If you travel far and wide
Keep Issy always by your side
And when you must turn out the light
You'll hear him softly say "good night!"

| Version | Issue Dates | Price Paid | Market Value |
|---|---|---|---|
| A. Through Retail Outlets, 47 Swing/Tush Tag Varieties | March 2001-Current | | Special Tag $_____ |
| B. Exclusive Through Four Seasons Hotel, New York | Dec. 2000-Current | | Special Tag $_____ |

155

## Jabber™

Parrot · #4197
Issued: May 30, 1998
Retired: December 23, 1999

Birthdate: October 10, 1997

Teaching Jabber to move his beak
A large vocabulary he now can speak
Jabber will repeat what you say
Teach him a new word everyday!

| Version | Issue Dates | Price Paid | Market Value |
|---|---|---|---|
| Original | May 1998-Dec. 1999 | | ❺ $9 |

| Page Totals | Price Paid | Market Value |
|---|---|---|
| | | |

## Jake™

156

Mallard Duck • #4199
Issued: May 30, 1998
Retired: December 23, 1999

Birthdate: April 16, 1997

Jake the drake likes to splash in a puddle
Take him home and give him a cuddle
Quack, Quack, Quack, he will say
He's so glad you're here to play!

| Version | Issue Dates | Price Paid | Market Value |
|---|---|---|---|
| Original | May 1998-Dec. 1999 | | ❺ $9 |

## Jester™

157

Clownfish • #4349
Issued: April 1, 2001
Current – Easy To Find

Birthdate: September 30, 2001

He loves to play in the sea
With his friend the anemone
Dancing is their favorite way
Of spending each and every day!

| Version | Issue Dates | Price Paid | Market Value |
|---|---|---|---|
| Original | April 2001-Current | | ❼ $________ |

## Jinglepup™

158

New!

Dog • #4394
Issued: October 1, 2001
Current – Just Released

Birthdate: December 3, 2000

Winter is the very best season
Yummy treats are just one reason
But gingerbread, cookies and candy, too
Can't beat cuddling up next to you!

| Version | Issue Dates | Price Paid | Market Value |
|---|---|---|---|
| Original | Oct. 2001-Current | | ❼ $________ |

159

## Jolly™

Walrus · #4082
Issued: May 11, 1997
Retired: May 1, 1998

Birthdate: December 2, 1996

Jolly the walrus is not very serious
He laughs and laughs until he's delirious
He often reminds me of my dad
Always happy, never sad!

| Version | Issue Dates | Price Paid | Market Value |
|---|---|---|---|
| Original | May 1997-May 1998 | | 5 $12 4 $12 |

160

## July™

**(Birthday Beanies Collection™)**

Bear · #4370
Issued: July 3, 2001
Retired: August 30, 2001

Birthdate: N/A

My nose is the color of my birthstone.
Ruby
It brings beauty, serenity and hope!

| Version | Issue Dates | Price Paid | Market Value |
|---|---|---|---|
| Original | July 2001-Aug. 2001 | | 7 $12 |

161

## Kaleidoscope™

Cat · #4348
Issued: January 30, 2001
Retired: March 14, 2001

Birthdate: June 24, 2000

I'm wild and crazy as you can see
Other cats want to be like me
Some may say I look like a clown
But I'm the coolest cat in town!

| Version | Issue Dates | Price Paid | Market Value |
|---|---|---|---|
| Original | Jan. 2001-March 2001 | | 7 $13 |

| Page Totals | Price Paid | Market Value |
|---|---|---|
| | | |

## Kicks™ 162

Bear • #4229
Issued: January 1, 1999
Retired: December 23, 1999

Birthdate: August 16, 1998

The world cup is his dream
Kicks the bear is the best on his team
He hopes that one day he'll be the pick
First he needs to improve his kick!

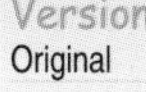

| Version | Issue Dates | Price Paid | Market Value |
|---|---|---|---|
| Original | Jan. 1999-Dec. 1999 | | (5) $12 |

## Kirby™ 163

New!

Dog • #4396
Issued: October 1, 2001
Current - Just Released

Birthdate: May 5, 2001

Prancing on the icy snow
I put on quite a funny show
Slipping and sliding all around
I hope my paws stay on the ground!

| Version | Issue Dates | Price Paid | Market Value |
|---|---|---|---|
| Original | Oct. 2001-Current | | (7) $________ |

## Kiwi™ 164

Toucan • #4070
Issued: June 3, 1995
Retired: January 1, 1997

Birthdate: September 16, 1995

Kiwi waits for the April showers
Watching a garden bloom with flowers
There trees grow with fruit that's sweet
I'm sure you'll guess his favorite treat!

| Version | Issue Dates | Price Paid | Market Value |
|---|---|---|---|
| Original | June 1995-Jan. 1997 | | (4) $90 (3) $110 |

165

## Knuckles™

Pig • #4247
Issued: April 14, 1999
Retired: December 23, 1999

Birthdate: March 25, 1999

In the kitchen working hard
Using ingredients from the yard
No one will eat it, can you guess why?
Her favorite recipe is for mud pie!

| Version | Issue Dates | Price Paid | Market Value |
|---|---|---|---|
| Original | April 1999-Dec. 1999 | | 5 $10 |

166

## Kooky™

Cat • #4357
Issued: May 1, 2001
Retired: July 12, 2001

Birthdate: October 24, 2000

If you want to have some fun
Kooky will be number one
This cat loves to dance around
To his favorite groovy sounds!

| Version | Issue Dates | Price Paid | Market Value |
|---|---|---|---|
| Original | May 2001-July 2001 | | 7 $11 |

167

## KuKu™

Cockatoo • #4192
Issued: May 30, 1998
Retired: December 23, 1999

Birthdate: January 5, 1997

This fancy bird loves to converse
He talks in poems, rhythms and verse
So take him home and give him some time
You'll be surprised how he can rhyme!

| Version | Issue Dates | Price Paid | Market Value |
|---|---|---|---|
| Original | May 1998-Dec. 1999 | | 5 $9 |

| Page Totals | Price Paid | Market Value |
|---|---|---|
| | | |

## Lefty™

168

Donkey • #4085
Issued: June 15, 1996
Retired: January 1, 1997

Birthdate: July 4, 1996

Donkeys to the left, elephants to the right
Often seems like a crazy sight
This whole game seems very funny
Until you realize they're spending
Your money!

| Version | Issue Dates | Price Paid | Market Value |
|---|---|---|---|
| Original | June 1996-Jan. 1997 | | ❹ $180 |

## Lefty 2000™

169

**(exclusive to the United States)**

Donkey • #4290
Issued: June 24, 2000
Retired: December 21, 2000

Birthdate: July 4, 2000

This November make a note
The time has come for you to vote
Pick me when you have to choose
I'm a Beanie, you can't lose!

| Version | Issue Dates | Price Paid | Market Value |
|---|---|---|---|
| Original | June 2000-Dec. 2000 | | ❻ $17 |

## Legs™

170

Frog • #4020
Issued: January 8, 1994
Retired: October 1, 1997

Birthdate: April 25, 1993

Legs lives in a hollow log
Legs likes to play leap frog
If you like to hang out at the lake
Legs will be the new friend you'll make!

| Version | Issue Dates | Price Paid | Market Value |
|---|---|---|---|
| Original | Jan. 1994-Oct. 1997 | | ❹ $15 ❸ $52<br>❷ $200 ❶ $370 |

| Page Totals | Price Paid | Market Value |
|---|---|---|
| | | |

171

## Libearty™

Bear • #4057
Issued: June 15, 1996
Retired: January 1, 1997

Birthdate: Summer 1996

I am called libearty
I wear the flag for all to see
Hope and freedom is my way
That's why I wear flag USA

| Version | Issue Dates | Price Paid | Market Value |
|---|---|---|---|
| Original | June 1996-Jan. 1997 | | 4 $270 |

172

## Lips™

Fish • #4254
Issued: Summer 1999
Retired: December 23, 1999

Birthdate: March 15, 1999

Did you ever see a fish like me?
I'm the most colorful in the sea
Traveling with friends in a school
Swimming all day is really cool!

| Version | Issue Dates | Price Paid | Market Value |
|---|---|---|---|
| Original | Summer 1999-Dec. 1999 | | 5 $12 |

173

## Lizzy™

Lizard • #4033
Issued: June 3, 1995
Retired: December 31, 1997

Birthdate: May 11, 1995

Lizzy loves Legs the frog
She hides with him under logs
Both of them search for flies
Underneath the clear blue skies!

| Version | Issue Dates | Price Paid | Market Value |
|---|---|---|---|
| A. Blue | Jan. 1996-Dec. 1997 | | 5 $16 4 $20 3 $130 |
| B. Ty-dye | June 1995-Jan. 1996 | | 3 $600 |

| Page Totals | Price Paid | Market Value |
|---|---|---|
| | | |

## Loosy™

174

Goose • #4206
Issued: September 30, 1998
Retired: September 1, 1999

Birthdate: March 29, 1998

A tale has been told
Of a goose that laid gold
But try as she might
Loosy's eggs are just white!

| Version | Issue Dates | Price Paid | Market Value |
|---|---|---|---|
| Original | Sept. 1998-Sept. 1999 | | (5) $8 |

## Lucky™

175

Ladybug • #4040
Issued: June 25, 1994
Retired: May 1, 1998

B · A · C

Birthdate: May 1, 1995

Lucky the lady bug loves the lotto
"Someone must win" that's her motto
But save your dimes and even a penny
Don't spend on the lotto and
You'll have many!

| Version | Issue Dates | Price Paid | Market Value |
|---|---|---|---|
| A. Approx. 11 Printed Spots | Feb. 1996-May 1998 | | (5) $18 (4) $18 |
| B. Approx. 21 Printed Spots | Est. Mid 1996-Late 1996 | | (4) $325 |
| C. Approx. 7 Felt Glued-On Spots | June 1994-Feb. 1996 | | (3) $160 (2) $300 (1) $475 |

## Luke™

176

Black Lab • #4214
Issued: January 1, 1999
Retired: December 23, 1999

Birthdate: June 15, 1998

After chewing on your favorite shoes
Luke gets tired, takes a snooze
Who wouldn't love a puppy like this?
Give him a hug, he'll give you a kiss!

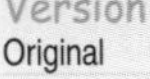

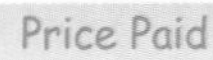

| Version | Issue Dates | Price Paid | Market Value |
|---|---|---|---|
| Original | Jan. 1999-Dec. 1999 | | (5) $11 |

| Page Totals | Price Paid | Market Value |
|---|---|---|
| | | |

177

## Lurkey™

Turkey • #4309
Issued: July 8, 2000
Retired: March 14, 2001

Birthdate: June 13, 2000

Thanksgiving is my special day
But there is something I must say
When you sit down with your fork
Make sure your plate is full of pork!

| Version | Issue Dates | Price Paid | Market Value |
|---|---|---|---|
| Original | July 2000-March 2001 | | 6 $9 |

178

## M.C. Beanie™

**(exclusive to participants in the Ty MasterCard Program)**

Bear • #4997
Issued: August 14, 2001
Current - Very Hard To Find

Birthdate: N/A

You shop and shop, so much to do
So little time, you're never through
Ty Mastercard will save the day
'Cause it's the easy way to pay!

| Version | Issue Dates | Price Paid | Market Value |
|---|---|---|---|
| Original | Aug. 2001-Current | | 7 $______ |

179

## Mac™

Cardinal • #4225
Issued: January 1, 1999
Retired: December 23, 1999

Birthdate: June 10, 1998

Mac tries hard to prove he's the best
Swinging his bat harder than the rest
Breaking records, enjoying the game
Hitting home runs is his claim to fame!

| Version | Issue Dates | Price Paid | Market Value |
|---|---|---|---|
| Original | Jan. 1999-Dec. 1999 | | 5 $9 |

| Page Totals | Price Paid | Market Value |
|---|---|---|
| | | |

# Magic™

**180**

Dragon · #4088
Issued: June 3, 1995
Retired: December 31, 1997

Birthdate: September 5, 1995

Magic the dragon lives in a dream
The most beautiful that you have ever seen
Through magic lands she likes to fly
Look up and watch her, way up high!

| Version | Issue Dates | Price Paid | Market Value |
|---|---|---|---|
| A. Pale Pink Thread | June 1995-Dec. 1997 | | (4) $36 (3) $95 |
| B. Hot Pink Thread | Est. Mid 1996-Early 1997 | | (4) $80 |

# Manny™

**181**

Manatee · #4081
Issued: January 7, 1996
Retired: May 11, 1997

Birthdate: June 8, 1995

Manny is sometimes called a sea cow
She likes to twirl and likes to bow
Manny sure is glad you bought her
Because it's so lonely under water!

| Version | Issue Dates | Price Paid | Market Value |
|---|---|---|---|
| Original | Jan. 1996-May 1997 | | (4) $95 (3) $125 |

# Maple™

**182**

**(exclusive to Canada)**

Bear · #4600
Issued: January 1, 1997
Retired: July 30, 1999

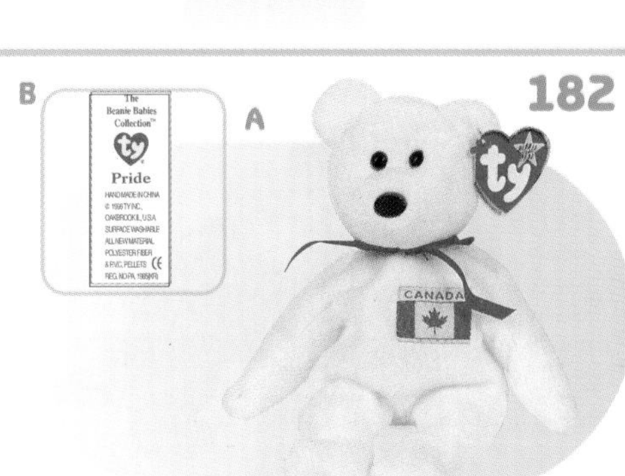


Birthdate: July 1, 1996

Maple the bear likes to ski
With his friends, he plays hockey.
He loves his pancakes and eats every crumb
Can you guess which country he's from?

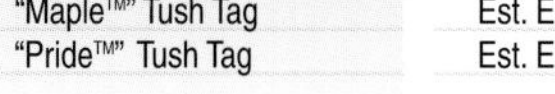

| Version | Issue Dates | Price Paid | Market Value (in U.S. market) |
|---|---|---|---|
| A. "Maple™" Tush Tag | Est. Early 1997-July 1999 | | (5) $80 (4) $100 |
| B. "Pride™" Tush Tag | Est. Early 1997 | | (4) $400 |

| Page Totals | Price Paid | Market Value |
|---|---|---|
| | | |

## 183

# Mel™

Koala • #4162
Issued: January 1, 1997
Retired: March 31, 1999

Birthdate: January 15, 1996

How do you name a Koala bear?
It's rather tough, I do declare!
It confuses me, I get into a funk
I'll name him Mel, after my favorite hunk!

| Version | Issue Dates | Price Paid | Market Value |
|---|---|---|---|
| Original | Jan. 1997-March 1999 | | 5 $9 4 $9 |

## 184

# Mellow™

Bear • #4344
Issued: March 1, 2001
Retired: May 21, 2001

Birthdate: December 7, 2000

My all time favorite thing to do
Is snuggle up real close to you
Take me home and you will see
How much fun a hug can be!

| Version | Issue Dates | Price Paid | Market Value |
|---|---|---|---|
| Original | March 2001-May 2001 | | 7 $14 |

## 185

# Midnight™

Black Panther • #4355
Issued: May 1, 2001
Current - Easy To Find

Birthdate: December 23, 2000

Walking silent through the street
Always keeping out of sight
Not a single noise or sound
This is how he moves around!

| Version | Issue Dates | Price Paid | Market Value |
|---|---|---|---|
| Original | May 2001-Current | | 7 $________ |

| Page Totals | Price Paid | Market Value |
|---|---|---|
| | | |

# Millennium™ 186

Bear • #4226
Issued: January 1, 1999
Retired: November 12, 1999

Birthdate: January 1, 1999

A brand new century has come to call
Health and happiness to one and all
Bring on the fireworks and all the fun
Let's keep the party going 'til 2001!

| Version | Issue Dates | Price Paid | Market Value |
|---|---|---|---|
| A. "Millennium™" On Both Tags | Early 1999-Nov. 1999 | | 5 $13 |
| B. "Millenium™" Swing Tag & "Millennium™" Tush Tag | Early 1999 | | 5 $15 |
| C. "Millenium™" On Both Tags | Jan. 1999-Early 1999 | | 5 $15 |

# Mistletoe™ 187

New!

Bear • #4500
Issued: October 1, 2001
Current - Just Released

Birthdate: December 18, 2000

If you see some mistletoe
Take a chance and stand below
The custom is that if you do
You might just get a kiss or two!

| Version | Issue Dates | Price Paid | Market Value |
|---|---|---|---|
| Original | Oct. 2001-Current | | 7 $________ |

# Monkey 188

**(Zodiac Collection™)**

Monkey • #4328
Issued: August 19, 2000
Retired: May 8, 2001

Years Of The Monkey: 1944, 1956, 1968, 1980, 1992, 2004

Intelligent and enthusiastic achiever
Easily able to influence people
Seek a dragon or rat
Avoid tigers!

| Version | Issue Dates | Price Paid | Market Value |
|---|---|---|---|
| Original | Aug. 2000-May 2001 | | 2 $9 |

| Page Totals | Price Paid | Market Value |
|---|---|---|
| | | |

189

## Mooch™

Spider Monkey • #4224
Issued: January 1, 1999
Retired: December 23, 1999

Birthdate: August 1, 1998

Look in the treetops, up towards the sky
Swinging from branches way up high
Tempt him with a banana or fruit
When he's hungry, he acts so cute!

| Version | Issue Dates | Price Paid | Market Value |
|---|---|---|---|
| Original | Jan. 1999-Dec. 1999 | | 5 $10 |

190

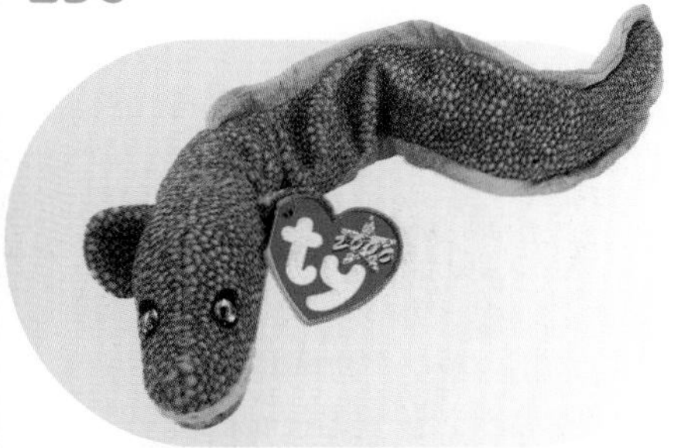

## Morrie™

Eel • #4282
Issued: February 13, 2000
Retired: December 15, 2000

Birthdate: February 20, 2000

Over, under, upside and down
Morrie loves to swim all around
He looks like a snake - could be a fish
To be your best friend is his only wish!

| Version | Issue Dates | Price Paid | Market Value |
|---|---|---|---|
| Original | Feb. 2000-Dec. 2000 | | 6 $10 |

191

## Mr.™

Bear • #4363
Issued: June 1, 2001
Current - Moderate To Find

Birthdate: N/A

All dressed up in black and white
Friends and family here tonight
Now our vows have all been said
With this ring, I thee wed!

| Version | Issue Dates | Price Paid | Market Value |
|---|---|---|---|
| Original | June 2001-Current | | 7 $________ |

| Page Totals | Price Paid | Market Value |
|---|---|---|
| | | |

## Mrs.™

192

Bear • #4364
Issued: June 1, 2001
Current – Moderate To Find

Birthdate: N/A

All dressed up in satin and lace
A special day, a special place
Let's begin our brand new life
As we're pronounced man and wife!

| Version | Issue Dates | Price Paid | Market Value |
|---|---|---|---|
| Original | June 2001-Current | | 7 $________ |

## Mystic™

193

Unicorn • #4007
Issued: June 25, 1994
Retired: May 18, 1999

Birthdate: May 21, 1994

Once upon a time so far away
A unicorn was born one day in May
Keep Mystic with you, she's a prize
You'll see the magic in her blue eyes!

B

C

D

A

| Version | Issue Dates | Price Paid | Market Value |
|---|---|---|---|
| A. Iridescent Horn/Fluffy Mane | Jan. 1999-May 1999 | | 5 $12 |
| B. Iridescent Horn/Coarse Mane | Oct. 1997-Dec. 1998 | | 5 $12  4 $12 |
| C. Brown Horn/Coarse Mane | Est. Late 1995-Oct. 1997 | | 4 $20  3 $90 |
| D. Brown Horn/Fine Mane | Est. June 1994-Late 1995 | | 3 $240  2 $340  1 $420 |

## Nana™

194

**(name changed to "Bongo™")**

Monkey • #4067
Issued: June 3, 1995
Retired: 1995

Birthdate: N/A

No Poem

| Version | Issue Dates | Price Paid | Market Value |
|---|---|---|---|
| Original | June 1995-1995 | | 3 $2,700 |

| Page Totals | Price Paid | Market Value |
|---|---|---|
| | | |

## 195

# Nanook™

Husky · #4104
Issued: May 11, 1997
Retired: March 31, 1999

Birthdate: November 21, 1996

Nanook is a dog that loves cold weather
To him a sled is light as a feather
Over the snow and through the slush
He runs at hearing the cry of "mush"!

| Version | Issue Dates | Price Paid | Market Value |
|---|---|---|---|
| Original | May 1997-March 1999 | | (5) $10 (4) $10 |

## 196

# Nectar™

Hummingbird · #4361
Issued: May 1, 2001
Retired: May 21, 2001

Birthdate: July 30, 2000

The smallest bird you'll ever see
Flies as swiftly as can be
You might miss her if you blink
She moves faster than you think!

| Version | Issue Dates | Price Paid | Market Value |
|---|---|---|---|
| Original | May 2001-May 2001 | | (7) $28 |

## 197

# Neon™

Seahorse · #4239
Issued: April 8, 1999
Retired: December 23, 1999

Birthdate: April 1, 1999

Born in shallow water in a sea grass bay
Their eyes can swivel and look every way
Walk down the beach on a bright sunny day
Jump into the sea and watch them play!

| Version | Issue Dates | Price Paid | Market Value |
|---|---|---|---|
| Original | April 1999-Dec. 1999 | | (5) $10 |

| Page Totals | Price Paid | Market Value |
|---|---|---|
| | | |

## Nibbler™ 198

Rabbit • #4216
Issued: January 1, 1999
Retired: July 9, 1999

Birthdate: April 6, 1998

Twitching her nose, she looks so sweet
Small in size, she's very petite
Soft and furry, hopping with grace
She'll visit your garden, her favorite place!

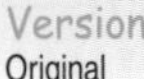

| Version | Issue Dates | Price Paid | Market Value |
|---|---|---|---|
| Original | Jan. 1999-July 1999 | | 5 $11 |

## Nibbly™ 199

Rabbit • #4217
Issued: January 1, 1999
Retired: July 20, 1999

Birthdate: May 7, 1998

Wonderful ways to spend a day
Bright and sunny in the month of May
Hopping around as trees sway
Looking for friends, out to play!

| Version | Issue Dates | Price Paid | Market Value |
|---|---|---|---|
| Original | Jan. 1999-July 1999 | | 5 $11 |

## Niles™ 200

Camel • #4284
Issued: February 13, 2000
Retired: March 14, 2001

Birthdate: February 1, 2000

The desert is a dry, hot land
Filled with lots and lots of sand
But I can still have so much fun
As long as we play in the sun!

| Version | Issue Dates | Price Paid | Market Value |
|---|---|---|---|
| Original | Feb. 2000-March 2001 | | 6 $8 |

## 201

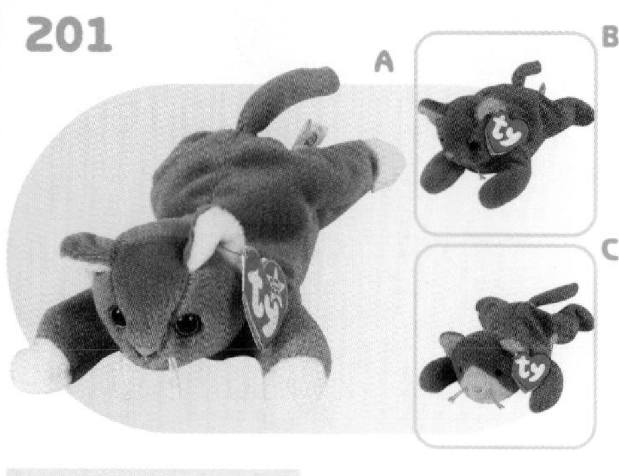


# Nip™

Cat • #4003
Issued: January 7, 1995
Retired: December 31, 1997

Birthdate: March 6, 1994

His name is Nipper, but we call him Nip
His best friend is a black cat named Zip
Nip likes to run in races for fun
He runs so fast he's always number one!

| Version | Issue Dates | Price Paid | Market Value |
|---|---|---|---|
| A. White Paws | March 1996-Dec. 1997 | | 5 $15 4 $15 3 $120 |
| B. All Gold | Jan. 1996-March 1996 | | 3 $500 |
| C. White Face | Jan. 1995-Jan. 1996 | | 3 $400 2 $440 |

## 202

# Nipponia™ ニッポニア™

**(exclusive to Japan)**

Bear • #4605
Issued: September 5, 2000
Retired: March 21, 2001
Birthdate: September 15, 2000

Poem Translation

The new morning has come
Let's get out from the small Island
And shine on the world with everybody

お誕生日：2000年9月15日
さぁ、新しい朝が来た
小さな島をとびだして
世界を照らそう
みんなと一緒に

| Version | Issue Dates | Price Paid | Market Value (in U.S. market) |
|---|---|---|---|
| Original | Sept. 2000-March 2001 | | 6 $100 |

## 203

New!

# November™

Bear • #4386
Issued: October 1, 2001
Current - Just Released

Birthdate: N/A

My nose is the color of my birthstone.
Topaz
It brings courage,
honor and optimism!

| Version | Issue Dates | Price Paid | Market Value |
|---|---|---|---|
| Original | Oct. 2001-Current | | 7 $________ |

| Page Totals | Price Paid | Market Value |
|---|---|---|
| | | |

# Nuts™

204

Squirrel · #4114
Issued: January 1, 1997
Retired: December 31, 1998

Birthdate: January 21, 1996

With his bushy tail, he'll scamper up a tree
The most cheerful critter you'll ever see,
He's nuts about nuts, and he loves to chat
Have you ever seen a squirrel like that?

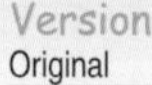

| Version | Issue Dates | Price Paid | Market Value |
|---|---|---|---|
| Original | Jan. 1997-Dec. 1998 | | 5 $9 4 $10 |

# Oats™

205

Horse · #4305
Issued: July 8, 2000
Retired: June 18, 2001

Birthdate: July 5, 2000

Hop on my back, we'll have a ball
Just hold on tight, so you won't fall
Over hills and trails we'll go
I won't stop 'till you say "whoa!"

| Version | Issue Dates | Price Paid | Market Value |
|---|---|---|---|
| Original | July 2000-June 2001 | | 6 $9 |

# October™

206

New!

**(Birthday Beanies Collection™)**

Bear · #4380
Issued: September 3, 2001
Current - Just Released

Birthdate: N/A

My nose is the color of my birthstone.
Opal
It brings sensitivity,
patience and innocence!

| Version | Issue Dates | Price Paid | Market Value |
|---|---|---|---|
| Original | Sept. 2001-Current | | 7 $________ |

| Page Totals | Price Paid | Market Value |
|---|---|---|
| | | |

207

## Osito™

**(exclusive to the United States)**

Bear • #4244
Issued: April 17, 1999
Retired: November 30, 1999

Birthdate: February 5, 1999

Across the waters of the Rio Grande
Lies a beautiful and mystic land
A place we all should plan to go
Known by all as Mexico!

| Version | Issue Dates | Price Paid | Market Value |
|---|---|---|---|
| Original | April 1999-Nov. 1999 | | 5 $15 |

208

## Ox

**(Zodiac Collection™)**

Ox • #4319
Issued: August 19, 2000
Retired: May 8, 2001

Years Of The Ox: 1937, 1949, 1961, 1973, 1985, 1997

Bright, patient and inspiring to others
Often makes an outstanding parent
Snake and rooster suit your temperament
The goat will bring you trouble!

| Version | Issue Dates | Price Paid | Market Value |
|---|---|---|---|
| Original | Aug. 2000-May 2001 | | 2 $9 |

209

A B

## Patriot™

**(exclusive to the United States)**

Bear • #4360
Issued: May 1, 2001
Retired: June 20, 2001

Birthdate: May 29, 2000

I'm proud to wear flag USA
I wear it each and every day
I think we all should celebrate
Because our country is so great!

| Version | Issue Dates | Price Paid | Market Value |
|---|---|---|---|
| A. Flag on left foot | May 2001-June 2001 | | 7 $18 |
| B. Flag on right foot | May 2001-June 2001 | | 7 $14 |

| Page Totals | Price Paid | Market Value |
|---|---|---|
| | | |

## Patti™

210

Platypus · #4025
Issued: January 8, 1994
Retired: May 1, 1998

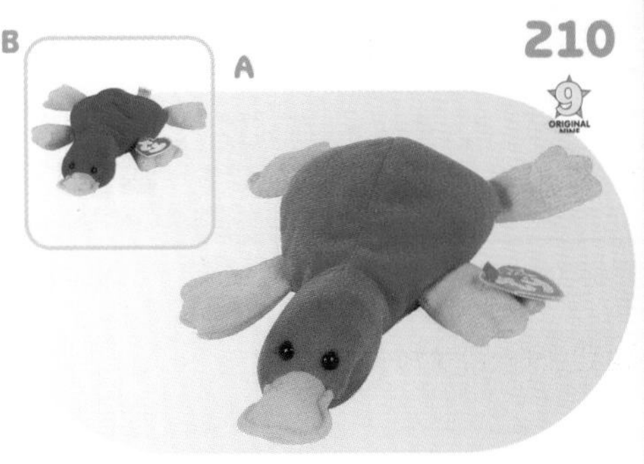


Birthdate: January 6, 1993

Ran into Patti one day while walking
Believe me she wouldn't stop talking
Listened and listened to her speak
That would explain her extra large beak!

| Version | Issue Dates | Price Paid | Market Value |
|---|---|---|---|
| A. Magenta | Feb. 1995-May 1998 | | ⑤ $16 ④ $20 ③ $115 |
| B. Maroon | Jan. 1994-Feb. 1995 | | ③ $450 ② $500 ① $600 |

## Paul™

211

Walrus · #4248
Issued: April 12, 1999
Retired: December 23, 1999

Birthdate: February 23, 1999

Traveling the ocean in a submarine
Singing and playing a tambourine
One day hoping to lead a band
First he needs to find dry land!

| Version | Issue Dates | Price Paid | Market Value |
|---|---|---|---|
| Original | April 1999-Dec. 1999 | | ⑤ $9 |

## Peace™

212

Bear · #4053
Issued: May 11, 1997
Retired: July 14, 1999

Birthdate: February 1, 1996

All races, all colors, under the sun
Join hands together and have some fun
Dance to the music, rock and roll is the sound
Symbols of peace and love abound!

| Version | Issue Dates | Price Paid | Market Value |
|---|---|---|---|
| Original | May 1997-July 1999 | | ⑤ $18 ④ $20 |

## 213

A B

### Peanut™

Elephant · #4062
Issued: June 3, 1995
Retired: May 1, 1998

Birthdate: January 25, 1995

Peanut the elephant walks on tip-toes
Quietly sneaking wherever she goes
She'll sneak up on you and a hug
You will get
Peanut is a friend you won't soon forget!

| Version | Issue Dates | Price Paid | Market Value |
|---|---|---|---|
| A. Light Blue | Oct. 1995-May 1998 | | (5) $18 (4) $22<br>(3) $360 |
| B. Dark Blue | June 1995-Oct. 1995 | | (3) $3,400 |

## 214

### Pecan™

Bear · #4251
Issued: April 8, 1999
Retired: December 23, 1999

Birthdate: April 15, 1999

In late fall, as wind gusts blow
Pecan hibernates before winter snow
In early spring, sweet scent of a flower
Wakes her up to take a shower!

| Version | Issue Dates | Price Paid | Market Value |
|---|---|---|---|
| Original | April 1999-Dec. 1999 | | (5) $9 |

## 215

### Peekaboo™

Turtle · #4303
Issued: June 24, 2000
Retired: April 19, 2001

Birthdate: April 11, 2000

Underneath my shell I hide
I try to keep my head inside
If you'll be my friend today
I'll come out so we can play!

| Version | Issue Dates | Price Paid | Market Value |
|---|---|---|---|
| Original | June 2000-April 2001 | | (6) $9 |

| Page Totals | Price Paid | Market Value |
|---|---|---|
| | | |

## Peking™ 216

Panda • #4013
Issued: June 25, 1994
Retired: January 7, 1996

Birthdate: N/A

No Poem

| Version | Issue Dates | Price Paid | Market Value |
|---|---|---|---|
| Original | June 1994-Jan 1996 | | (3) $1,000 (2) $1,150 (1) $1,500 |

## Pellet™ 217

Hamster • #4313
Issued: July 8, 2000
Retired: June 20, 2001

Birthdate: July 29, 2000

I have many things to do
But it seems I'm never through
On my wheel I spin all day
That is how I love to play!

| Version | Issue Dates | Price Paid | Market Value |
|---|---|---|---|
| Original | July 2000-June 2001 | | (6) $10 |

## Periwinkle™ 218

E-Beanie • #4400
Issued: December 1, 2000
Retired: December 8, 2000

Birthdate: February 8, 2000

Into cyberspace I go
Where I'll end up, I don't know
It's such a thrill, a wild ride
I'll keep Periwinkle by my side!

| Version | Issue Dates | Price Paid | Market Value |
|---|---|---|---|
| Original | Dec. 2000-Dec. 2000 | | (6) $20 |

219

## Pierre™

**(exclusive to Canada)**

Bear • #4607
Issued: August 13, 2001
Current - Impossible To Find

Birthdate: May 4, 2001

I am Pierre the Canadian bear
My country's flag I proudly wear
My hope for all from sea to sea:
That Canadians live in harmony!

| Version | Issue Dates | Price Paid | Market Value (in U.S. market) |
| --- | --- | --- | --- |
| Original | Aug. 2001-Current | | 7 $70 |

220

## Pig

**(Zodiac Collection™)**

Pig • #4327
Issued: August 19, 2000
Retired: May 11, 2001

Years Of The Pig: 1947, 1959, 1971, 1983, 1995, 2007

Often noble and chivalrous
Your friends will be life-long
Marry a rabbit or goat
The snake is your enemy!

| Version | Issue Dates | Price Paid | Market Value |
| --- | --- | --- | --- |
| Original | Aug. 2000-May 2001 | | 2 $9 |

221

A

B

The Beanie Babies Collection
Punchers ™ style 4026
© 1993 Ty Inc. Oakbrook, IL. USA
All Rights Reserved. Caution:
Remove this tag before giving
toy to a child. For ages 5 and up.
Handmade in Korea.
Surface
Wash.

## Pinchers™

Lobster • #4026
Issued: January 8, 1994
Retired: May 1, 1998

Birthdate: June 19, 1993

This lobster loves to pinch
Eating his food inch by inch
Balancing carefully with his tail
Moving forward slow as a snail!

| Version | Issue Dates | Price Paid | Market Value |
| --- | --- | --- | --- |
| A. "Pinchers™" Swing Tag | Jan. 1994-May 1998 | | 5 $16, 4 $16, 3 $80, 2 $350, 1 $600 |
| B. "Punchers™" Swing Tag | Est. Early 1994 | | 1 $2,200 |

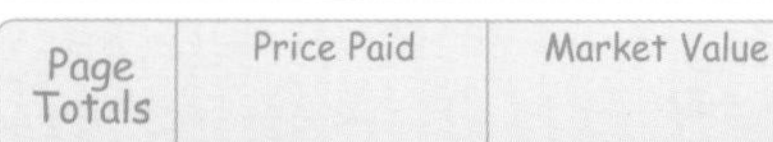

## Pinky™

222

Flamingo · #4072
Issued: June 3, 1995
Retired: December 31, 1998

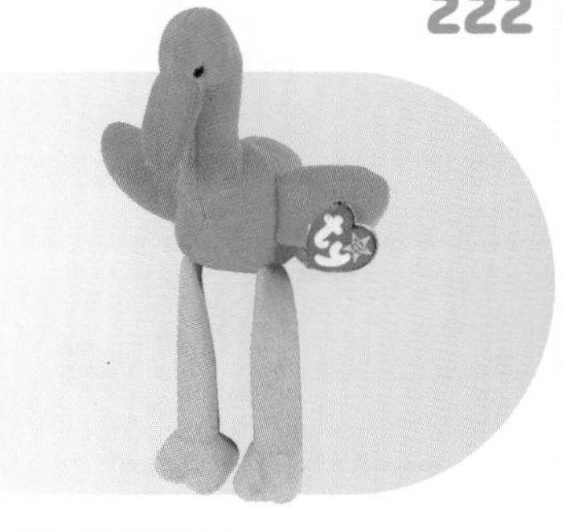

Birthdate: February 13, 1995

Pinky loves the everglades
From the hottest pink she's made
With floppy legs and big orange beak
She's the Beanie that you seek!

| Version | Issue Dates | Price Paid | Market Value |
|---|---|---|---|
| Original | June 1995-Dec. 1998 | | 5 $9 4 $9 3 $75 |

## Poopsie™

223

Bear · #4381
Issued: July 31, 2001
Current - Hard To Find

Birthdate: March 31, 2001

I'm a bear who's sweet as honey
I'm also cute and very funny
Take me home, we'll laugh and play
'Cause by your side is where I'll stay!

| Version | Issue Dates | Price Paid | Market Value |
|---|---|---|---|
| Original | July 2001-Current | | 7 $________ |

## Poseidon™

224

Whale Shark · #4356
Issued: May 1, 2001
Retired: July 25, 2001

Birthdate: September 14, 2000

He sports a rather silly grin
Wearing spots from head to fin
Look around and you'll agree
Nothing's bigger in the sea!

| Version | Issue Dates | Price Paid | Market Value |
|---|---|---|---|
| Original | May 2001-July 2001 | | 7 $11 |

225

## Pouch™

Kangaroo · #4161
Issued: January 1, 1997
Retired: March 31, 1999

Birthdate: November 6, 1996

My little pouch is handy I've found
It helps me carry my baby around
I hop up and down without any fear
Knowing my baby is safe and near.

| Version | Issue Dates | Price Paid | Market Value |
|---|---|---|---|
| Original | Jan. 1997-March 1999 | | 5 $10 4 $10 |

226

## Pounce™

Cat · #4122
Issued: December 31, 1997
Retired: March 31, 1999

Birthdate: August 28, 1997

Sneaking and slinking down the hall
To pounce upon a fluffy yarn ball
Under the tables, around the chairs
Through the rooms and down the stairs!

| Version | Issue Dates | Price Paid | Market Value |
|---|---|---|---|
| Original | Dec. 1997-March 1999 | | 5 $9 |

227

## Prance™

Cat · #4123
Issued: December 31, 1997
Retired: March 31, 1999

Birthdate: November 20, 1997

She darts around and swats the air
Then looks confused when nothing's there
Pick her up and pet her soft fur
Listen closely, and you'll hear her purr!

| Version | Issue Dates | Price Paid | Market Value |
|---|---|---|---|
| Original | Dec. 1997-March 1999 | | 5 $9 |

| Page Totals | Price Paid | Market Value |
|---|---|---|
| | | |

## Prickles™ 228

Hedgehog · #4220
Issued: January 1, 1999
Retired: December 23, 1999

Birthdate: February 19, 1998

Prickles the hedgehog loves to play
She rolls around the meadow all day
Tucking under her feet and head
Suddenly she looks like a ball instead!

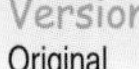
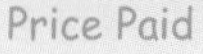

| Version | Issue Dates | Price Paid | Market Value |
|---|---|---|---|
| Original | Jan. 1999-Dec. 1999 | | ⑤ $9 |

## Prince™ 229

Frog · #4312
Issued: July 8, 2000
Retired: June 20, 2001

Birthdate: July 3, 2000

Sitting on a lily pad
I'm all alone and feeling sad
So won't you be a friend to me
And let me jump upon your knee!

| Version | Issue Dates | Price Paid | Market Value |
|---|---|---|---|
| Original | July 2000-June 2001 | | ⑥ $9 |

## Princess™ 230

Bear · #4300
Issued: October 29, 1997
Retired: April 13, 1999

Birthdate: N/A

Like an angel, she came from heaven above
She shared her compassion, her pain, her love
She only stayed with us long enough to teach
The world to share, to give, to reach.

| Version | Issue Dates | Price Paid | Market Value |
|---|---|---|---|
| A. "P.E. Pellets" On Tush Tag | Est. Late 1997-April 1999 | | ④ $23 |
| B. "P.V.C. Pellets" On Tush Tag | Est. Late 1997 | | ④ $50 |

| Page Totals | Price Paid | Market Value |
|---|---|---|
| | | |

231

## Propeller™

Flying Fish • #4366
Issued: June 1, 2001
Retired: July 12, 2001

Birthdate: August 8, 2000

In the water and the air
He can go most anywhere
Propelling out into the sky
We can watch him sail on by!

| Version | Issue Dates | Price Paid | Market Value |
|---|---|---|---|
| Original | June 2001-July 2001 | | 7 $11 |

232

## Puffer™

Puffin • #4181
Issued: December 31, 1997
Retired: September 18, 1998

Birthdate: November 3, 1997

What in the world does a puffin do?
We're sure that you would like to know too
We asked Puffer how she spends her days
Before she answered, she flew away!

| Version | Issue Dates | Price Paid | Market Value |
|---|---|---|---|
| Original | Dec. 1997-Sept. 1998 | | 5 $9 |

233

## Pugsly™

Pug Dog • #4106
Issued: May 11, 1997
Retired: March 31, 1999

Birthdate: May 2, 1996

Pugsly is picky about what he will wear
Never a spot, a stain or a tear
Image is something of which he'll gloat
Until he noticed his wrinkled coat!

| Version | Issue Dates | Price Paid | Market Value |
|---|---|---|---|
| Original | May 1997-March 1999 | | 5 $12  4 $12 |

| Page Totals | Price Paid | Market Value |
|---|---|---|
| | | |

## Purr™ 234

Kitten · #4346
Issued: March 1, 2001
Retired: June 18, 2001

Birthdate: March 18, 2000

Today feels like a lazy day
I don't even want to play
I won't try to catch a mouse
I'll just lay around the house.

| Version | Issue Dates | Price Paid | Market Value |
|---|---|---|---|
| Original | March 2001-June 2001 | | (7) $12 |

## Pumkin'™ 235

Pumpkin · #4205
Issued: September 30, 1998
Retired: December 31, 1998

Birthdate: October 31, 1998

Ghost and goblins are out tonight
Witches try hard to cause fright
This little pumpkin is very sweet
He only wants to trick or treat!

| Version | Issue Dates | Price Paid | Market Value |
|---|---|---|---|
| Original | Sept. 1998-Dec. 1998 | | (5) $20 |

## Quackers™ 236

Duck · #4024
Issued: June 25, 1994
Retired: May 1, 1998

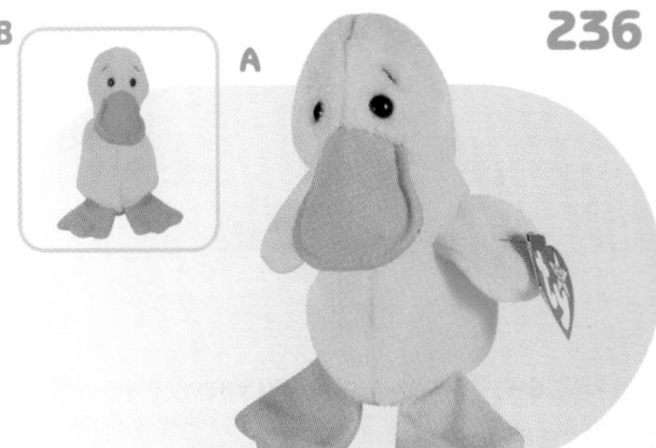

Birthdate: April 19, 1994

There is a duck by the name of Quackers
Every night he eats animal crackers
He swims in a lake that's clear and blue
But he'll come to the shore to be with you!

| Version | Issue Dates | Price Paid | Market Value |
|---|---|---|---|
| A. "Quackers™" With Wings | Jan. 1995-May 1998 | | (5) $14 (4) $14 (3) $68 (2) $415 |
| B. "Quacker™" Without Wings | June 1994-Jan. 1995 | | (2) $1,100 (1) $1,500 |

| Page Totals | Price Paid | Market Value |
|---|---|---|
| | | |

## 237

## Radar™

Bat • #4091
Issued: September 1, 1995
Retired: May 11, 1997

Birthdate: October 30, 1995

Radar the bat flies late at night
He can soar to an amazing height
If you see something as high as a star
Take a good look, it might be Radar!

| Version | Issue Dates | Price Paid | Market Value |
|---|---|---|---|
| Original | Sept. 1995-May 1997 | | (4) $88 (3) $125 |

## 238

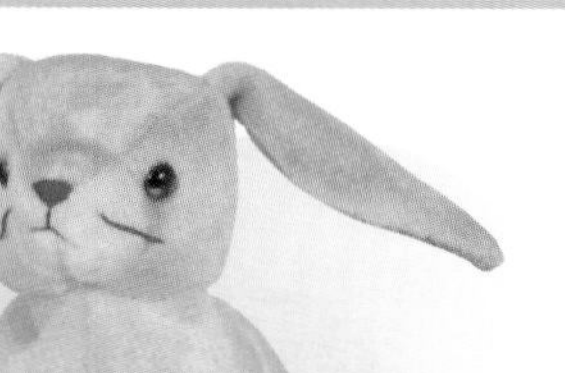

## Rabbit

**(Zodiac Collection™)**

Rabbit • #4321
Issued: August 19, 2000
Retired: May 24, 2001

Years Of The Rabbit: 1939, 1951, 1963, 1975, 1987, 1999

You are the luckiest of all signs
Talented, affectionate yet shy
Marry a goat or pig
The rooster is your enemy!

| Version | Issue Dates | Price Paid | Market Value |
|---|---|---|---|
| Original | Aug. 2000-May 2001 | | (2) $9 |

## 239

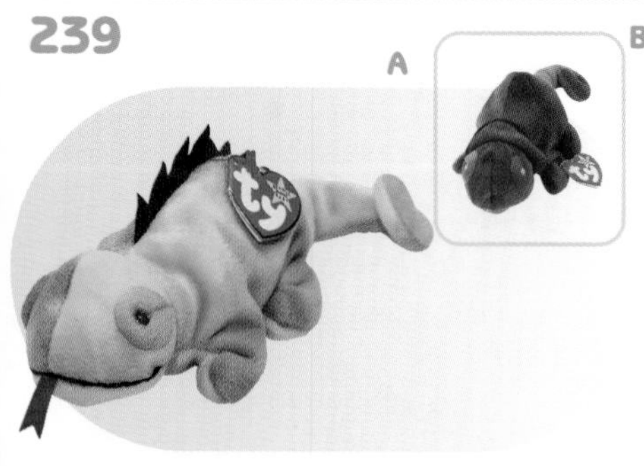


## Rainbow™

Chameleon • #4037
Issued: December 31, 1997
Retired: March 31, 1999

Birthdate: October 14, 1997

Red, green, blue and yellow
This chameleon is a colorful fellow.
A blend of colors, his own unique hue
Rainbow was made especially for you!

| Version | Issue Dates | Price Paid | Market Value |
|---|---|---|---|
| A. Ty-dye/With Tongue | Mid 1998-March 1999 | | (5) $12 |
| B. Blue/No Tongue | Dec. 1997-Mid 1998 | | (5) $11 |

| Page Totals | Price Paid | Market Value |
|---|---|---|
| | | |

# Rat

240

**(Zodiac Collection™)**

Rat • #4318
Issued: August 19, 2000
Retired: May 29, 2001

Years Of The Rat: 1936, 1948, 1960, 1972, 1984, 1996

Ambitious yet honest
Prone to spend freely
Seldom makes lasting friendships
Marry a dragon or monkey
Avoid horses!

| Version | Issue Dates | Price Paid | Market Value |
|---|---|---|---|
| Original | Aug. 2000-May 2001 | | 2 $9 |

# Regal™

241

King Charles Spaniel • #4358
Issued: May 1, 2001
Retired: October 8, 2001

Birthdate: November 11, 2000

It's not easy being King
I just want to do my thing
I would rather jump and play
Than sit on my throne today!

| Version | Issue Dates | Price Paid | Market Value |
|---|---|---|---|
| Original | May 2001-Oct. 2001 | | 7 $10 |

# Rex™

242

Tyrannosaurus • #4086
Issued: June 3, 1995
Retired: June 15, 1996

Birthdate: N/A

No Poem

| Version | Issue Dates | Price Paid | Market Value |
|---|---|---|---|
| Original | June 1995-June 1996 | | 3 $500 |

243

## Righty™

Elephant · #4086
Issued: June 15, 1996
Retired: January 1, 1997

Birthdate: July 4, 1996

Donkeys to the left, elephants to the right
Often seems like a crazy sight
This whole game seems very funny
Until you realize they're spending
Your money!

| Version | Issue Dates | Price Paid | Market Value |
|---|---|---|---|
| Original | June 1996-Jan. 1997 | | ④ $170 |

244

## Righty 2000™

**(exclusive to the United States)**

Elephant · #4289
Issued: June 24, 2000
Retired: December 21, 2000

Birthdate: July 4, 2000

On and on the race will go
Who will win we just don't know
No matter how this all will end
You will always be my friend!

| Version | Issue Dates | Price Paid | Market Value |
|---|---|---|---|
| Original | June 2000-Dec. 2000 | | ⑥ $17 |

245

## Ringo™

Raccoon · #4014
Issued: January 7, 1996
Retired: September 16, 1998

Birthdate: July 14, 1995

Ringo hides behind his mask
He will come out, if you should ask
He loves to chitter. He loves to chatter
Just about anything, it doesn't matter!

| Version | Issue Dates | Price Paid | Market Value |
|---|---|---|---|
| Original | Jan. 1996-Sept. 1998 | | ⑤ $11 ④ $13 ③ $60 |

| Page Totals | Price Paid | Market Value |
|---|---|---|
| | | |

## Roam™ 246

Buffalo · #4209
Issued: September 30, 1998
Retired: December 23, 1999

Birthdate: September 27, 1998

Once roaming wild on American land
Tall and strong, wooly and grand
So rare and special is this guy
Find him quickly, he's quite a buy!

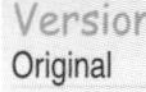

| Version | Issue Dates | Price Paid | Market Value |
|---|---|---|---|
| Original | Sept. 1998-Dec. 1999 | | ⑤ $9 |

## Roary™ 247

Lion · #4069
Issued: May 11, 1997
Retired: December 31, 1998

Birthdate: February 20, 1996

Deep in the jungle they crowned him king
But being brave is not his thing
A cowardly lion some may say
He hears his roar and runs away!

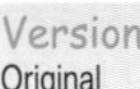

| Version | Issue Dates | Price Paid | Market Value |
|---|---|---|---|
| Original | May 1997-Dec. 1998 | | ⑤ $11 ④ $13 |

## Rocket™ 248

Blue Jay · #4202
Issued: May 30, 1998
Retired: December 23, 1999

Birthdate: March 12, 1997

Rocket is the fastest blue jay ever
He flies in all sorts of weather
Aerial tricks are his specialty
He's so entertaining for you and me!

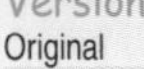

| Version | Issue Dates | Price Paid | Market Value |
|---|---|---|---|
| Original | May 1998-Dec. 1999 | | ⑤ $10 |

| Page Totals | Price Paid | Market Value |
|---|---|---|
| | | |

249

## Rooster
**(Zodiac Collection™)**

Rooster • #4325
Issued: August 19, 2000
Retired: May 11, 2001

Years Of The Rooster: 1945, 1957, 1969, 1981, 1993, 2005

You are intelligent and devoted to work
Can be selfish and eccentric
Snakes and oxen are good for you
Rabbits are trouble!

| Version | Issue Dates | Price Paid | Market Value |
|---|---|---|---|
| Original | Aug. 2000-May 2001 | | (2) $9 |

250

## Rover™

Dog • #4101
Issued: June 15, 1996
Retired: May 1, 1998

Birthdate: May 30, 1996

This dog is red and his name is Rover
If you call him he is sure to come over
He barks and plays with all his might
But worry not, he won't bite!

| Version | Issue Dates | Price Paid | Market Value |
|---|---|---|---|
| Original | June 1996-May 1998 | | (5) $15 (4) $19 |

251

A B

## Roxie™

Reindeer • #4334
Issued: September 28, 2000
Retired: December 12, 2000

Birthdate: December 1, 2000

Once every year I pull a sleigh
Come with me on that special day
We will soar high in the sky
Because you know reindeer can fly!

| Version | Issue Dates | Price Paid | Market Value |
|---|---|---|---|
| A. Red Nose | Sept. 2000-Dec. 2000 | | (6) $20 |
| B. Black Nose | Sept. 2000-Dec. 2000 | | (6) $14 |

| Page Totals | Price Paid | Market Value |
|---|---|---|
| | | |

## Rufus™

252

Dog · #4280
Issued: February 13, 2000
Retired: June 11, 2001

Birthdate: February 28, 2000

Smart and friendly as can be
I'm really cute as you can see
Play with me, we'll have some fun
Throw a ball and watch me run!

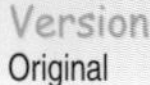

| Version | Issue Dates | Price Paid | Market Value |
|---|---|---|---|
| Original | Feb. 2000-June 2001 | | 6 $9 |

## Runner™

253

Mustelidae · #4304
Issued: June 24, 2000
Retired: April 11, 2001

B

A

Birthdate: May 25, 2000

A ferret, mongoose, weasel or mink
What am I . . . what do you think?
Find a book, look and see
I'm whatever you want me to be!

| Version | Issue Dates | Price Paid | Market Value |
|---|---|---|---|
| A. Authorized Poem | June 2000-April 2001 | | 6 $10 |
| B. Unauthorized Poem | June 2000-June 2000 | | 6 $20 |

## Sakura™ さくら™

254

**(exclusive to Japan)**

Bear · #4602
Issued: March 17, 2000
Retired: May 24, 2000

Birthdate: March 25, 2000

わたしは日本の宝物
あなたに春と愛を運んでくるよ
抱きしめられたら心が暖まって
ほら、花が咲いた

Poem Translation

I'm the treasure of Japan
I will bring spring and love to you
A hug will warm my heart
As you watch my flower bloom

| Version | Issue Dates | Price Paid | Market Value (in U.S. market) |
|---|---|---|---|
| Original | March 2000-May 2000 | | 6 $135 |

Beanie Babies®

255

## Sammy®

Bear • #4215
Issued: January 1, 1999
Retired: December 23, 1999

Birthdate: June 23, 1998

As Sammy steps up to the plate
The crowd gets excited, can hardly wait
We know Sammy won't let us down
He makes us the happiest fans in town!

| Version | Issue Dates | Price Paid | Market Value |
|---|---|---|---|
| Original | Jan. 1999-Dec. 1999 | | 5 $10 |

256

## Santa™

Santa • #4203
Issued: September 30, 1998
Retired: December 31, 1998

Birthdate: December 6, 1998

Known by all in his suit of red
Piles of presents on his sled
Generous and giving, he brings us joy
Peace and love, plus this special toy!

| Version | Issue Dates | Price Paid | Market Value |
|---|---|---|---|
| Original | Sept. 1998-Dec. 1998 | | 5 $25 |

257

## Sarge™

German Shepherd • #4277
Issued: February 13, 2000
Retired: April 4, 2001

Birthdate: February 14, 2000

I defend you, so count on me
To stay by your side, that's where I'll be
Protect and serve is what I do
For just a little hug from you!

| Version | Issue Dates | Price Paid | Market Value |
|---|---|---|---|
| Original | Feb. 2000-April 2001 | | 6 $10 |

| Page Totals | Price Paid | Market Value |
|---|---|---|
| | | |

## Scaly™

258

Lizard • #4263
Issued: August 31, 1999
Retired: December 23, 1999

Birthdate: February 9, 1999

I love to lie, basking in the sun
Living in the desert sure is fun
Climbing up cactus, avoiding a spike
I'm the Beanie you're sure to like!

| Version | Issue Dates | Price Paid | Market Value |
|---|---|---|---|
| Original | Aug. 1999-Dec. 1999 | | 5 $10 |

## Scary™

259

New!

Witch • #4378
Issued: September 3, 2001
Current – Just Released

Birthdate: October 25, 2000

Flying around on Halloween night
Trying so hard to give you a fright
She will not cast a spell on you
She'll just play a trick or two!

| Version | Issue Dates | Price Paid | Market Value |
|---|---|---|---|
| Original | Sept. 2001-Current | | 7 $_______ |

## Scat™

260

Cat • #4231
Issued: January 1, 1999
Retired: December 23, 1999

Birthdate: May 27, 1998

Newborn kittens require lots of sleep
Shhh . . . it's naptime, don't make a peep
Touch her fur, it feels like silk
Wake her up to drink mother's milk!

| Version | Issue Dates | Price Paid | Market Value |
|---|---|---|---|
| Original | Jan. 1999-Dec. 1999 | | 5 $9 |

261

## Schweetheart™

Orangutan • #4252
Issued: April 11, 1999
Retired: December 23, 1999

Birthdate: January 23, 1999

Of all the jungles filled with vines
Traveling about, you came to mine
Because of all the things you said
I can't seem to get you outta my head!

| Version | Issue Dates | Price Paid | Market Value |
|---|---|---|---|
| Original | April 1999-Dec. 1999 | | ⑤ $10 |

262

## Scoop™

Pelican • #4107
Issued: June 15, 1996
Retired: December 31, 1998

Birthdate: July 1, 1996

All day long he scoops up fish
To fill his bill, is his wish
Diving fast and diving low
Hoping those fish are very slow!

| Version | Issue Dates | Price Paid | Market Value |
|---|---|---|---|
| Original | June 1996-Dec. 1998 | | ⑤ $10 ④ $11 |

263

## Scorch™

Dragon • #4210
Issued: September 30, 1998
Retired: December 23, 1999

Birthdate: July 31, 1998

A magical mystery with glowing wings
Made by wizards and other things
Known to breathe fire with lots of smoke
Scorch is really a friendly ol' bloke!

| Version | Issue Dates | Price Paid | Market Value |
|---|---|---|---|
| Original | Sept. 1998-Dec. 1999 | | ⑤ $11 |

| Page Totals | Price Paid | Market Value |
|---|---|---|
| | | |

## Scottie™ 264

Scottish Terrier • #4102
Issued: June 15, 1996
Retired: May 1, 1998

Birthdate: June 3, 1996 or June 15, 1996

Scottie is a friendly sort
Even though his legs are short
He is always happy as can be
His best friends are you and me!

| Version | Issue Dates | Price Paid | Market Value |
|---|---|---|---|
| Original | June 1996-May 1998 | | ⑤ $16 ④ $16 |

## Scurry™ 265

Beetle • #4281
Issued: February 13, 2000
Retired: December 15, 2000

Birthdate: January 18, 2000

I play in the cellar with all of my friends
We laugh, we sing, the fun never ends
I hurry and scurry and hide most of the day
But if you come down, I'll stay out and play!

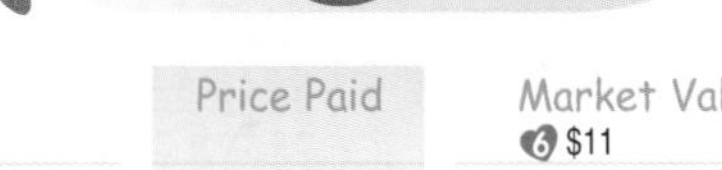

| Version | Issue Dates | Price Paid | Market Value |
|---|---|---|---|
| Original | Feb. 2000-Dec. 2000 | | ⑥ $11 |

## Seamore™ 266

Seal • #4029
Issued: June 25, 1994
Retired: October 1, 1997

Birthdate: December 14, 1996

Seamore is a little white seal
Fish and clams are her favorite meal
Playing and laughing in the sand
She's the happiest seal in the land!

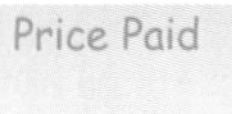

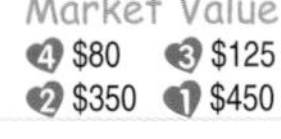

| Version | Issue Dates | Price Paid | Market Value |
|---|---|---|---|
| Original | June 1994-Oct. 1997 | | ④ $80 ③ $125 ② $350 ① $450 |

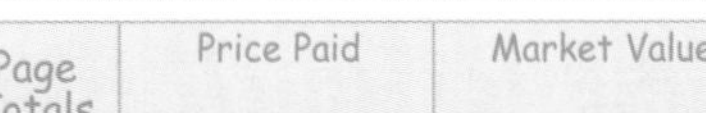

| Page Totals | Price Paid | Market Value |
|---|---|---|
| | | |

267

## Seaweed™

Otter · #4080
Issued: January 7, 1996
Retired: September 19, 1998

Birthdate: March 19, 1996

Seaweed is what she likes to eat
It's supposed to be a delicious treat
Have you tried a treat from the water
If you haven't, maybe you "otter"!

| Version | Issue Dates | Price Paid | Market Value |
|---|---|---|---|
| Original | Jan. 1996-Sept. 1998 | | 5 $16 4 $16 3 $72 |

268

## September™

**(Birthday Beanies Collection™)**

Bear · #4372
Issued: July 3, 2001
Current - Moderate To Find

Birthdate: N/A

My nose is the color of my birthstone.
Sapphire
It brings good luck and lots of $$!

| Version | Issue Dates | Price Paid | Market Value |
|---|---|---|---|
| Original | July 2001-Current | | 7 $________ |

269

## Shamrock™

Bear · #4338
Issued: January 1, 2001
Retired: March 6, 2001

Birthdate: March 17, 2000

I wear a shamrock on my chest
With good luck I have been blessed
I will share my luck with you
So all your dreams will come true!

| Version | Issue Dates | Price Paid | Market Value |
|---|---|---|---|
| Original | Jan. 2001-March 2001 | | 7 $18 |

| Page Totals | Price Paid | Market Value |
|---|---|---|
| | | |

## Sheets™ 270

Ghost • #4260
Issued: August 31, 1999
Retired: December 23, 1999

Birthdate: October 31, 1999

Living alone in a haunted house
Friend to the spider, bat and mouse
Often heard, but never seen
Waiting to wish you "Happy Halloween!"

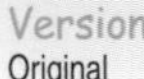

| Version | Issue Dates | Price Paid | Market Value |
|---|---|---|---|
| Original | Aug. 1999-Dec. 1999 | | (5) $10 |

## Siam™ 271

Siamese Cat • #4369
Issued: July 3, 2001
Current – Easy To Find

Birthdate: October 19, 2000

She has a rather regal air
Other cats cannot compare
Standing straight and full of pride
You can't resist her deep blue eyes!

| Version | Issue Dates | Price Paid | Market Value |
|---|---|---|---|
| Original | July 2001-Current | | (7) $________ |

## Silver™ 272

Cat • #4242
Issued: April 21, 1999
Retired: December 23, 1999

Birthdate: February 11, 1999

Curled up, sleeping in the sun
He's worn out from having fun
Chasing dust specks in the sunrays
This is how he spends his days!

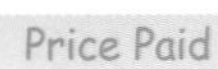

| Version | Issue Dates | Price Paid | Market Value |
|---|---|---|---|
| Original | April 1999-Dec. 1999 | | (5) $10 |

273

## Slayer™

Frilled Dragon • #4307
Issued: July 8, 2000
Retired: April 4, 2001

Birthdate: September 26, 2000

If you want to have some fun
Try to make Slayer run
Tickle his tail, then you'll know
Just how fast he can go!

| Version | Issue Dates | Price Paid | Market Value |
|---|---|---|---|
| Original | July 2000-April 2001 | | 6 $10 |

274

## Slippery™

Seal • #4222
Issued: January 1, 1999
Retired: December 23, 1999

Birthdate: January 17, 1998

In the ocean, near a breaking wave
Slippery the seal acts very brave
On his surfboard, he sees a swell
He's riding the wave! Oooops . . . he fell!

| Version | Issue Dates | Price Paid | Market Value |
|---|---|---|---|
| Original | Jan. 1999-Dec. 1999 | | 5 $10 |

275

## Slither™

Snake • #4031
Issued: June 25, 1994
Retired: June 15, 1995

Birthdate: N/A

No Poem

| Version | Issue Dates | Price Paid | Market Value |
|---|---|---|---|
| Original | June 1994-June 1995 | | 3 $900 2 $1,110 1 $1,300 |

| Page Totals | Price Paid | Market Value |
|---|---|---|
| | | |

## Slowpoke™

276

Sloth · #4261
Issued: August 31, 1999
Retired: December 23, 1999

Birthdate: May 20, 1999

Look up in the sky to the top of the tree
What in the world is that you see?
A little sloth as sweet as can be
Munching on leaves very slowly!

| Version | Issue Dates | Price Paid | Market Value |
|---|---|---|---|
| Original | Aug. 1999-Dec. 1999 | | (5) $9 |

## Sly™

277

Fox · #4115
Issued: June 15, 1996
Retired: September 22, 1998

B

A

Birthdate: September 12, 1996

Sly is a fox and tricky is he
Please don't chase him, let him be
If you want him, just say when
He'll peek out from his den!

| Version | Issue Dates | Price Paid | Market Value |
|---|---|---|---|
| A. White Belly | Aug. 1996-Sept. 1998 | | (5) $13 (4) $13 |
| B. Brown Belly | June 1996-Aug. 1996 | | (4) $90 |

## Smart™

278

Owl · #4353
Issued: April 1, 2001
Retired: May 30, 2001

Birthdate: June 7, 2000

A special song they will play
On your graduation day
Relax and smile, you're finally done
Congratulations . . . class of 2001!

| Version | Issue Dates | Price Paid | Market Value |
|---|---|---|---|
| Original | April 2001-May 2001 | | (7) $12 |

## 279

### Smooch™

Bear • #4335
Issued: January 1, 2001
Retired: February 14, 2001

Birthdate: February 14, 2000

Chocolate candy and flowers are fine
They help to say, "Will you be mine?"
But there's a better thing to do
Let me deliver kisses for you!

| Version | Issue Dates | Price Paid | Market Value |
|---|---|---|---|
| Original | Jan. 2001-Feb. 2001 | | 7 $32 |

## 280

### Smoochy™

Frog • #4039
Issued: December 31, 1997
Retired: March 31, 1999

Birthdate: October 1, 1997

Is he a frog or maybe a prince?
This confusion makes him wince
Find the answer, help him with this
Be the one to give him a kiss!

| Version | Issue Dates | Price Paid | Market Value |
|---|---|---|---|
| Original | Dec. 1997-March 1999 | | 5 $10 |

## 281

### Snake

**(Zodiac Collection™)**

Snake • #4323
Issued: August 19, 2000
Retired: May 17, 2001

Years Of The Snake: 1941, 1953, 1965, 1977, 1989, 2001

Wise, intense and very attractive
Can be vain and high tempered
Rooster and ox are your best signs
The pig is your enemy!

| Version | Issue Dates | Price Paid | Market Value |
|---|---|---|---|
| Original | Aug. 2000-May 2001 | | 2 $9 |



| Page Totals | Price Paid | Market Value |
|---|---|---|
| | | |

## Sneaky™

**282**

Leopard • #4278
Issued: February 13, 2000
Retired: April 4, 2001

Birthdate: February 22, 2000

A shadow in the dark you'll see
Don't be afraid, it's only me
My spots will hide me 'til I see
That you are just the friend for me!

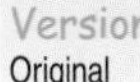

| Version | Issue Dates | Price Paid | Market Value |
|---|---|---|---|
| Original | Feb. 2000-April 2001 | | (6) $10 |

## Sniffer™

**283**

Beagle • #4299
Issued: June 24, 2000
Retired: April 24, 2001

Birthdate: May 6, 2000

When I run fast, my ears will flap
When I get tired, I sit in your lap
All through the night, I'll tickle your toes
And say I love you by licking your nose!

| Version | Issue Dates | Price Paid | Market Value |
|---|---|---|---|
| Original | June 2000-April 2001 | | (6) $10 |

## Snip™

**284**

Siamese Cat • #4120
Issued: January 1, 1997
Retired: December 31, 1998

Birthdate: October 22, 1996

Snip the cat is Siamese
She'll be your friend if you please
So toss her a toy or a piece of string
Playing with you is her favorite thing!

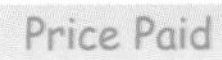

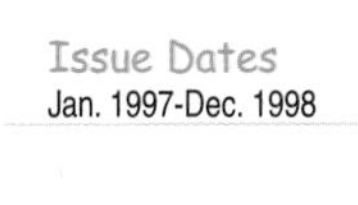

| Version | Issue Dates | Price Paid | Market Value |
|---|---|---|---|
| Original | Jan. 1997-Dec. 1998 | | (5) $10 (4) $10 |

| Page Totals | Price Paid | Market Value |
|---|---|---|
| | | |

## 285

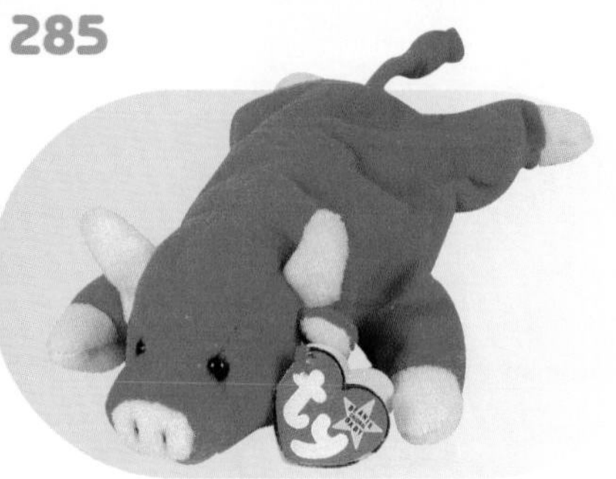

## Snort™

Bull • #4002
Issued: January 1, 1997
Retired: September 15, 1998

Birthdate: May 15, 1995

Although Snort is not so tall
He loves to play basketball
He is a star player in his dreams
Can you guess his favorite team?

| Version | Issue Dates | Price Paid | Market Value |
|---|---|---|---|
| Original | Jan. 1997-Sept. 1998 | | 5 $11 4 $13 |

## 286

## Snowball™

Snowman • #4201
Issued: October 1, 1997
Retired: December 31, 1997

Birthdate: December 22, 1996

There is a snowman, I've been told
That plays with Beanies out in the cold
What is better in a winter wonderland
Than a Beanie snowman in your hand!

| Version | Issue Dates | Price Paid | Market Value |
|---|---|---|---|
| Original | Oct. 1997-Dec. 1997 | | 4 $22 |

## 287

## Snowgirl™

Snowgirl • #4333
Issued: September 28, 2000
Retired: December 12, 2000

Birthdate: November 30, 2000

Look outside that's where I'm at
Wearing a warm scarf and hat
So even though the wind gusts blow
We can still play in the snow!

| Version | Issue Dates | Price Paid | Market Value |
|---|---|---|---|
| Original | Sept. 2000-Dec. 2000 | | 6 $16 |

| Page Totals | Price Paid | Market Value |
|---|---|---|
| | | |

## Spangle™

288

Bear • #4245
Issued: April 24, 1999
Retired: December 23, 1999

Birthdate: June 14, 1999

Stars and stripes he wears proudly
Everywhere he goes he says loudly
"Hip hip hooray, for the land of the free
There's no place on earth I'd rather be!"

| Version | Issue Dates | Price Paid | Market Value |
|---|---|---|---|
| A. White Face | Aug. 1999-Dec. 1999 | | 5 $21 |
| B. Blue Face | June 1999-Dec. 1999 | | 5 $40 |
| C. Red Face | April 1999-Dec. 1999 | | 5 $21 |

## Sparky™

289

Dalmatian • #4100
Issued: June 15, 1996
Retired: May 11, 1997

Birthdate: February 27, 1996

Sparky rides proud on the fire truck
Ringing the bell and pushing his luck
He gets under foot when trying to help
He often gets stepped on and
Lets out a yelp!

| Version | Issue Dates | Price Paid | Market Value |
|---|---|---|---|
| Original | June 1996-May 1997 | | 4 $78 |

## Speckles™

290

**(available exclusively on-line)**

e-Beanie • #4402
Issued: June 28, 2000
Current - Very Hard To Find

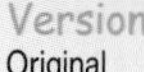

Birthdate: February 17, 2000

Surfing on the Internet
I think of friends I've never met
They're 'round the world both near and far
I hope they know how dear they are!

| Version | Issue Dates | Price Paid | Market Value |
|---|---|---|---|
| Original | June 2000-Current | | 6 $_________ |

## 291

## Speedy™

Turtle · #4030
Issued: June 25, 1994
Retired: October 1, 1997

Birthdate: August 14, 1994

Speedy ran marathons in the past
Such a shame, always last
Now Speedy is a big star
After he bought a racing car!

| Version | Issue Dates | Price Paid | Market Value |
|---|---|---|---|
| Original | June 1994-Oct. 1997 | | (4) $20 (3) $65 (2) $225 (1) $355 |

## 292

## Spike™

Rhinoceros · #4060
Issued: June 15, 1996
Retired: December 31, 1998

Birthdate: August 13, 1996

Spike the rhino likes to stampede
He's the bruiser that you need
Gentle to birds on his back and spike
You can be his friend if you like!

| Version | Issue Dates | Price Paid | Market Value |
|---|---|---|---|
| Original | June 1996-Dec. 1998 | | (5) $9 (4) $9 |

## 293

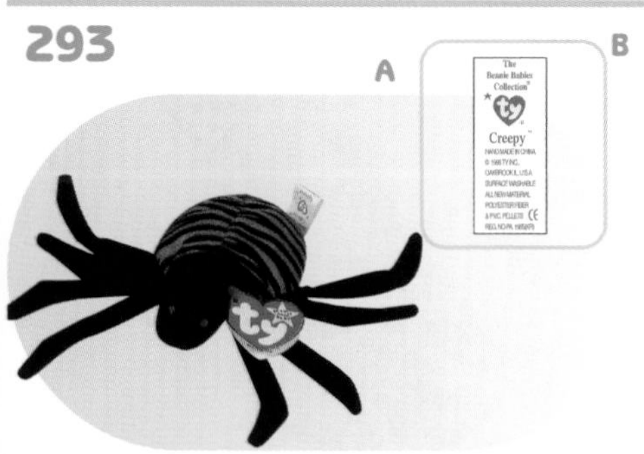


## Spinner™

Spider · #4036
Issued: October 1, 1997
Retired: September 19, 1998

Birthdate: October 28, 1996

Does this spider make you scared?
Among many people that feeling is shared
Remember spiders have feelings too
In fact, this spider really likes you!

| Version | Issue Dates | Price Paid | Market Value |
|---|---|---|---|
| A. "Spinner™" Tush Tag | Oct. 1997-Sept. 1998 | | (5) $9 (4) $9 |
| B. "Creepy™" Tush Tag | Est. Late 1997-Sept. 1998 | | (5) $35 |

| Page Totals | Price Paid | Market Value |
|---|---|---|
| | | |

## Splash™

294

Whale · #4022
Issued: January 8, 1994
Retired: May 11, 1997

Birthdate: July 8, 1993

Splash loves to jump and dive
He's the fastest whale alive
He always wins the 100 yard dash
With a victory jump he'll make a splash!

| Version | Issue Dates | Price Paid | Market Value |
|---|---|---|---|
| Original | Jan. 1994-May 1997 | | (4) $80 (3) $105 (2) $295 (1) $400 |

## Spooky™

295

Ghost · #4090
Issued: September 1, 1995
Retired: December 31, 1997

B

Spook ™ style 4090
to
from
with
love

A

Birthdate: October 31, 1995

Ghosts can be a scary sight
But don't let Spooky bring you any fright
Because when you're alone, you will see
The best friend that Spooky can be!

| Version | Issue Dates | Price Paid | Market Value |
|---|---|---|---|
| A. "Spooky™" Swing Tag | Est. Late 1995-Dec. 1997 | | (4) $26 (3) $115 |
| B. "Spook™" Swing Tag | Est. Sept. 1995-Late 1995 | | (3) $380 |

## Spot™

296

Dog · #4000
Issued: January 8, 1994
Retired: October 1, 1997

B

A

Birthdate: January 3, 1993

See Spot sprint, see Spot run
You and Spot will have lots of fun
Watch out now, because he's not slow
Just stand back and watch him go!

| Version | Issue Dates | Price Paid | Market Value |
|---|---|---|---|
| A. With Spot | April 1994-Oct. 1997 | | (4) $32 (3) $85 (2) $380 |
| B. Without Spot | Jan. 1994-April 1994 | | (2) $1,050 (1) $1,250 |

| Page Totals | Price Paid | Market Value |
|---|---|---|
| | | |

## 297

## Springy™

Bunny · #4272
Issued: February 13, 2000
Retired: July 14, 2000

Birthdate: February 29, 2000

Hopping and jumping all around
I never stay long on the ground
I might be gone for just a while
But I'll be back and make you smile!

| Version | Issue Dates | Price Paid | Market Value |
|---|---|---|---|
| Original | Feb. 2000-July 2000 | | (6) $11 |

## 298

## Spunky™

Cocker Spaniel · #4184
Issued: December 31, 1997
Retired: March 31, 1999

Birthdate: January 14, 1997

Bouncing around without much grace
To jump on your lap and lick your face
But watch him closely he has no fears
He'll run so fast he'll trip over his ears

| Version | Issue Dates | Price Paid | Market Value |
|---|---|---|---|
| Original | Dec. 1997-March 1999 | | (5) $12 |

## 299

## Squealer™

Pig · #4005
Issued: January 8, 1994
Retired: May 1, 1998

Birthdate: April 23, 1993

Squealer likes to joke around
He is known as class clown
Listen to his stories awhile
There is no doubt he'll make you smile!

| Version | Issue Dates | Price Paid | Market Value |
|---|---|---|---|
| Original | Jan. 1994-May 1998 | | (5) $15 (4) $19 (3) $67 (2) $225 (1) $375 |

| Page Totals | Price Paid | Market Value |
|---|---|---|
| | | |

## Squirmy™ 300

Worm · #4302
Issued: June 24, 2000
Retired: December 15, 2000

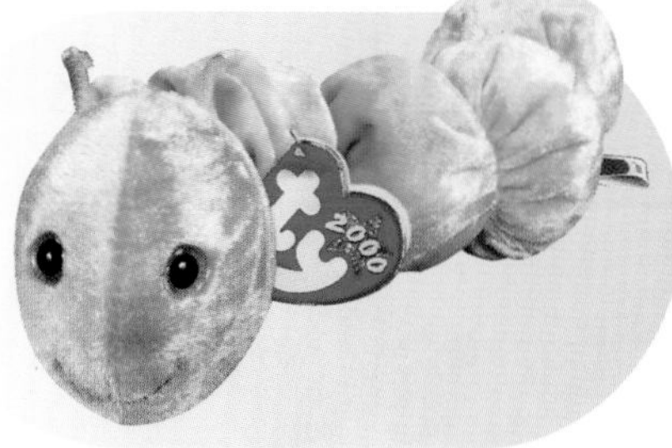

Birthdate: April 13, 2000

I can't sit still, it's just too hard
I roll and wiggle in the yard
They try to tell me not to squirm
But I can't help it, I'm a worm!

| Version | Issue Dates | Price Paid | Market Value |
|---|---|---|---|
| Original | June 2000-Dec. 2000 | | 6 $10 |

## Starlett™ 301

Kitten · #4382
Issued: July 31, 2001
Current - Hard To Find

Birthdate: January 9, 2001

Curled up snugly in your lap
Is where I'll take a little nap
And if you pet my long white fur
You'll be sure to hear me purr!

| Version | Issue Dates | Price Paid | Market Value |
|---|---|---|---|
| Original | July 2001-Current | | 7 $________ |

## Steg™ 302

Stegosaurus · #4087
Issued: June 3, 1995
Retired: June 15, 1996

Birthdate: N/A

No Poem

| Version | Issue Dates | Price Paid | Market Value |
|---|---|---|---|
| Original | June 1995-June 1996 | | 3 $500 |

303

## Stilts™

Stork · #4221
Issued: January 1, 1999
Retired: May 31, 1999

Birthdate: June 16, 1998

Flying high over mountains and streams
Fulfilling wishes, hopes and dreams
The stork brings parents bundles of joy
The greatest gift, a girl or boy!

| Version | Issue Dates | Price Paid | Market Value |
|---|---|---|---|
| Original | Jan. 1999-May 1999 | | (5) $9 |

304

## Sting™

Stingray · #4077
Issued: June 3, 1995
Retired: January 1, 1997

Birthdate: August 27, 1995

I'm a manta ray and my name is Sting
I'm quite unusual and this is the thing
Under the water I glide like a bird
Have you ever seen something so absurd?

| Version | Issue Dates | Price Paid | Market Value |
|---|---|---|---|
| Original | June 1995-Jan. 1997 | | (4) $85 (3) $110 |

305

## Stinger™

Scorpion · #4193
Issued: May 30, 1998
Retired: December 31, 1998

Birthdate: September 29, 1997

Stinger the scorpion will run and dart
But this little fellow is really all heart
So if you see him don't run away
Say hello and ask him to play!

| Version | Issue Dates | Price Paid | Market Value |
|---|---|---|---|
| Original | May 1998-Dec. 1998 | | (5) $9 |



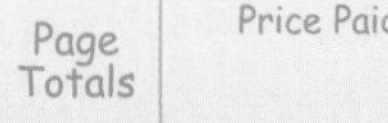

| Page Totals | Price Paid | Market Value |
|---|---|---|
| | | |

## Stinky™

306

Skunk • #4017
Issued: June 3, 1995
Retired: September 28, 1998

Birthdate: February 13, 1995

Deep in the woods he lived in a cave
Perfume and mints were the gifts he gave
He showered every night in the kitchen sink
Hoping one day he wouldn't stink!

| Version | Issue Dates | Price Paid | Market Value |
|---|---|---|---|
| Original | June 1995-Sept. 1998 | | 5: $11 4: $12 3: $65 |

## Stretch™

307

Ostrich • #4182
Issued: December 31, 1997
Retired: March 31, 1999

Birthdate: September 21, 1997

She thinks when her head is underground
The rest of her body can't be found
The Beanie Babies think it's absurd
To play hide and seek with this bird!

| Version | Issue Dates | Price Paid | Market Value |
|---|---|---|---|
| Original | Dec. 1997-March 1999 | | 5: $9 |

## Stripes™

308

Tiger • #4065
Issued: Est. June 3, 1995
Retired: May 1, 1998

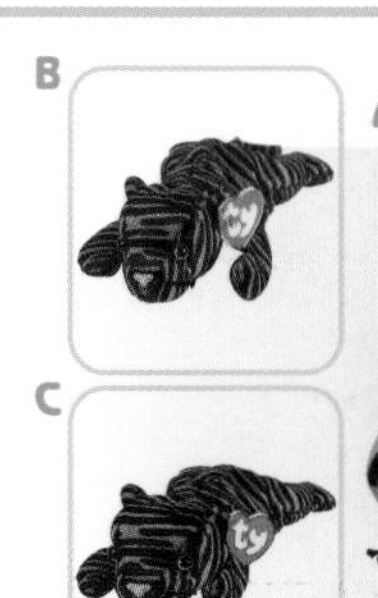

B

C

A

Birthdate: June 11, 1995

Stripes was never fierce nor strong
So with tigers, he didn't get along
Jungle life was hard to get by
So he came to his friends at Ty!

| Version | Issue Dates | Price Paid | Market Value |
|---|---|---|---|
| A. Light w/Fewer Stripes | June 1996-May 1998 | | 5: $13 4: $15 |
| B. Dark w/Fuzzy Belly | Est. Early 1996-June 1996 | | 3: $620 |
| C. Dark w/More Stripes | Est. June 1995-Early 1996 | | 3: $290 |

309

## Strut™

**(name changed from "Doodle™")**

Rooster • #4171
Issued: July 12, 1997
Retired: March 31, 1999

Birthdate: March 8, 1996

Listen closely to "cock-a-doodle-doo"
What's the rooster saying to you?
Hurry, wake up sleepy head
We have lots to do, get out of bed!

| Version | Issue Dates | Price Paid | Market Value |
|---|---|---|---|
| Original | July 1997-March 1999 | | 5 $10 4 $13 |

310

## Sunny™

e-Beanie • #4401
Issued: December 1, 2000
Retired: December 8, 2000

Birthdate: February 13, 2000

There's some mail waiting for me
A real surprise - a mystery
It's a message just from you
Telling me secrets I never knew!

| Version | Issue Dates | Price Paid | Market Value |
|---|---|---|---|
| Original | Dec. 2000-Dec. 2000 | | 6 $20 |

311

## Swampy™

Alligator • #4273
Issued: February 13, 2000
Retired: March 23, 2001

Birthdate: January 24, 2000

Through the murky swamps I glide
My yellow eyes I try to hide
I drift as silent as a log
A friend to you and every frog!

| Version | Issue Dates | Price Paid | Market Value |
|---|---|---|---|
| Original | Feb. 2000-March 2001 | | 6 $9 |

| Page Totals | Price Paid | Market Value |
|---|---|---|
| | | |

## Swirly™

**312**

Snail • #4249
Issued: April 14, 1999
Retired: December 23, 1999

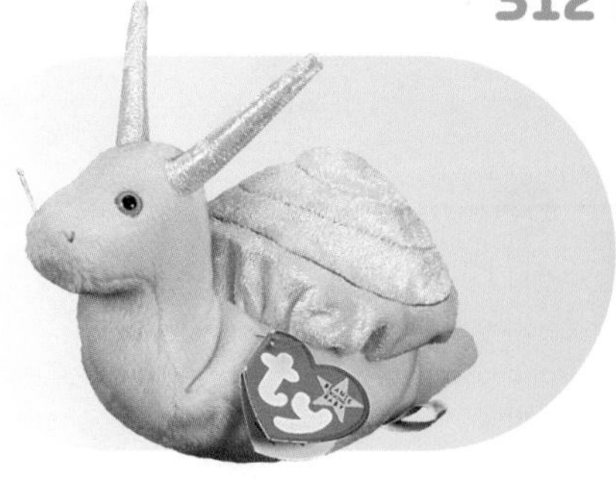

Birthdate: March 10, 1999

Carefully traveling, leaving a trail
I'm not very fast, for I am a snail
Although I go my own plodding pace
Slow and steady, wins the race!

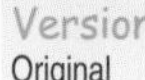

| Version | Issue Dates | Price Paid | Market Value |
|---|---|---|---|
| Original | April 1999-Dec. 1999 | | (5) $11 |

## Swoop™

**313**

Pterodactyl • #4268
Issued: February 13, 2000
Retired: June 11, 2001

Birthdate: February 24, 2000

Gliding through the summer sky
Looking low and looking high
Now I think my quest can end
I've found you, my special friend!

| Version | Issue Dates | Price Paid | Market Value |
|---|---|---|---|
| Original | Feb. 2000-June 2001 | | (6) $9 |

## Tabasco™

**314**

Bull • #4002
Issued: June 3, 1995
Retired: January 1, 1997

Birthdate: May 15, 1995

Although Tabasco is not so tall
He loves to play basketball
He is a star player in his dream
Can you guess his favorite team?

| Version | Issue Dates | Price Paid | Market Value |
|---|---|---|---|
| Original | June 1995-Jan. 1997 | | (4) $75 (3) $110 |

## 315 Tank™

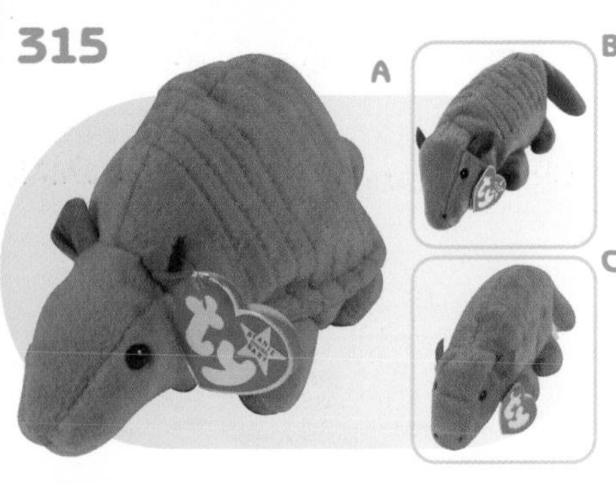

Armadillo · #4031
Issued: Est. January 7, 1996
Retired: October 1, 1997

Birthdate: February 22, 1995

This armadillo lives in the South
Shoving Tex-Mex in his mouth
He sure loves it south of the border
Keeping his friends in good order!

| Version | Issue Dates | Price Paid | Market Value |
|---|---|---|---|
| A. 9 Plates/With Shell | Est. Late 1996-Oct. 1997 | | (4) $55 |
| B. 9 Plates/Without Shell | Est. Mid 1996-Late 1996 | | (4) $225 |
| C. 7 Plates/Without Shell | Est. Jan. 1996-Mid 1996 | | (3) $180 |

## 316 Teddy™ (brown)

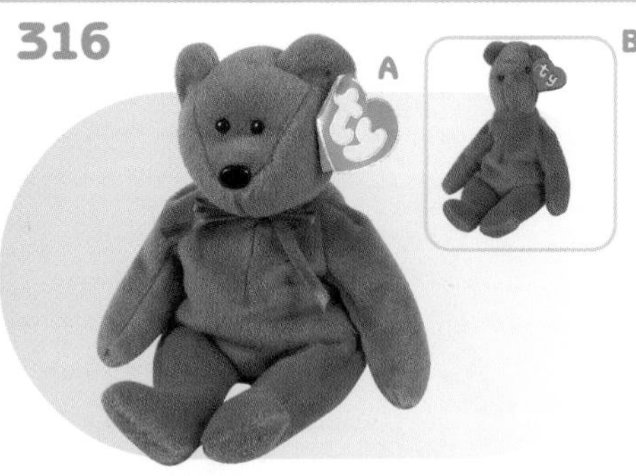

Bear · #4050
Issued: June 25, 1994
Retired: October 1, 1997

Birthdate: November 28, 1995

Teddy wanted to go out today
All of his friends went out to play
But he'd rather help whatever you do
After all, his best friend is you!

| Version | Issue Dates | Price Paid | Market Value |
|---|---|---|---|
| A. New Face | Jan. 1995-Oct. 1997 | | (4) $68 (3) $200 (2) $500 |
| B. Old Face | June 1994-Jan. 1995 | | (2) $1,200 (1) $1,400 |

## 317 Teddy™ (cranberry)

Bear · #4052
Issued: June 25, 1994
Retired: January 7, 1996

Birthdate: N/A

No Poem

| Version | Issue Dates | Price Paid | Market Value |
|---|---|---|---|
| A. New Face | Jan. 1995-Jan. 1996 | | (3) $800 (2) $1,000 |
| B. Old Face | June 1994-Jan. 1995 | | (2) $800 (1) $1,000 |

| Page Totals | Price Paid | Market Value |
|---|---|---|
| | | |

## Teddy™ (jade)

Bear • #4057
Issued: June 25, 1994
Retired: January 7, 1996

318

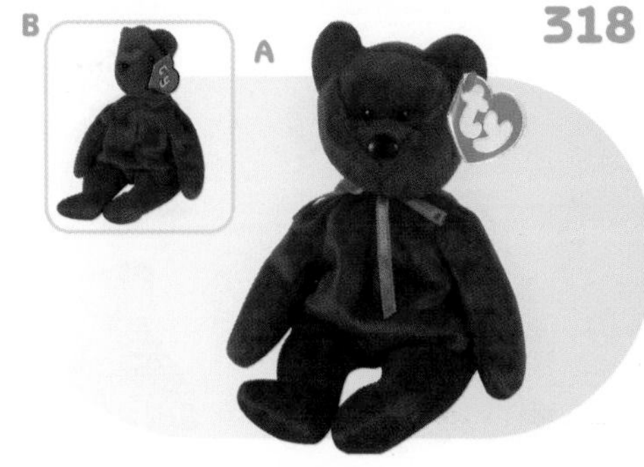

Birthdate: N/A

No Poem

| Version | Issue Dates | Price Paid | Market Value |
|---|---|---|---|
| A. New Face | Jan. 1995-Jan. 1996 | | ③ $800 ② $1,000 |
| B. Old Face | June 1994-Jan. 1995 | | ② $800 ① $1,000 |

## Teddy™ (magenta)

Bear • #4056
Issued: June 25, 1994
Retired: January 7, 1996

319

Birthdate: N/A

No Poem

| Version | Issue Dates | Price Paid | Market Value |
|---|---|---|---|
| A. New Face | Jan. 1995-Jan. 1996 | | ③ $800 ② $1,000 |
| B. Old Face | June 1994-Jan. 1995 | | ② $800 ① $1,000 |

## Teddy™ (teal)

Bear • #4051
Issued: June 25, 1994
Retired: January 7, 1996

320

Birthdate: N/A

No Poem

| Version | Issue Dates | Price Paid | Market Value |
|---|---|---|---|
| A. New Face | Jan. 1995-Jan. 1996 | | ③ $800 ② $1,000 |
| B. Old Face | June 1994-Jan. 1995 | | ② $800 ① $1,000 |

## 321

A

B

C

### Teddy™ (violet)

Bear • #4055
Issued: June 25, 1994
Retired: January 7, 1996

Birthdate: N/A

No Poem

| Version | Issue Dates | Price Paid | Market Value |
|---|---|---|---|
| A. New Face | Jan. 1995-Jan. 1996 | | (3) $800 (2) $1,000 |
| B. New Face/Employee Bear, Rec Tush Tag (Green or Red Ribbon) | Sept. 1996 | | No Swing Tag $2,600 |
| C. Old Face | June 1994-Jan. 1995 | | (2) $800 (1) $1,00 |

## 322

### Thank You Bear™

**(exclusive gift to authorized Ty retailers)**

Bear • #4330
Issued: December 29, 2000
Not Available In Retail Stores

Birthdate: N/A

Dedication Appearing On Special Tag

Thanks for everything you've done
Because of you we're #1
We're a great team you and me
Thanks again for your loyalty!

| Version | Issue Dates | Price Paid | Market Value |
|---|---|---|---|
| Original | Dec. 2000 | | Special Tag $400 |

## 323

### The Beginning™

Bear • #4267
Issued: February 13, 2000
Retired: May 10, 2000

Birthdate: January 1, 2000

Beanie Babies can never end
They'll always be our special friends
Start the fun because we're here
To bring you hope, love and cheer!

| Version | Issue Dates | Price Paid | Market Value |
|---|---|---|---|
| Original | Feb. 2000-May 2000 | | (6) $26 |

| Page Totals | Price Paid | Market Value |
|---|---|---|
| | | |

## The End™ 324

Bear • #4265
Issued: August 31, 1999
Retired: December 23, 1999

Birthdate: N/A

All good things come to an end
It's been fun for everyone
Peace and hope are never gone
Love you all and say, "So long!"

| Version | Issue Dates | Price Paid | Market Value |
|---|---|---|---|
| Original | Aug. 1999-Dec. 1999 | | (5) $24 |

## Tiger 325

**(Zodiac Collection™)**

Tiger • #4320
Issued: August 19, 2000
Retired: May 24, 2001

Years Of The Tiger: 1938, 1950, 1962, 1974, 1986, 1998

You are aggressive and courageous
Often candid and sensitive
Look to the dog and horse for happiness
Beware of the monkey!

| Version | Issue Dates | Price Paid | Market Value |
|---|---|---|---|
| Original | Aug. 2000-May 2001 | | (2) $9 |

## Tiny™ 326

Chihuahua • #4234
Issued: January 1, 1999
Retired: December 23, 1999

Birthdate: September 8, 1998

South of the Border, in the sun
Tiny the Chihuahua is having fun
Attending fiestas, breaking piñatas
Eating a taco, or some enchiladas!

| Version | Issue Dates | Price Paid | Market Value |
|---|---|---|---|
| Original | Jan. 1999-Dec. 1999 | | (5) $11 |

## 327

## Tiptoe™

Mouse • #4241
Issued: April 16, 1999
Retired: October 21, 1999

Birthdate: January 8, 1999

Creeping quietly along the wall
Little foot prints fast and small
Tiptoeing through the house with ease
Searching for a piece of cheese!

| Version | Issue Dates | Price Paid | Market Value |
|---|---|---|---|
| Original | Apr. 1999-Oct. 1999 | | 5 $11 |

## 328

## Tracker™

Basset Hound • #4198
Issued: May 30, 1998
Retired: November 26, 1999

Birthdate: June 5, 1997

Sniffing and tracking and following trails
Tracker the basset always wags his tail
It doesn't matter what you do
He's always happy when he's with you!

| Version | Issue Dates | Price Paid | Market Value |
|---|---|---|---|
| Original | May 1998-Nov. 1999 | | 5 $10 |

## 329

## Tradee™

**(available exclusively on-line)**

e-Beanie • #4403
Issued: June 26, 2001
Current - Very Hard To Find

Birthdate: June 29, 2000

Now the trading has begun
Check it out, it's lots of fun
Come along and play with me
I have some things that you must see!

| Version | Issue Dates | Price Paid | Market Value |
|---|---|---|---|
| Original | June 2001-Current | | 7 $________ |

| Page Totals | Price Paid | Market Value |
|---|---|---|
| | | |

## Trap™

330

Mouse • #4042
Issued: June 25, 1994
Retired: June 15, 1995

Birthdate: N/A

No Poem

| Version | Issue Dates | Price Paid | Market Value |
|---|---|---|---|
| Original | June 1994-June 1995 | | ③ $680 ② $875 ① $975 |

## Tricks™

331

Dog • #4311
Issued: July 8, 2000
Retired: June 18, 2001

Birthdate: May 14, 2000

Some games that we always play
Are fetch and sit, give paw and stay
Teach me other tricks to do
And I'll have found a friend in you!

| Version | Issue Dates | Price Paid | Market Value |
|---|---|---|---|
| Original | July 2000-June 2001 | | ⑥ $9 |

## Trumpet™

332

Elephant • #4276
Issued: February 13, 2000
Retired: April 19, 2001

Birthdate: February 11, 2000

Trumpet uses his trunk to spray
Be careful you don't get in his way
He plays in mud - he never forgets
Give him some peanuts, he'll be your pet!

| Version | Issue Dates | Price Paid | Market Value |
|---|---|---|---|
| Original | Feb. 2000-April 2001 | | ⑥ $9 |

## 333

### Tuffy™

Terrier • #4108
Issued: May 11, 1997
Retired: December 31, 1998

Birthdate: October 12, 1996

Taking off with a thunderous blast
Tuffy rides his motorcycle fast
The Beanies roll with laughs and squeals
He never took off his training wheels!

| Version | Issue Dates | Price Paid | Market Value |
|---|---|---|---|
| Original | May 1997-Dec. 1998 | | 5 $11 4 $11 |

## 334

A

B

### Tusk™

Walrus • #4076
Issued: Est. June 3, 1995
Retired: January 1, 1997

Birthdate: September 18, 1995

Tusk brushes his teeth everyday
To keep them shiny, it's the only way
Teeth are special, so you must try
And they will sparkle when
You say "Hi"!

| Version | Issue Dates | Price Paid | Market Value |
|---|---|---|---|
| A. "Tusk™" Swing Tag | Est. June 1995-Jan. 1997 | | 4 $80 3 $110 |
| B. "Tuck™" Swing Tag | Est. Early 1996-Jan. 1997 | | 4 $80 |

## 335

### Twigs™

Giraffe • #4068
Issued: January 7, 1996
Retired: May 1, 1998

Birthdate: May 19, 1995

Twigs has his head in the clouds
He stands tall, he stands proud
With legs so skinny they wobble and shake
What an unusual friend he will make!

| Version | Issue Dates | Price Paid | Market Value |
|---|---|---|---|
| Original | Jan. 1996-May 1998 | | 5 $17 4 $19 3 $70 |

| Page Totals | Price Paid | Market Value |
|---|---|---|
| | | |

## Ty 2K™

336

Bear • #4262
Issued: August 31, 1999
Retired: December 23, 1999

Birthdate: January 1, 2000

Red, yellow, green and blue
Let's have some fun me and you
So join the party, and let's all say
"Happy New Millennium", from Ty 2K!

| Version | Issue Dates | Price Paid | Market Value |
|---|---|---|---|
| Original | Aug. 1999-Dec. 1999 | | 5 $19 |

## USA™

337

**(exclusive to the United States)**

Bear • #4287
Issued: June 6, 2000
Retired: April 6, 2001

Birthdate: July 4, 2000

From this land of liberty
Come this bear for you and me
Proud to wear red, white and blue
He'll be a special friend for you!

| Version | Issue Dates | Price Paid | Market Value |
|---|---|---|---|
| Original | June 2000-April 2001 | | 6 $15 |

## Unity™

338

**(exclusive to Europe)**

Bear • #4606
Issued: April 20, 2001
Current - Impossible To Find

Birthdate: September 28, 2000

The EU finally came to be
That's why I'm named Unity
Our countries now unite as one
A brand new era has begun!

| Version | Issue Dates | Price Paid | Market Value (in U.S. market) |
|---|---|---|---|
| Original | April 2000-Current | | 7 $50 |

339

## Valentina™

Bear • #4233
Issued: January 1, 1999
Retired: December 23, 1999

Birthdate: February 14, 1998

Flowers, candy and hearts galore
Sweet words of love for those you adore
With this bear comes love that's true
On Valentine's Day and all year through!

| Version | Issue Dates | Price Paid | Market Value |
|---|---|---|---|
| Original | Jan. 1999-Dec. 1999 | | ⑤ $15 |

340

## Valentino™

Bear • #4058
Issued: January 7, 1995
Retired: December 31, 1998

Birthdate: February 14, 1994

His heart is red and full of love
He cares for you so give him a hug
Keep him close when feeling blue
Feel the love he has for you!

| Version | Issue Dates | Price Paid | Market Value |
|---|---|---|---|
| Original | Jan. 1995-Dec. 1998 | | ⑤ $17 ④ $20 ③ $120 ② $345 |

341

## Velvet™

Panther • #4064
Issued: June 3, 1995
Retired: October 1, 1997

Birthdate: December 16, 1995

Velvet loves to sleep in the trees
Lulled to dreams by the buzz of the bees
She snoozes all day and plays all night
Running and jumping in the moonlight!

| Version | Issue Dates | Price Paid | Market Value |
|---|---|---|---|
| Original | June 1995-Oct. 1997 | | ④ $21 ③ $72 |



| Page Totals | Price Paid | Market Value |
|---|---|---|
| | | |

## Waddle™ 342

Penguin • #4075
Issued: June 3, 1995
Retired: May 1, 1998

Birthdate: December 19, 1995

Waddle the Penguin likes to dress up
Every night he wears his tux
When Waddle walks, it never fails
He always trips over his tails!

| Version | Issue Dates | Price Paid | Market Value |
|---|---|---|---|
| Original | June 1995-May 1998 | | 5 $15 4 $16 3 $65 |

## Wallace™ 343

Bear • #4264
Issued: August 31, 1999
Retired: December 23, 1999

Birthdate: January 25, 1999

Castles rise from misty glens
Shielding bands of warrior men
Wearing tartan of their clan
Red, green and a little tan!

| Version | Issue Dates | Price Paid | Market Value |
|---|---|---|---|
| Original | Aug. 1999-Dec. 1999 | | 5 $16 |

## Waves™ 344

Whale • #4084
Issued: May 11, 1997
Retired: May 1, 1998

Birthdate: December 8, 1996

Join him today on the Internet
Don't be afraid to get your feet wet
He taught all the Beanies how to surf
Our web page is his home turf!

| Version | Issue Dates | Price Paid | Market Value |
|---|---|---|---|
| Original | May 1997-May 1998 | | 5 $12 4 $12 |

345

## Web™

Spider • #4041
Issued: June 25, 1994
Retired: January 7, 1996

Birthdate: N/A

No Poem

| Version | Issue Dates | Price Paid | Market Value |
|---|---|---|---|
| Original | June 1994-Jan. 1996 | | ③ $650 ② $800 ① $925 |

346

## Weenie™

Dachshund • #4013
Issued: January 7, 1996
Retired: May 1, 1998

Birthdate: July 20, 1995

Weenie the dog is quite a sight
Long of body and short of height
He perches himself high on a log
And considers himself to be top dog!

| Version | Issue Dates | Price Paid | Market Value |
|---|---|---|---|
| Original | Jan. 1996-May 1998 | | ⑤ $20 ④ $22 ③ $85 |

347

## Whiskers™

Dog • #4317
Issued: July 8, 2000
Retired: April 11, 2001

Birthdate: August 6, 2000

Sometimes when we jump and play
I can't stop when you say "stay"
I'm very frisky, this is true.
But I'll never run away from you!

| Version | Issue Dates | Price Paid | Market Value |
|---|---|---|---|
| Original | July 2000-April 2001 | | ⑥ $9 |

| Page Totals | Price Paid | Market Value |
|---|---|---|
| | | |

## Whisper™

348

Deer • #4194
Issued: May 30, 1998
Retired: December 23, 1999

Birthdate: April 5, 1997

She's very shy as you can see
When she hides behind a tree
With big brown eyes and soft to touch
This little fawn will love you so much!

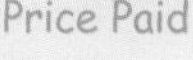

| Version | Issue Dates | Price Paid | Market Value |
|---|---|---|---|
| Original | May 1998-Dec. 1999 | | ❺ $9 |

## Wiggly™

349

Octopus • #4275
Issued: February 13, 2000
Retired: March 27, 2001

Birthdate: January 25, 2000

Under the sea I travel with ease
I flip and flop - do whatever I please
Being a squid can be lots of fun
Because I swim faster than anyone!

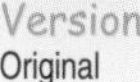

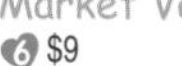

| Version | Issue Dates | Price Paid | Market Value |
|---|---|---|---|
| Original | Feb. 2000-March 2001 | | ❻ $9 |

## Wise™

350

Owl • #4187
Issued: May 30, 1998
Retired: December 31, 1998

Birthdate: May 31, 1997

Wise is at the head of the class
With A's and B's he'll always pass
He's got his diploma and feels really great
Meet the newest graduate: Class of '98!

| Version | Issue Dates | Price Paid | Market Value |
|---|---|---|---|
| Original | May 1998-Dec. 1998 | | ❺ $13 |

| Page Totals | Price Paid | Market Value |
|---|---|---|
| | | |

351

## Wiser™

Owl • #4238
Issued: April 22, 1999
Retired: August 27, 1999

Birthdate: June 4, 1999

Waking daily to the morning sun
Learning makes school so much fun
Looking great and feeling fine
The newest graduate, "Class of 99!"

| Version | Issue Dates | Price Paid | Market Value |
|---|---|---|---|
| Original | April 1999-Aug. 1999 | | ❺ $14 |

352

## Wisest™

Owl • #4286
Issued: May 1, 2000
Retired: December 15, 2000

Birthdate: June 6, 2000

I always try to do my best
And study hard for all my tests
Now it's time to celebrate
Because at last I graduate!

| Version | Issue Dates | Price Paid | Market Value |
|---|---|---|---|
| Original | May 2000-Dec. 2000 | | ❻ $12 |

353

## Wrinkles™

Bulldog • #4103
Issued: June 15, 1996
Retired: September 22, 1998

Birthdate: May 1, 1996

This little dog is named Wrinkles
His nose is soft and often crinkles
Likes to climb up on your lap
He's a cheery sort of chap!

| Version | Issue Dates | Price Paid | Market Value |
|---|---|---|---|
| Original | June 1996-Sept. 1998 | | ❺ $11 ❹ $11 |

| Page Totals | Price Paid | Market Value |
|---|---|---|
| | | |

## Zero™

354

Penguin • #4207
Issued: September 30, 1998
Retired: December 31, 1998

Birthdate: January 2, 1998

Penguins love the ice and snow
Playing in weather twenty below
Antarctica is where I love to be
Splashing in the cold, cold sea!

| Version | Issue Dates | Price Paid | Market Value |
| --- | --- | --- | --- |
| Original | Sept. 1998-Dec. 1998 | | ⑤ $16 |

## Ziggy™

355

Zebra • #4063
Issued: June 3, 1995
Retired: May 1, 1998

Birthdate: December 24, 1995

Ziggy likes soccer - he's a referee
That way he watches the games for free
The other Beanies don't think it's fair
But Ziggy the Zebra doesn't care!

| Version | Issue Dates | Price Paid | Market Value |
| --- | --- | --- | --- |
| Original | June 1995-May 1998 | | ⑤ $13 ④ $16 ③ $70 |

## Zip™

356

Cat • #4004
Issued: January 7, 1995
Retired: May 1, 1998

B

C

A

Birthdate: March 28, 1994

Keep Zip by your side all the day through
Zip is good luck, you'll see it's true
When you have something you need to do
Zip will always believe in you!

| Version | Issue Dates | Price Paid | Market Value |
| --- | --- | --- | --- |
| A. White Paws | March 1996-May 1998 | | ⑤ $18 ④ $22 ③ $205 |
| B. All Black | Jan. 1996-March 1996 | | ③ $700 |
| C. White Face | Jan. 1995-Jan. 1996 | | ③ $350 ② $440 |

# Beanie Buddies®

The *Beanie Buddies* collection has grown to include over 150 pieces. Many popular, retired Beanie Babies designs have "returned" in this line of larger plush animals, sometimes with interesting modifications.

1

New!

## 1997 Holiday Teddy™

Bear · #9426
Issued: October 1, 2001
Current – Just Released

Beanie Buddies® Fact
This 1997 Beanie Baby was the first of the Holiday Teddy series!

| Version | Price Paid | Market Value |
|---|---|---|
| Original | | ❷ $________ |

2

## 2000 Signature Bear™

Bear · #9348
Issued: January 4, 2000
Retired: April 3, 2000

Beanie Buddies® Fact
2000 Ty Signature Bear Beanie Baby did not exist. This bear represents the future!

| Version | Price Paid | Market Value |
|---|---|---|
| Original | | ❷ $40 |

3

New!

## 2001 Holiday Teddy™

Bear · #9427
Issued: October 1, 2001
Current – Just Released

Beanie Buddies® Fact
The 2001 Beanie and Buddy are the first Holiday Teddies to be introduced at the same time!

| Version | Price Paid | Market Value |
|---|---|---|
| Original | | ❷ $________ |

| Page Totals | Price Paid | Market Value |
|---|---|---|
| | | |

## Almond™ 4

Bear • #9425
Issued: July 31, 2001
Retired: October 16, 2001

Beanie Buddies® Fact
Almond the Beanie Baby was introduced with a friend named "Pecan"!

| Version | Price Paid | Market Value |
|---|---|---|
| Original | | ❷ $17 |

## Amber™ 5

Cat • #9341
Issued: August 31, 1999
Retired: May 19, 2000

Beanie Buddies® Fact
Amber and Silver the Beanie Babies were modeled after two orphaned kittens found by Ty Warner!

| Version | Price Paid | Market Value |
|---|---|---|
| Original | | ❷ $14<br>❶ $22 |

## Ariel™ 6

Bear • #9409
Issued: April 1, 2001
Current - Moderate To Find

Beanie Buddies® Fact
The flowers embroidered on the Ariel Beanie Baby and Beanie Buddy were based on a drawing by Ariel Glaser.

| Version | Price Paid | Market Value |
|---|---|---|
| Original | | ❷ $________ |

## B.B. Bear™ 7

Bear • #9398
Issued: January 1, 2001
Current - Moderate To Find

Beanie Buddies® Fact
B.B. Bear the Beanie Baby was the first Beanie Baby created without a birthday.

| Version | Price Paid | Market Value |
|---|---|---|
| Original | | ❷ $________ |



| Page Totals | Price Paid | Market Value |
|---|---|---|
| | | |

8

## Baldy™

Bald Eagle • #9408
Issued: April 1, 2001
Retired: April 26, 2001

Beanie Buddies® Fact
Baldy the Beanie Baby originally had a different name which was changed at the last minute.

| Version | Price Paid | Market Value |
|---|---|---|
| Original | | 2 $20 |

9

## Bananas™

Orangutan • #9402
Issued: January 1, 2001
Retired: June 14, 2001

Beanie Buddies® Fact
Bananas the Beanie Baby's beard was three different colors before it was made yellow.

| Version | Price Paid | Market Value |
|---|---|---|
| Original | | 2 $19 |

10

A B

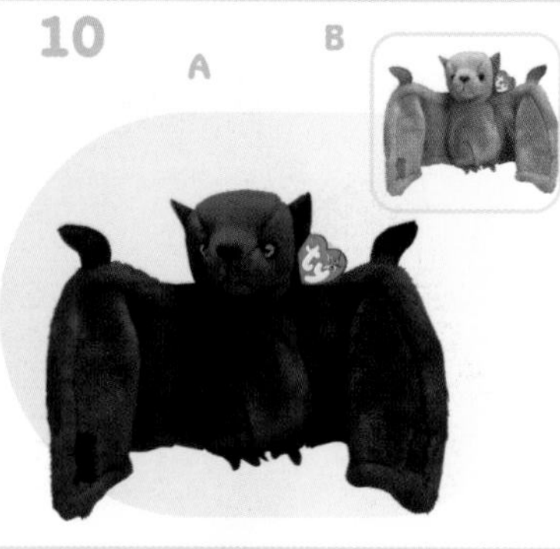

## Batty™

Bat • #9379
Issued: June 24, 2000
Current – Easy To Find (Mocha Rose)
Very Hard To Find (Black)

Beanie Buddies® Fact
Batty the Beanie Baby was the second bat made by Ty. Batty came in two colors, mocha rose and Ty-dyed!

| Version | Price Paid | Market Value |
|---|---|---|
| A. Black | | 2 $______ |
| B. Mocha Rose | | 2 $______ |

11

## Beak™

Kiwi • #9301
Issued: September 30, 1998
Retired: March 31, 1999

Beanie Buddies® Fact
Beak the Beanie Baby and Beak the Beanie Buddy are the first to be released as a set!

| Version | Price Paid | Market Value |
|---|---|---|
| Original | | 1 $28 |

| Page Totals | Price Paid | Market Value |
|---|---|---|
| | | |

## Bones™ 12

Dog • #9377
Issued: June 24, 2000
Current - Easy To Find

Beanie Buddies® Fact
Bones the Beanie Baby was one of the longest running and most popular Beanies ever made!

| Version | Price Paid | Market Value |
|---|---|---|
| Original | | ❷ $________ |

## Bongo™ 13

Monkey • #9312
Issued: January 1, 1999
Retired: December 11, 1999

Beanie Buddies® Fact
Bongo the Beanie Baby was first named Nana. Ty Warner liked the name Bongo better because he plays the Bongos!

| Version | Price Paid | Market Value |
|---|---|---|
| Original | | ❶ $20 |

## Britannia™ 14

**(exclusive to the United Kingdom)**

Bear • #9601
Issued: August 31, 1999
Retired: May 24, 2000

Beanie Buddies® Fact
Britannia the Beanie Baby was the first international bear to have an embroidered flag rather than a patch!

| Version | Price Paid | Market Value (in U.S. market) |
|---|---|---|
| Original | | ❷ $90<br>❶ $135 |

## Bronty™ 15

Brontosaurus • #9353
Issued: January 4, 2000
Retired: April 6, 2000

Beanie Buddies® Fact
Bronty the Beanie Baby was one of the dinosaur trio. This trio is highly prized by collectors!

| Version | Price Paid | Market Value |
|---|---|---|
| Original | | ❷ $32 |

16

## Bubbles™

Fish • #9323
Issued: January 1, 1999
Retired: November 29, 1999

Beanie Buddies® Fact
Bubbles the Beanie Baby made in the swimming position was quite a challenge to manufacture.

| Version | Price Paid | Market Value |
|---|---|---|
| Original | | 1 $18 |

17

## Bushy™

Lion • #9382
Issued: June 24, 2000
Current – Easy To Find

Beanie Buddies® Fact
Bushy the Beanie Baby's fabric has a total of 4 colors: pink, orange, yellow and green. This fabric is very difficult and expensive to 'oduce!

| Version | Price Paid | Market Value |
|---|---|---|
| Original | | 2 $________ |

18

## Cassie™

Collie • #9405
Issued: April 1, 2001
Retired: July 17, 2001

Beanie Buddies® Fact
Cassie is the first Beanie Baby dog designed with long fur.

| Version | Price Paid | Market Value |
|---|---|---|
| Original | | 2 $15 |

19

## Celebrate™

Bear • #9423
Issued: June 23, 2001
Retired: October 11, 2001

Beanie Buddies® Fact
Celebrate the Beanie Baby was the first bear to commemorate our Company's birthday!

| Version | Price Paid | Market Value |
|---|---|---|
| Original | | 2 $19 |

| Page Totals | Price Paid | Market Value |
|---|---|---|
| | | |

## Chilly™ 20

Polar Bear • #9317
Issued: January 1, 1999
Retired: November 24, 1999

Beanie Buddies® Fact
Chilly the Beanie Baby was introduced in June of 1994 and retired in January of 1996 making him one of the most sought after!

| Version | Price Paid | Market Value |
|---|---|---|
| Original | | 1 $20 |

## Chip™ 21

Cat • #9318
Issued: January 1, 1999
Retired: December 12, 1999

Beanie Buddies® Fact
Chip the Beanie Baby due to the variety of colors and pattern shapes, is one of the most difficult to produce. It takes over 20 pieces to make Chip!

| Version | Price Paid | Market Value |
|---|---|---|
| Original | | 1 $18 |

## Chocolate™ 22

Moose • #9349
Issued: January 4, 2000
Retired: October 27, 2000

Beanie Buddies® Fact
Chocolate the Beanie Baby was the last of the Original Nine to be retired!

| Version | Price Paid | Market Value |
|---|---|---|
| Original | | 2 $18 |

## Chops™ 23

Lamb • #9394
Issued: January 1, 2001
Retired: April 16, 2001

Beanie Buddies® Fact
Chops the Beanie Baby was the very first Beanie Baby lamb created by Ty.

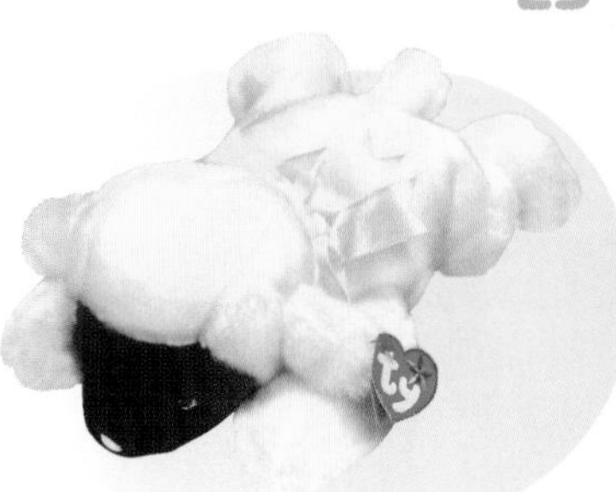

| Version | Price Paid | Market Value |
|---|---|---|
| Original | | 2 $15 |

24

## Clubby® (Club exclusive)

Bear • #9990
Issued: August 9, 1999
Retired: N/A

Beanie Buddies® Fact
Clubby the Beanie Baby was not only the first BBOC Bear, but also the first to wear a button!

| Version | Price Paid | Market Value |
|---|---|---|
| Original | | 1 $32 |

25

## Clubby II™ (Club exclusive)

Bear • #9991
Issued: August 9, 1999
Retired: N/A

Beanie Buddies® Fact
Clubby II the Beanie Baby was the first to be included in a BBOC Kit!

| Version | Price Paid | Market Value |
|---|---|---|
| Original | | 1 $24 |

26

Set includes Beanie Baby® & Beanie Buddy®

## Clubby III™ (set/2, Club exclusive)

Bear • #9993
Issued: September 18, 2000
Retired: December 10, 2000

Beanie Buddies® Fact
Clubby III the Beanie Baby is the first BBOC Beanie Baby to be introduced along with its Buddy counterpart!

| Version | Price Paid | Market Value |
|---|---|---|
| Original | | 2 $40 (set) |

27

New!

## Clubby IV™ (Club exclusive)

Bear • #9994
Issued: September 24, 2001
Current - Just Released

Beanie Buddies® Fact
Clubby IV Beanie Baby was the first to have several different versions of the BBOC button!

| Version | Price Paid | Market Value |
|---|---|---|
| Original | | 2 $________ |

| Page Totals | Price Paid | Market Value |
|---|---|---|
| | | |

## Congo™

28

Gorilla • #9361
Issued: January 4, 2000
Retired: November 10, 2000

Beanie Buddies® Fact
Congo the Beanie Baby was inspired by the Ty plush gorilla George!

| Version | Price Paid | Market Value |
|---|---|---|
| Original | | ❷ $16 |

## Coral™

29

Fish • #9381
Issued: June 24, 2000
Current - Easy To Find

Beanie Buddies® Fact
Coral the Beanie Baby shares its birthday with Ty Warner's secretary!

| Version | Price Paid | Market Value |
|---|---|---|
| Original | | ❷ $________ |

## Digger™

30

Crab • #9351
Issued: January 4, 2000
Retired: June 21, 2000

Beanie Buddies® Fact
Digger the Beanie Baby was originally made in orange and then changed to red!

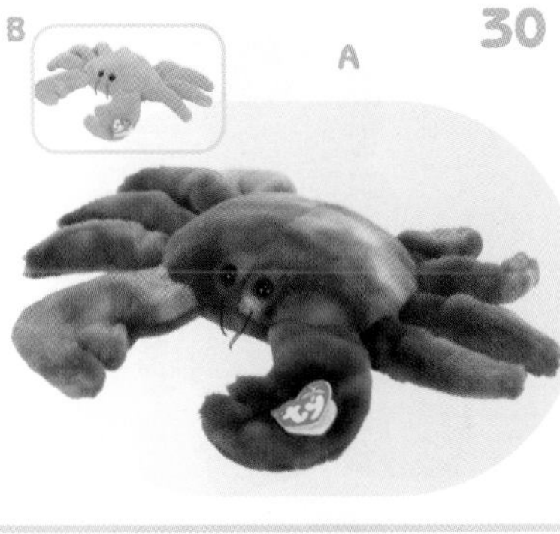


| Version | Price Paid | Market Value |
|---|---|---|
| A. Ty-Dye | | ❷ $55 |
| B. Orange | | ❷ $18 |

## Dotty™

31

Dalmatian • #9364
Issued: January 4, 2000
Retired: July 21, 2000

Beanie Buddies® Fact
Dotty the Beanie Baby was the second Dalmatian produced by Ty and still remains a favorite with collectors!

| Version | Price Paid | Market Value |
|---|---|---|
| Original | | ❷ $22 |

32

## Dragon™

Dragon · #9365
Issued: January 4, 2000
Retired: June 13, 2000

Beanie Buddies® Fact
Scorch the Beanie Baby was one of the first Beanies to feature the ty-dyed curly fabric!

| Version | Price Paid | Market Value |
|---|---|---|
| Original | | 2 $16 |

33

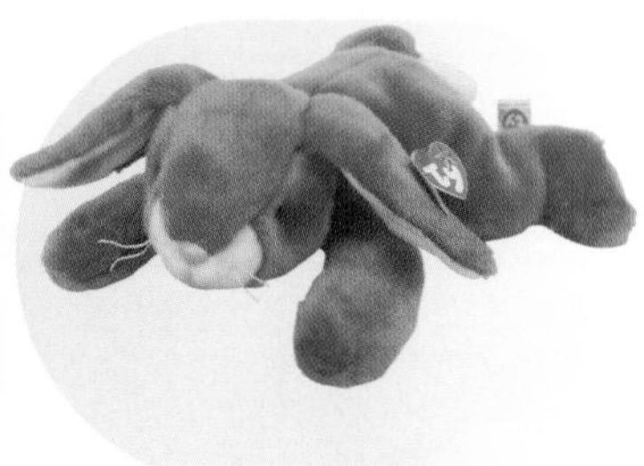

## Ears™

Bunny · #9388
Issued: January 1, 2001
Current - Easy To Find

Beanie Buddies® Fact
Ears the Beanie Baby was the only Beanie Baby bunny ever created laying down.

| Version | Price Paid | Market Value |
|---|---|---|
| Original | | 2 $________ |

34

## Employee Bear™

Bear · #9373
Issued: June 24, 2000
Current - Easy To Find

Beanie Buddies® Fact
The Employee Bear Beanie was the only Beanie produced without a hang tag!

| Version | Price Paid | Market Value |
|---|---|---|
| Original | | 2 $________ |

35

## Erin™

Bear · #9309
Issued: January 1, 1999
Retired: November 19, 1999

Beanie Buddies® Fact
Erin the Beanie Baby is the first bear to represent a country but not wear the country's flag!

| Version | Price Paid | Market Value |
|---|---|---|
| Original | | 1 $25 |

| Page Totals | Price Paid | Market Value |
|---|---|---|
| | | |

## Eucalyptus™

36

Koala Bear • #9363
Issued: January 4, 2000
Retired: July 18, 2000

Beanie Buddies® Fact
Eucalyptus the Beanie Baby was the second koala to be made by Ty. He was made due to the popularity of Mel!

| Version | Price Paid | Market Value |
|---|---|---|
| Original | | ❷ $18 |

## Extra Large 1997 Holiday Teddy™

37

New!

Bear • #9054
Issued: October 1, 2001
Current - Just Released

Beanie Buddies® Fact
This Beanie Baby and one other were the first introduced to represent the holiday season!

| Version | Price Paid | Market Value |
|---|---|---|
| Original | | ❷ $________ |

## Extra Large Dotty™

38

Dalmatian • #9052
Issued: January 1, 2001
Current - Moderate To Find

Beanie Buddies® Fact
This Beanie Buddy is so big, you might mistake him for a real dog!

| Version | Price Paid | Market Value |
|---|---|---|
| Original | | ❷ $________ |

## Extra Large Ears™

39

Bunny • #9047
Issued: January 1, 2001
Retired: March 29, 2001

Beanie Buddies® Fact
Only time will tell if a new all white Ears Beanie Baby will appear!

| Version | Price Paid | Market Value |
|---|---|---|
| Original | | ❷ $50 |

40

## Extra Large Hippie™

Bunny · #9038
Issued: January 4, 2000
Retired: April 25, 2000

Beanie Buddies® Fact
The length of the ear on the extra large Hippie is the same length as the Hippie Buddy!

| Version | Price Paid | Market Value |
|---|---|---|
| Original | | ❷ $85 |

41

## Extra Large Libearty™

Bear · #9042
Issued: June 24, 2000
Retired: January 12, 2001

Beanie Buddies® Fact
This extra large Libearty weighs as much as a dozen Beanie Babies!

| Version | Price Paid | Market Value |
|---|---|---|
| Original | | ❷ $70 |

42

## Extra Large Peace™

Bear · #9036
Issued: January 4, 2000
Current – Moderate To Find

Beanie Buddies® Fact
The amount of pellets used to fill one extra large Buddy can fill 75 Beanie Babies!

| Version | Price Paid | Market Value |
|---|---|---|
| Original | | ❷ $________ |

43

## Extra Large Schweetheart™

Orangutan · #9044
Issued: June 24, 2000
Current – Moderate To Find

Beanie Buddies® Fact
This extra large Schweetheart is almost the same size as a real orangutan!

| Version | Price Paid | Market Value |
|---|---|---|
| Original | | ❷ $________ |

| Page Totals | Price Paid | Market Value |
|---|---|---|
| | | |

## Extra Large Valentina™ 44

Bear • #9049
Issued: January 1, 2001
Retired: March 16, 2001

Beanie Buddies® Fact
Extra Large Valentina's heart is twice as large as Valentina the Beanie Baby's heart!

| Version | Price Paid | Market Value |
|---|---|---|
| Original | | (2) $65 |

## Fetch™ 45

Golden Retriever • #9338
Issued: August 31, 1999
Retired: March 10, 2000

Beanie Buddies® Fact
Fetch the Beanie Baby was introduced in May of 1998 and retired in December of 1998 when he was less than one year old!

| Version | Price Paid | Market Value |
|---|---|---|
| Original | | (2) $22<br>(1) $32 |

## Flip™ 46

Cat • #9359
Issued: January 4, 2000
Retired: January 12, 2001

Beanie Buddies® Fact
Flip the Beanie Baby was reminiscent of the first item produced by Ty. A white cat named Kashmir!

| Version | Price Paid | Market Value |
|---|---|---|
| Original | | (2) $18 |

## Flippity™ 47

Bunny • #9358
Issued: January 4, 2000
Retired: April 5, 2000

Beanie Buddies® Fact
Flippity the Beanie Baby was never made. He is Floppity's missing twin!

| Version | Price Paid | Market Value |
|---|---|---|
| Original | | (2) $23 |

| Page Totals | Price Paid | Market Value |
|---|---|---|
| | | |

48

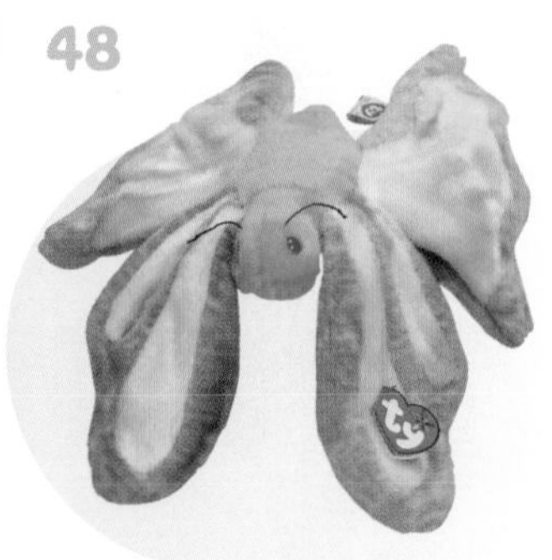

## Flitter™

Butterfly • #9384
Issued: June 24, 2000
Current - Easy To Find

Beanie Buddies® Fact
Flitter the Beanie Baby was a 1999 summer show exclusive. This exclusivity makes Flitter very collectible!

| Version | Price Paid | Market Value |
|---|---|---|
| Original | | ❷ $________ |

49

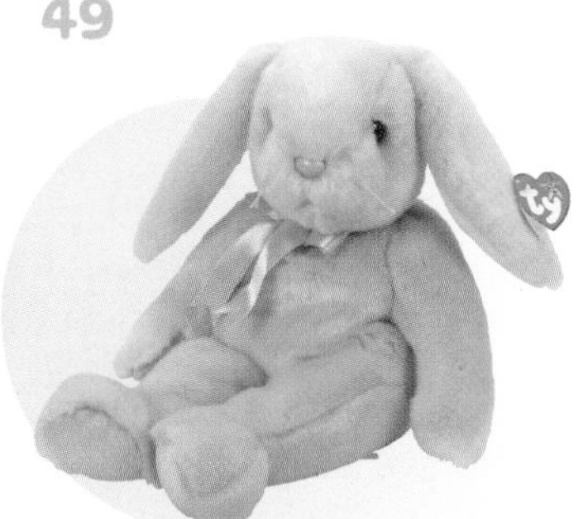

## Floppity™

Bunny • #9390
Issued: January 1, 2001
Retired: April 25, 2001

Beanie Buddies® Fact
Floppity the Beanie Baby was one of the "Bunny Trio" that included Hippity and Hoppity.

| Version | Price Paid | Market Value |
|---|---|---|
| Original | | ❷ $17 |

50

## Fuzz™

Bear • #9328
Issued: May 1, 1999
Retired: April 12, 2000

Beanie Buddies® Fact
Fuzz the Beanie Baby is made with Tylon that is crimped under extremely high temperature.

| Version | Price Paid | Market Value |
|---|---|---|
| Original | | ❷ $19<br>❶ $24 |

51

## Germania™

**(exclusive to Germany)**

Bear • #9063
Issued: February 18, 2000
Retired: February 7, 2001

Beanie Buddies® Fact
Germania the Beanie Baby was the first Beanie Baby to have its poem in a language other than English!

| Version | Price Paid | Market Value (in U.S. market) |
|---|---|---|
| Original | | ❷ $100 |



| Page Totals | Price Paid | Market Value |
|---|---|---|
| | | |

## Glory™ 52

**(exclusive to the United States)**

Bear • #9410
Issued: May 1, 2001
Retired: June 22, 2001

Beanie Buddies® Fact
The flag on Glory the Beanie Baby has 12 stars and 13 stripes.

| Version | Price Paid | Market Value |
| --- | --- | --- |
| Original | | ❷ $33 |

## Gobbles™ 53

Turkey • #9333
Issued: August 31, 1999
Retired: December 12, 1999

Beanie Buddies® Fact
Gobbles the Beanie Baby had several different types of waddles, including single and double felt!

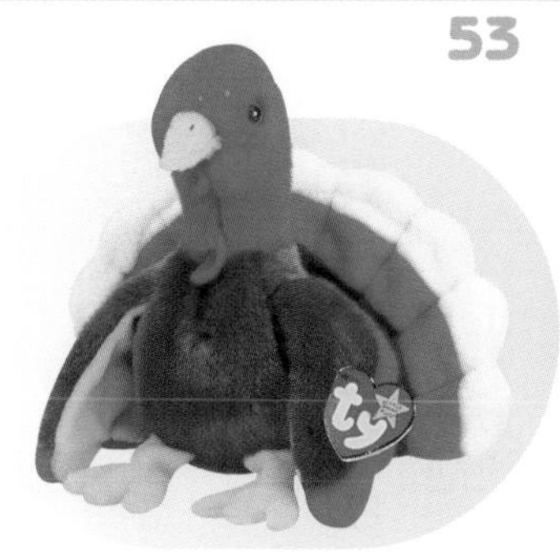

| Version | Price Paid | Market Value |
| --- | --- | --- |
| Original | | ❶ $18 |

## Goochy™ 54

Jelly Fish • #9362
Issued: January 4, 2000
Retired: June 13, 2000

Beanie Buddies® Fact
Goochy the Beanie Baby's fabric was one of the most expensive to produce. The shine on the fabric makes the ty-dying process more difficult!

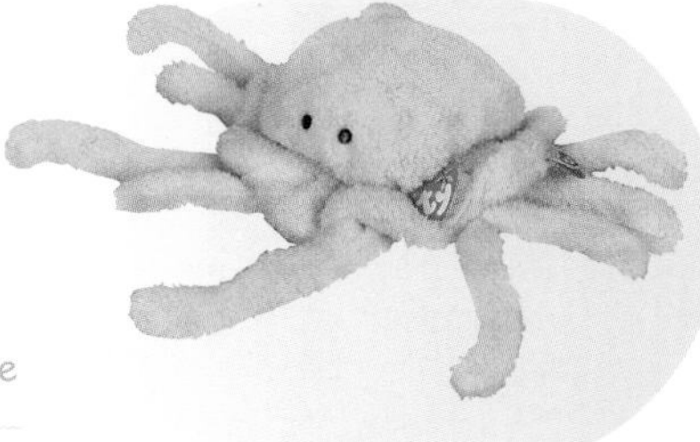

| Version | Price Paid | Market Value |
| --- | --- | --- |
| Original | | ❷ $14 |

## Grace™ 55

Bunny • #9389
Issued: January 1, 2001
Retired: April 16, 2001

Beanie Buddies® Fact
Grace the Beanie Baby was one of only two Beanies to be featured in a prayerful position.

| Version | Price Paid | Market Value |
| --- | --- | --- |
| Original | | ❷ $16 |

| Page Totals | Price Paid | Market Value |
| --- | --- | --- |
| | | |

56

## Groovy™

Bear • #9345
Issued: January 4, 2000
Retired: September 29, 2000

Beanie Buddies® Fact
Groovy the Beanie Baby was the first bear to have a colored-flocked nose!

| Version | Price Paid | Market Value |
|---|---|---|
| Original | | ② $22 |

57

## Halo™

Angel Bear • #9337
Issued: August 31, 1999
Retired: June 8, 2000

Beanie Buddies® Fact
Halo the Beanie Baby is made from a special fabric that shimmers. This fabric makes Halo even more heavenly!

| Version | Price Paid | Market Value |
|---|---|---|
| Original | | ② $19<br>① $26 |

58

## Halo II™

Angel Bear • #9386
Issued: September 28, 2000
Retired: February 28, 2001

Beanie Buddies® Fact
Halo II the Beanie Baby's fabric is one of the most expensive to make, due to its special iridescent sparkle!

| Version | Price Paid | Market Value |
|---|---|---|
| Original | | ② $22 |

59

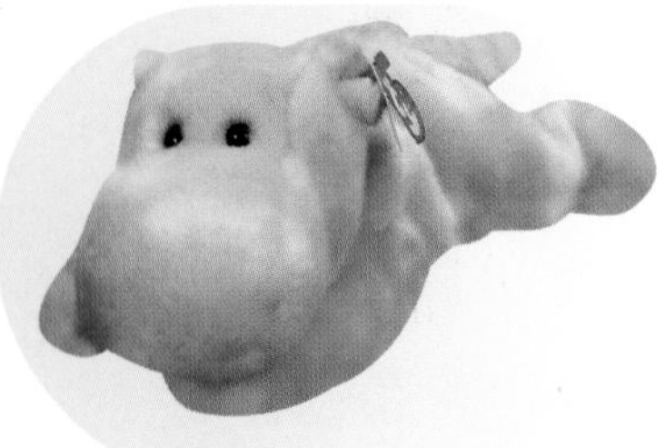

## Happy™

Hippopotamus • #9375
Issued: June 24, 2000
Current - Easy To Find

Beanie Buddies® Fact
Happy the Beanie Baby was originally made in gray. The gray version is very rare and is highly prized by collectors!

| Version | Price Paid | Market Value |
|---|---|---|
| Original | | ② $________ |

| Page Totals | Price Paid | Market Value |
|---|---|---|
| | | |

## Hippie™

60

Bunny · #9357
Issued: January 4, 2000
Retired: April 4, 2000

Beanie Buddies® Fact
Hippie the Beanie Baby
was the first bunny to be ty-dyed!

| Version | Price Paid | Market Value |
|---|---|---|
| Original | | ② $24 |

## Hippity™

61

Bunny · #9324
Issued: January 1, 1999
Retired: December 11, 1999

Beanie Buddies® Fact
Hippity the Beanie Baby
is a shade of green called Spring Mint.
This custom color is very difficult
to maintain throughout production.

| Version | Price Paid | Market Value |
|---|---|---|
| Original | | ① $22 |

## Hope™

62

Bear · #9327
Issued: May 1, 1999
Retired: March 23, 2000

Beanie Buddies® Fact
Hope the Beanie Baby
is the first Beanie Baby to be modeled after
one of Ty's plush bears!

| Version | Price Paid | Market Value |
|---|---|---|
| Original | | ② $17<br>① $21 |

## Hornsly™

63

Triceratops · #9407
Issued: April 1, 2001
Current - Easy To Find

Beanie Buddies® Fact
Hornsly is the first Beanie Baby
dinosaur created with horns.

| Version | Price Paid | Market Value |
|---|---|---|
| Original | | ② $________ |

| Page Totals | Price Paid | Market Value |
|---|---|---|
| | | |

64

## Humphrey™

Camel • #9307
Issued: September 30, 1998
Retired: December 11, 1999

Beanie Buddies® Fact
Humphrey the Beanie Baby was one of the first to be retired. Very few were produced, making him highly collectable!

| Version | Price Paid | Market Value |
|---|---|---|
| Original | | 1 $38 |

65

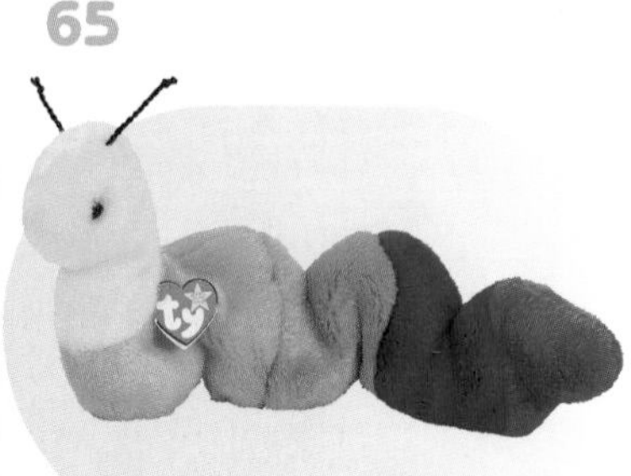

## Inch™

Inchworm • #9331
Issued: Summer 1999
Retired: January 31, 2000

Beanie Buddies® Fact
Inch the Beanie Baby was available with both felt and yarn antennas!

| Version | Price Paid | Market Value |
|---|---|---|
| Original | | 1 $18 |

66

## India™

Tiger • #9406
Issued: April 1, 2001
Current - Easy To Find

Beanie Buddies® Fact
India the Beanie Baby is one of only three tiger styles ever created.

| Version | Price Paid | Market Value |
|---|---|---|
| Original | | 2 $________ |

67

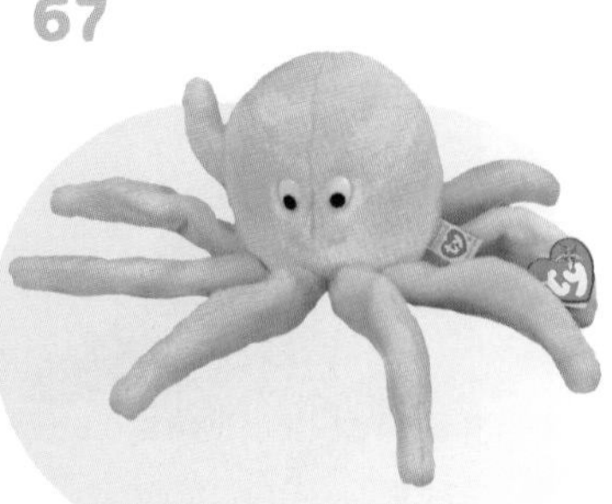

## Inky™

Octopus • #9404
Issued: April 1, 2001
Retired: April 26, 2001

Beanie Buddies® Fact
Inky the Beanie Baby was made in two colors: can you name them?

| Version | Price Paid | Market Value |
|---|---|---|
| Original | | 2 $15 |

| Page Totals | Price Paid | Market Value |
|---|---|---|
| | | |

## Jabber™

68

Parrot • #9326
Issued: May 1, 1999
Retired: December 12, 1999

Beanie Buddies® Fact
Jabber the Beanie Baby has 6 colors of fabric and 17 pattern pieces which make him one of the most difficult Beanies to produce!

| Version | Price Paid | Market Value |
|---|---|---|
| Original | | 1 $19 |

## Jake™

69

Mallard Duck • #9304
Issued: September 30, 1998
Retired: December 10, 1999

Beanie Buddies® Fact
Jake the Beanie Baby due to his numerous colors was difficult to manufacture making him one of the most sought after!

| Version | Price Paid | Market Value |
|---|---|---|
| Original | | 1 $22 |

## Jumbo Peace™

70

Bear • #9035
Issued: January 4, 2000
Current - Moderate To Find

Beanie Buddies® Fact
It takes the same amount of fabric to produce one jumbo Buddy as it does to make 25 regular Buddies!

| Version | Price Paid | Market Value |
|---|---|---|
| Original | | 2 $________ |

## Jumbo Schweetheart™

71

Orangutan • #9045
Issued: June 24, 2000
Current - Moderate To Find

Beanie Buddies® Fact
Ty hadn't originally planned to make Schweetheart this big, but his staff insisted that he try it! What do you think?

| Version | Price Paid | Market Value |
|---|---|---|
| Original | | 2 $________ |

| Page Totals | Price Paid | Market Value |
|---|---|---|
| | | |

72

## Jumbo Valentina™

Bear • #9050
Issued: January 1, 2001
Retired: March 16, 2001

Beanie Buddies® Fact
Jumbo Valentina is so large that she is shipped in her own box!

| Version | Price Paid | Market Value |
|---|---|---|
| Original | | 2 $95 |

73

## Kicks™

Bear • #9343
Issued: January 4, 2000
Retired: June 15, 2000

Beanie Buddies® Fact
Kicks the Beanie Baby was the first bear to represent a sport!

| Version | Price Paid | Market Value |
|---|---|---|
| Original | | 2 $24 |

74

New!

## Large 1997 Holiday Teddy™

Bear • #9053
Issued: October 1, 2001
Current – Just Released

Beanie Buddies® Fact
This was the first Beanie Baby to wear a Santa hat!

| Version | Price Paid | Market Value |
|---|---|---|
| Original | | 2 $_______ |

75

## Large Dotty™

Dalmatian • #9051
Issued: January 1, 2001
Current – Moderate To Find

Beanie Buddies® Fact
There were two Dalmatian Beanie Babies created: one with black ears and one with spotted ears.

| Version | Price Paid | Market Value |
|---|---|---|
| Original | | 2 $_______ |

| Page Totals | Price Paid | Market Value |
|---|---|---|
| | | |

## Large Ears™ 76

Bunny • #9046
Issued: January 1, 2001
Retired: March 29, 2001

Beanie Buddies® Fact
Ears the Beanie Baby was never manufactured in a solid white color.

| Version | Price Paid | Market Value |
|---|---|---|
| Original | | ② $40 |

## Large Fuzz™ 77

Bear • #9040
Issued: January 4, 2000
Retired: July 26, 2000

Beanie Buddies® Fact
In order for Fuzz to maintain the proper proportions, longer Tylon had to be used. The longer the fur the more difficult it is to distress!

| Version | Price Paid | Market Value |
|---|---|---|
| Original | | ② $48 |

## Large Hippie™ 78

Bunny • #9039
Issued: January 4, 2000
Retired: April 24, 2000

Beanie Buddies® Fact
One large Hippie is the same size as four Hippie Buddies!

| Version | Price Paid | Market Value |
|---|---|---|
| Original | | ② $55 |

## Large Libearty™ 79

**(exclusive to the United States)**

Bear • #9041
Issued: June 24, 2000
Retired: January 12, 2001

Beanie Buddies® Fact
Libearty the Beanie Baby was the only Beanie to have a few of his hang tags attached with a white rather than red tag pin!

| Version | Price Paid | Market Value |
|---|---|---|
| Original | | ② $50 |

80

## Large Peace™

Bear • #9037
Issued: January 4, 2000
Retired: September 7, 2000

Beanie Buddies® Fact
The larger the Buddy, the longer the fur and the more difficult it is to ty-dye the fabric!

| Version | Price Paid | Market Value |
|---|---|---|
| Original | | 2 $55 |

81

## Large Schweetheart™

Orangutan • #9043
Issued: June 24, 2000
Current - Moderate To Find

Beanie Buddies® Fact
Schweetheart's hand-painted eyes are very distinctive. The larger the eye, the more skillful the painter must be!

| Version | Price Paid | Market Value |
|---|---|---|
| Original | | 2 $_______ |

82

## Large Valentina™

Bear • #9048
Issued: January 1, 2001
Retired: March 16, 2001

Beanie Buddies® Fact
Valentina the Beanie Baby was born on Valentine's Day.

| Version | Price Paid | Market Value |
|---|---|---|
| Original | | 2 $45 |

83

## Lefty™

**(exclusive to the United States)**

Donkey • #9370
Issued: June 24, 2000
Retired: November 29, 2000

Beanie Buddies® Fact
Lefty and Righty the Beanie Babies were the first two different Beanies to share a poem!

| Version | Price Paid | Market Value |
|---|---|---|
| Original | | 2 $17 |

| Page Totals | Price Paid | Market Value |
|---|---|---|
| | | |

## Libearty™ 84

**(exclusive to the United States)**

Bear • #9371
Issued: June 24, 2000
Retired: January 12, 2001

Beanie Buddies® Fact
Libearty the Beanie Baby was the first bear to wear a flag!

| Version | Price Paid | Market Value |
|---|---|---|
| Original | | ② $23 |

## Lips™ 85

Fish • #9355
Issued: January 4, 2000
Retired: September 21, 2001

Beanie Buddies® Fact
Lips the Beanie Baby was one of the first summer show exclusives. This makes him very rare and valuable!

| Version | Price Paid | Market Value |
|---|---|---|
| Original | | ② $15 |

## Lizzy™ 86

Lizard • #9366
Issued: January 4, 2000
Retired: May 9, 2000

Beanie Buddies® Fact
Lizzy the Beanie Baby made with ty-dyed fabric was only produced for six months, making her one of the most valuable Beanies!

| Version | Price Paid | Market Value |
|---|---|---|
| Original | | ② $19 |

## Loosy™ 87

New!

Goose • #9428
Issued: October 1, 2001
Current - Just Released

Beanie Buddies® Fact
Loosy the Beanie Baby was created to represent the Canadian geese that live in the United States!

| Version | Price Paid | Market Value |
|---|---|---|
| Original | | ② $________ |

88

## Lucky™

Lady Bug • #9354
Issued: January 4, 2000
Retired: June 13, 2000

Beanie Buddies® Fact
Lucky the Beanie Baby was produced with three varieties of spots; 7 felt spots, 11 printed spots and 21 printed spots. Collectors are very lucky if they have all three!

| Version | Price Paid | Market Value |
|---|---|---|
| Original | | ❷ $16 |

89

## Luke™

Dog • #9412
Issued: July 3, 2001
Current - Moderate To Find

Beanie Buddies® Fact
Luke the Beanie Baby was the first Beanie Baby to have a checkered ribbon!

| Version | Price Paid | Market Value |
|---|---|---|
| Original | | ❷ $________ |

90

## Maple™

**(exclusive to Canada)**

Bear • #9600
Issued: August 31, 1999
Retired: September 29, 2000

Beanie Buddies® Fact
Maple the Beanie Baby was the first exclusive international bear!

| Version | Price Paid | Market Value (in U.S. market) |
|---|---|---|
| Original | | ❷ $65 ❶ $90 |

91

## Mellow™

Bear • #9411
Issued: July 3, 2001
Current - Moderate To Find

Beanie Buddies® Fact
Do you know if Mellow the Beanie Baby was produced both with and without eyebrows?

| Version | Price Paid | Market Value |
|---|---|---|
| Original | | ❷ $________ |

| Page Totals | Price Paid | Market Value |
|---|---|---|
| | | |

## Millennium™

92

Bear • #9325
Issued: May 1, 1999
Retired: November 19, 1999

Beanie Buddies® Fact
Millennium the Beanie Baby commemorates a once in a lifetime event, making it a once in a lifetime Beanie Baby!

| Version | Price Paid | Market Value |
|---|---|---|
| Original | | 1 $28 |

## Mooch™

93

Monkey • #9416
Issued: July 31, 2001
Retired: September 13, 2001

Beanie Buddies® Fact
Mooch the Beanie Baby was created in response to repeated requests from fans for Spider Monkeys!

| Version | Price Paid | Market Value |
|---|---|---|
| Original | | 2 $ |

## Mystic™

94

Unicorn • #9396
Issued: January 1, 2001
Current - Easy To Find

Beanie Buddies® Fact
Mystic the Beanie Baby was produced with two different colored horns.

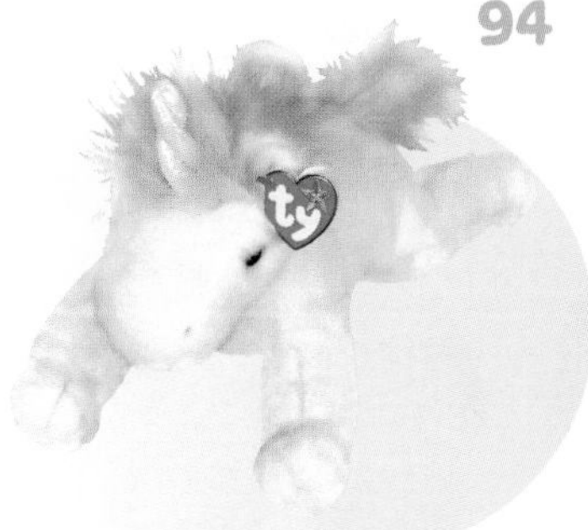

| Version | Price Paid | Market Value |
|---|---|---|
| Original | | 2 $________ |

## Nanook™

95

Husky • #9350
Issued: January 4, 2000
Retired: October 27, 2000

Beanie Buddies® Fact
Nanook the Beanie Baby was the first Beanie to feature blue eyes rather than black!

| Version | Price Paid | Market Value |
|---|---|---|
| Original | | 2 $20 |

96

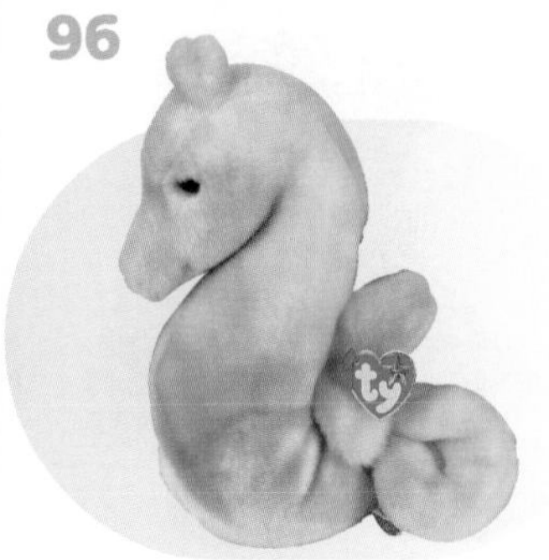

## Neon™

Seahorse • #9417
Issued: July 31, 2001
Retired: September 20, 2001

Beanie Buddies® Fact
Neon the Beanie Baby
was specifically designed to balance on his tail!

| Version | Price Paid | Market Value |
|---|---|---|
| Original | | 2 $17 |

97

## Oats™

Horse • #9392
Issued: January 1, 2001
Retired: May 15, 2001

Beanie Buddies® Fact
Oats the Beanie Baby
was the first horse
made into a Beanie Buddy!

| Version | Price Paid | Market Value |
|---|---|---|
| Original | | 2 $14 |

98

## Osito™

**(exclusive to the United States)**

Bear • #9344
Issued: January 4, 2000
Retired: October 25, 2000

Beanie Buddies® Fact
Osito the Beanie Baby
was the first USA exclusive that
did not have a US Flag!

| Version | Price Paid | Market Value |
|---|---|---|
| Original | | 2 $20 |

99

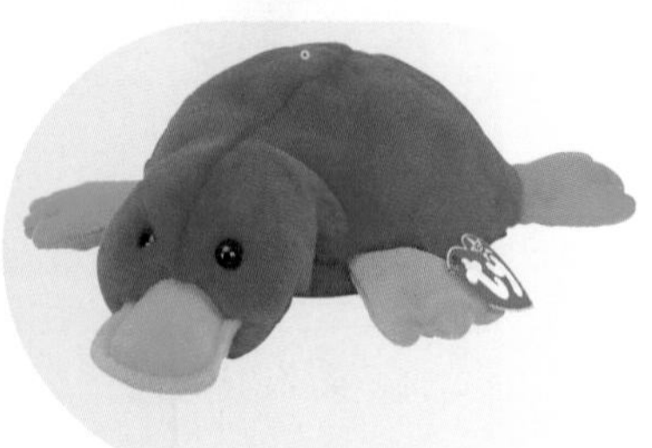

## Patti™

Platypus • #9320
Issued: January 1, 1999
Retired: July 27, 1999

Beanie Buddies® Fact
Patti the Beanie Baby
was one of the original nine.
Patti was available in both maroon
and magenta!

| Version | Price Paid | Market Value |
|---|---|---|
| Original | | 1 $18 |

| Page Totals | Price Paid | Market Value |
|---|---|---|
| | | |

## Peace™

100

Bear • #9335
Issued: August 31, 1999
Retired: June 23, 2000

Beanie Buddies® Fact
Peace the Beanie Baby was the first Beanie Baby with an embroidered emblem. This Ty-dye technique on a soft toy is the first in the World!

| Version | Price Paid | Market Value |
|---|---|---|
| Original | | 2 $25 1 $32 |

## Peanut™

101

Elephant • #9300
Issued: September 30, 1998
Retired: February 10, 2000

Beanie Buddies® Fact
Peanut the Beanie Baby made in this royal blue color is extremely rare and very valuable!

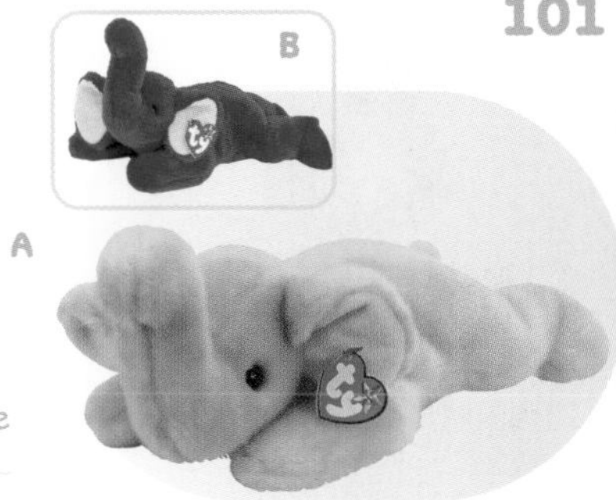


| Version | Price Paid | Market Value |
|---|---|---|
| A. Light Blue | | 2 $45 |
| B. Royal Blue | | 2 $23 1 $27 |

## Peking™

102

Panda • #9310
Issued: January 1, 1999
Retired: December 10, 1999

Beanie Buddies® Fact
Peking the Beanie Baby was the first panda made by Ty. He was retired after only six months making him highly collectible!

| Version | Price Paid | Market Value |
|---|---|---|
| Original | | 1 $21 |

## Periwinkle™

103

Bear • #9415
Issued: July 3, 2001
Current – Moderate To Find

Beanie Buddies® Fact
Collectors disagree as to whether Sunny and Periwinkle the Beanie Babies were originally planned to be sold via the Internet!

| Version | Price Paid | Market Value |
|---|---|---|
| Original | | 2 $_______ |

| Page Totals | Price Paid | Market Value |
|---|---|---|
| |  | 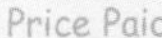 |

104

## Pinchers™

Lobster • #9424
Issued: July 31, 2001
Retired: September 20, 2001

Beanie Buddies® Fact
Pinchers the Beanie Baby was one of the original nine to be introduced in 1993!

| Version | Price Paid | Market Value |
|---|---|---|
| Original | | ② $13 |

105

## Pinky™

Flamingo • #9316
Issued: January 1, 1999
Retired: December 12, 1999

Beanie Buddies® Fact
Pinky the Beanie Baby was a manufacturing challenge because of her long neck!

| Version | Price Paid | Market Value |
|---|---|---|
| Original | | ① $14 |

106

## Pouch™

Kangaroo • #9380
Issued: June 24, 2000
Current – Easy To Find

Beanie Buddies® Fact
Pouch the Beanie Baby's pattern was used to create this kangaroo's "joey"!

| Version | Price Paid | Market Value |
|---|---|---|
| Original | | ② $______ |

107

## Prince™

Frog • #9401
Issued: January 1, 2001
Retired: September 21, 2001

Beanie Buddies® Fact
Prince the Beanie Baby is twice as big as Legs.

| Version | Price Paid | Market Value |
|---|---|---|
| Original | | ② $15 |

| Page Totals | Price Paid | Market Value |
|---|---|---|
| | | |

## Princess™ 108

Bear • #9329
Issued: May 1, 1999
Retired: April 10, 2000

Beanie Buddies® Fact
N/A

| Version | Price Paid | Market Value |
|---|---|---|
| Original | | ❷ $22 ❶ $32 |

## Pugsly™ 109

Dog • #9413
Issued: July 3, 2001
Retired: August 6, 2001

Beanie Buddies® Fact
Pugsly the Beanie Baby was difficult to produce because of the wrinkles in his face!

| Version | Price Paid | Market Value |
|---|---|---|
| Original | | ❷ $15 |

## Pumkin'™ 110

Pumpkin • #9332
Issued: August 31, 1999
Retired: November 29, 1999

Beanie Buddies® Fact
Pumkin' the Beanie Baby was the first Beanie to represent a vegetable!

| Version | Price Paid | Market Value |
|---|---|---|
| Original | | ❶ $22 |

## Quackers™ 111

B A

Duck • #9302
Issued: September 30, 1998
Retired: July 21, 1999

Beanie Buddies® Fact
Quackers the Beanie Baby retired in May 1998, was once made without wings!

| Version | Price Paid | Market Value |
|---|---|---|
| A. Without Wings | | ❶ $250 |
| B. With Wings | | ❶ $23 |

## 112

New!

### Radar™

Bat • #9422
Issued: September 3, 2001
Current – Just Released

Beanie Buddies® Fact
Radar is the first Beanie Baby whose name is a palindrome!

| Version | Price Paid | Market Value |
|---|---|---|
| Original | | ❷ $________ |

## 113

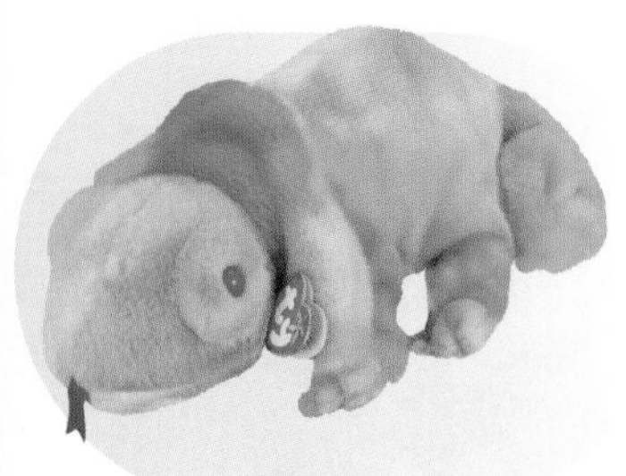

### Rainbow™

Chameleon • #9367
Issued: January 4, 2000
Current – Easy To Find

Beanie Buddies® Fact
Rainbow the Beanie Baby and his friend Iggy loved to switch tags and colors, making them the most confusing pair to date!

| Version | Price Paid | Market Value |
|---|---|---|
| Original | | ❷ $________ |

## 114

### Rex™

Tyrannosaurus • #9368
Issued: May 1, 2000
Retired: June 21, 2000

Beanie Buddies® Fact
Rex the Beanie Baby was one of the dinosaur trio. The poem and birthday for this item have yet to be discovered!

| Version | Price Paid | Market Value |
|---|---|---|
| Original | | ❷ $28 |

## 115

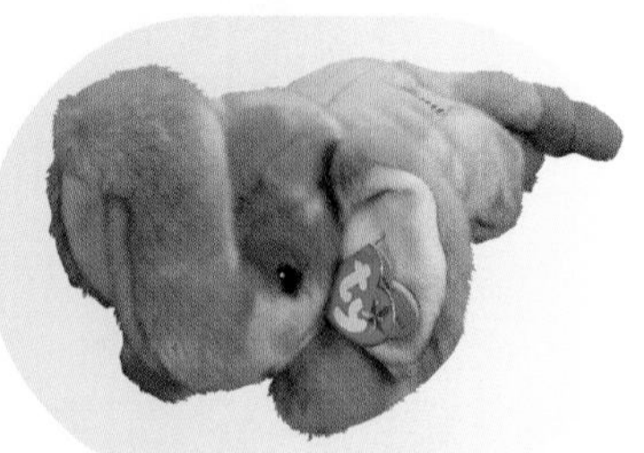

### Righty™
**(exclusive to the United States)**

Elephant • #9369
Issued: June 24, 2000
Retired: November 29, 2000

Beanie Buddies® Fact
Lefty and Righty the Beanie Babies were the first two different Beanies to share a poem!

| Version | Price Paid | Market Value |
|---|---|---|
| Original | | ❷ $17 |

| Page Totals | Price Paid | Market Value |
|---|---|---|
| | | |

## Roam™ 116

Buffalo · #9378
Issued: June 24, 2000
Current - Easy To Find

Beanie Buddies® Fact
The only Beanie Buddy created in the likeness of an original Beanie Baby - but in a different color!

| Version | Price Paid | Market Value |
|---|---|---|
| Original | | 2 $________ |

## Rover™ 117

Dog · #9305
Issued: September 30, 1998
Retired: December 12, 1999

Beanie Buddies® Fact
Rover the Beanie Baby was the first non-breed dog. Introduced in the summer of 1996 this red color set him apart!

| Version | Price Paid | Market Value |
|---|---|---|
| Original | | 1 $25 |

## Rufus™ 118

Dog · #9393
Issued: January 1, 2001
Retired: September 13, 2001

Beanie Buddies® Fact
Rufus the Beanie Baby was inspired by a puppy that Ty remembered as a child.

| Version | Price Paid | Market Value |
|---|---|---|
| Original | | 2 $ |

## Sakura™ 119

**(exclusive to Japan)**

Bear · #9608
Issued: February 19, 2001
Retired: July 26, 2001

Beanie Buddies® Fact
Sakura, created as a Japanese exclusive, was the first all pink Beanie Baby bear.

| Version | Price Paid | Market Value (in U.S. market) |
|---|---|---|
| Original | | 2 $45 |

120

## Santa™

Santa • #9385
Issued: September 28, 2000
Retired: November 17, 2000

Beanie Buddies® Fact
Santa the Beanie Baby has shed his green mittens and changed the color of the trim on his hat!

| Version | Price Paid | Market Value |
|---|---|---|
| Original | | ❷ $25 |

121

## Schweetheart™

Orangutan • #9330
Issued: June 26, 1999
Retired: January 31, 2000

Beanie Buddies® Fact
Schweetheart the Beanie Baby has fabric that is tip dyed. It is made with a special dying process where only the very tips are dyed a separate color. It is a very costly and difficult process!

| Version | Price Paid | Market Value |
|---|---|---|
| Original | | ❶ $24 |

122

## Seal™

Seal • #9419
Issued: July 3, 2001
Current – Easy To Find

Beanie Buddies® Fact
This Beanie Baby was the first and youngest of two Beanie Baby seals made by Ty!

| Version | Price Paid | Market Value |
|---|---|---|
| Original | | ❷ $________ |

123

## Silver™

Cat • #9340
Issued: August 31, 1999
Retired: May 19, 2000

Beanie Buddies® Fact
Silver and Amber the Beanie Babies were modeled after two orphaned kittens found by Ty Warner!

| Version | Price Paid | Market Value |
|---|---|---|
| Original | | ❷ $15 ❶ $20 |

| Page Totals | Price Paid | Market Value |
|---|---|---|
| | | |

## Slither™ 124

Snake • #9339
Issued: August 31, 1999
Retired: May 26, 2000

Beanie Buddies® Fact
Slither the Beanie Baby was the first snake made by Ty. Since his retirement in 1995 he has learned how to coil!

| Version | Price Paid | Market Value |
|---|---|---|
| Original | | 2 $15 1 $20 |

## Smoochy™ 125

Frog • #9315
Issued: January 1, 1999
Retired: November 24, 1999

Beanie Buddies® Fact
Smoochy the Beanie Baby is the second Beanie Baby frog made by Ty!

| Version | Price Paid | Market Value |
|---|---|---|
| Original | | 1 $19 |

## Sneaky™ 126

Leopard • #9376
Issued: June 24, 2000
Current - Easy To Find

Beanie Buddies® Fact
Sneaky the Beanie Baby has very detailed paws. This attention to detail makes Sneaky very difficult to manufacture!

| Version | Price Paid | Market Value |
|---|---|---|
| Original | | 2 $_______ |

## Snort™ 127

Bull • #9311
Issued: January 1, 1999
Retired: December 12, 1999

Beanie Buddies® Fact
Snort the Beanie Baby is the second bull made by Ty. The first bull did not have hooves!

| Version | Price Paid | Market Value |
|---|---|---|
| Original | | 1 $17 |

| Page Totals | Price Paid | Market Value |
|---|---|---|
| | | |

128

New!

## Snowball™

Snowman • #9429
Issued: October 1, 2001
Current – Just Released

Beanie Buddies® Fact
Snowball is one of the few Beanie Babies wearing a scarf instead of a ribbon. Do you know the others?

| Version | Price Paid | Market Value |
|---|---|---|
| Original | |  $________ |

129

## Snowboy™

Snowboy • #9342
Issued: August 31, 1999
Retired: December 12, 1999

Beanie Buddies® Fact
Snowboy the Beanie Baby was never made. This is the first and only time this pattern will be used!

| Version | Price Paid | Market Value |
|---|---|---|
| Original | | 1 $25 |

130

## Spangle™

Bear • #9336
Issued: August 31, 1999
Retired: June 15, 2000

Beanie Buddies® Fact
Spangle the Beanie Baby is the first Beanie to feature two distinct patterned fabrics and three different head colors!

| Version | Price Paid | Market Value |
|---|---|---|
| Original | | 2 $22 1 $30 |

131

## Speedy™

Turtle • #9352
Issued: January 4, 2000
Retired: May 9, 2000

Beanie Buddies® Fact
Speedy the Beanie Baby was one of the first Beanie Babies to feature printed fabric!

| Version | Price Paid | Market Value |
|---|---|---|
| Original | | 2 $17 |

| Page Totals | Price Paid | Market Value |
|---|---|---|
| | | |

Beanie Buddies®

## Spinner™ 132

Spider • #9334
Issued: August 31, 1999
Retired: December 12, 1999

Beanie Buddies® Fact
Spinner the Beanie Baby was the second spider to be made by Ty. The attention to detail includes a tiger striped body and red eyes!

| Version | Price Paid | Market Value |
| --- | --- | --- |
| Original | | 1 $16 |

## Spooky™ 133

New!

Ghost • #9421
Issued: September 3, 2001
Current - Just Released

Beanie Buddies® Fact
Spooky the Beanie Baby was made in two versions: with and without his red felt mouth!

| Version | Price Paid | Market Value |
| --- | --- | --- |
| Original | | 2 $________ |

## Spunky™ 134

Cocker Spaniel • #9400
Issued: January 1, 2001
Retired: June 14, 2001

Beanie Buddies® Fact
Spunky the Beanie Baby got his name because of the "spunky" nature of Cocker Spaniels.

| Version | Price Paid | Market Value |
| --- | --- | --- |
| Original | | 2 $17 |

## Squealer™ 135

Pig • #9313
Issued: January 1, 1999
Retired: November 24, 1999

Beanie Buddies® Fact
Squealer the Beanie Baby was one of the original nine. Squealer was so popular that he didn't retire for over four years!

| Version | Price Paid | Market Value |
| --- | --- | --- |
| Original | | 1 $16 |

136

## Steg™

Stegosaurus • #9383
Issued: June 24, 2000
Retired: August 30, 2000

Beanie Buddies® Fact
Steg the Beanie Baby was part of the dino trio. He is highly sought after and very collectable!

| Version | Price Paid | Market Value |
|---|---|---|
| Original | | 2 $20 |

137

## Stretch™

Ostrich • #9303
Issued: September 30, 1998
Retired: December 12, 1999

Beanie Buddies® Fact
Stretch the Beanie Baby is one of the most difficult to produce due to her long neck and numerous parts!

| Version | Price Paid | Market Value |
|---|---|---|
| Original | | 1 $18 |

138

## Sunny™

Bear • #9414
Issued: July 3, 2001
Current - Moderate To Find

Beanie Buddies® Fact
Sunny and Periwinkle the Beanie Babies were introduced and then retired only one week later!

| Version | Price Paid | Market Value |
|---|---|---|
| Original | | 2 $________ |

139

## Swoop™

Pterodactyl • #9391
Issued: January 1, 2001
Current - Easy To Find

Beanie Buddies® Fact
Swoop the Beanie Baby was the fourth dinosaur Beanie Baby made by Ty.

| Version | Price Paid | Market Value |
|---|---|---|
| Original | | 2 $________ |

| Page Totals | Price Paid | Market Value |
|---|---|---|
| | | |

## Tangerine™ 140

Bear • #9418
Issued: September 3, 2001
Current - Just Released

Beanie Buddies® Fact

Will there ever be a Tangerine the Beanie Baby?

| Version | Price Paid | Market Value |
|---|---|---|
| A. Terry Cloth | | 2 $________ |
| B. Plush | | 2 $________ |

## Teddy™ (cranberry) 141

Bear • #9306
Issued: September 30, 1998
Retired: November 17, 1999

Beanie Buddies® Fact
Teddy the Beanie Baby was made in six colors. A very limited number were produced in this special cranberry color!

| Version | Price Paid | Market Value |
|---|---|---|
| Original | | 1 $33 |

## Teddy™ (teal) 142

Bear • #9372
Issued: June 24, 2000
Current - Moderate To Find

Beanie Buddies® Fact
The Teddy teal Beanie Baby was produced with this style face. Commonly referred to as an "old faced" teddy, his value continues to grow!

| Version | Price Paid | Market Value |
|---|---|---|
| Original | | 2 $________ |

## The Beginning Bear™ 143

Bear • #9399
Issued: January 1, 2001
Retired: April 16, 2001

Beanie Buddies® Fact
The Beginning Bear Beanie Baby marked the beginning of a new millennium of Beanie Babies.

| Version | Price Paid | Market Value |
|---|---|---|
| Original | | 2 $22 |

144

## The Cardinal™

Bird • #9395
Issued: January 1, 2001
Retired: May 15, 2001

Beanie Buddies® Fact
The cardinal Beanie Baby's wings were originally designed to be black tipped.

| Version | Price Paid | Market Value |
|---|---|---|
| Original | | 2 $14 |

145

## Tracker™

Basset Hound • #9319
Issued: January 1, 1999
Retired: November 29, 1999

Beanie Buddies® Fact
Tracker the Beanie Baby has the most expressive eyes. Close attention to this detail means limited production.

| Version | Price Paid | Market Value |
|---|---|---|
| Original | | 1 $18 |

146

## Trumpet™

Elephant • #9403
Issued: April 1, 2001
Retired: August 6, 2001

Beanie Buddies® Fact
Trumpet the Beanie Baby was the first elephant made in a sitting position.

| Version | Price Paid | Market Value |
|---|---|---|
| Original | | 2 $15 |

147

## Twigs™

Giraffe • #9308
Issued: September 30, 1998
Retired: January 1, 1999

Beanie Buddies® Fact
Twigs the Beanie Baby was manufactured in fabric created exclusively for Ty and was retired in May 1998!

| Version | Price Paid | Market Value |
|---|---|---|
| Original | | 1 $150 |

| Page Totals | Price Paid | Market Value |
|---|---|---|
| | | |

## Ty 2K™ 148

Bear • #9346
Issued: January 4, 2000
Retired: March 8, 2000

Beanie Buddies® Fact
Ty 2K the Beanie Baby's name was the result of a play on words with Y2K!

| Version | Price Paid | Market Value |
|---|---|---|
| Original | | 2 $40 |

## Unity™ 149

**(exclusive to Europe)**

New!

Bear • #9609
Issued: October 1, 2001
Current - Just Released

Beanie Buddies® Fact
The twelve stars on Unity's chest represent the original twelve member countries in the European Union!

| Version | Price Paid | Market Value |
|---|---|---|
| Original | | 2 $______ |

## Valentina™ 150

Bear • #9397
Issued: January 1, 2001
Retired: March 16, 2001

Beanie Buddies® Fact
Valentina the Beanie Baby is the true love of Valentino.

| Version | Price Paid | Market Value |
|---|---|---|
| Original | | 2 $19 |

## Valentino™ 151

Bear • #9347
Issued: January 4, 2000
Retired: June 8, 2000

Beanie Buddies® Fact
Valentino the Beanie Baby was the first bear to feature embroidery!

| Version | Price Paid | Market Value |
|---|---|---|
| Original | | 2 $23 |

152

## Waddle™

Penguin • #9314
Issued: January 1, 1999
Retired: December 12, 1999

Beanie Buddies® Fact
Waddle the Beanie Baby was the first of two penguins to be made by Ty. He was retired in April of 1998!

| Version | Price Paid | Market Value |
| --- | --- | --- |
| Original | | 1 $17 |

153

## Wallace™

Bear • #9387
Issued: September 28, 2000
Retired: January 12, 2001

Beanie Buddies® Fact
Wallace the Beanie Baby wore a tartan plaid scarf. Can you guess which clan?

| Version | Price Paid | Market Value |
| --- | --- | --- |
| Original | | 2 $20 |

154

## Weenie™

Dachshund • #9356
Issued: January 4, 2000
Retired: May 26, 2000

Beanie Buddies® Fact
Weenie the Beanie Baby was the first Beanie to stand on all four paws!

| Version | Price Paid | Market Value |
| --- | --- | --- |
| Original | | 2 $22 |

155

## White Tiger™

Tiger • #9374
Issued: June 24, 2000
Current – Easy To Find

Beanie Buddies® Fact
The White Tiger Beanie Baby's name was inspired by the winter weather in Chicago!

| Version | Price Paid | Market Value |
| --- | --- | --- |
| Original | | 2 $________ |

| Page Totals | Price Paid | Market Value |
| --- | --- | --- |
| | | |

## Zip™

156

Cat • #9360
Issued: January 4, 2000
Retired: February 27, 2001

Beanie Buddies® Fact
Zip the Beanie Baby was made in three styles; all white, black and white and all black!

| Version | Price Paid | Market Value |
|---|---|---|
| Original | | ❷ $14 |

# Beanie Boppers™

This new Ty collection debuted in 2001, and currently features 13 super-hip girls and three sports-loving boys. The *Beanie Boppers* are a little bit bigger in size than the *Beanie Kids*.

1

LE-18,000, available exclusively at New York Yankees game, 8/5/01

## Bronx Bomber™

Bopper · #0100
Issued: August 5, 2001
Retired: August 7, 2001

Birthdate: August 5
Hometown: Bronx, New York
Favorites: Playing baseball and cheering for the Yankees

| Version | Price Paid | Market Value |
|---|---|---|
| Original | | $125 |

2

New!

## Bubbly Betty™

Bopper · #0207
Issued: October 1, 2001
Current - Just Released

Birthdate: May 29
Hometown: Golden, Colorado
Favorites: Snow boarding, pepperoni pizza, scary movies

| Version | Price Paid | Market Value |
|---|---|---|
| Original | | $______ |

3

New!

## Cuddly Crystal™ (Club exclusive)

Bopper · #0109
Issued: September 24, 2001
Current - Just Released

Birthdate: May 29
Hometown: St. Cloud, Minnesota
Favorites: Reading my BBOC newsletter, joining clubs, collecting Beanie Babies

| Version | Price Paid | Market Value |
|---|---|---|
| Original | | $______ |

| Page Totals | Price Paid | Market Value |
|---|---|---|
| | | |

## Dazzlin' Destiny™ 4

New!

Bopper · #0206
Issued: September 3, 2001
Current - Just Released

Birthdate: August 23
Hometown: Redmond, Washington
Favorites: Chatting on-line, surfin' the net, teen mags

| Version | Price Paid | Market Value |
|---|---|---|
| Original | | $_______ |

## Footie™ 5

**(exclusive to the United Kingdom)**

Bopper · #0102
Issued: August 15, 2001
Current - Impossible To Find
Birthdate: August 18
Hometown: England
Favorites: A kick around the park, dreaming of winning the World Cup

| Version | Price Paid | Market Value (in U.S. market) |
|---|---|---|
| Original | | $25 |

## Holiday Heidi™ 6

New!

Bopper · #0212
Issued: October 1, 2001
Current - Just Released

Birthdate: September 2
Hometown: Ann Arbor, Michigan
Favorites: Holiday shopping, making snowmen and wrapping presents

| Version | Price Paid | Market Value |
|---|---|---|
| Original | | $_______ |

## Huggable Holly™ 7

Bopper · #0203
Issued: July 3, 2001
Current - Moderate To Find

Birthdate: February 3
Hometown: Overland Park, Kansas
Favorites: Soccer, body glitter and drawing

| Version | Price Paid | Market Value |
|---|---|---|
| Original | | $_______ |

8

New!

LE-10,000, available exclusively at Chicago Cubs game, 9/30/01

## Ivy Leaguer™

Bopper • #0101
Issued: September 30, 2001
Retired: October 1, 2001

Birthdate: September 30
Hometown: Chicago, Illinois
Favorites: Playing baseball and cheering for the Cubs

| Version | Price Paid | Market Value |
|---|---|---|
| Original | | $80 |

9

New!

## Jazzy Jessie™

Bopper • #0209
Issued: October 1, 2001
Current - Just Released

Birthdate: January 30
Hometown: Queens, New York
Favorites: Jumping rope, visiting my grandma and watching videos

| Version | Price Paid | Market Value |
|---|---|---|
| Original | | $______ |

10

New!

## Jolly Janie™

Bopper • #0210
Issued: October 1, 2001
Current - Just Released

Birthdate: March 30
Hometown: Scottsdale, Arizona
Favorites: Baking holiday cookies, caroling and trimming the tree

| Version | Price Paid | Market Value |
|---|---|---|
| Original | | $______ |

11

## Kooky Kandy™

Bopper • #0202
Issued: July 3, 2001
Current - Moderate To Find

Birthdate: May 20
Hometown: Walnut Creek, California
Favorites: Boys, pink lip gloss, talking on the phone

| Version | Price Paid | Market Value |
|---|---|---|
| Original | | $______ |

| Page Totals | Price Paid | Market Value |
|---|---|---|
| | | |

## Loveable Lulu™ 12

Bopper • #0204
Issued: July 3, 2001
Current - Moderate To Find

Birthdate: July 17
Hometown: Naperville, Illinois
Favorites: Popcorn, unicorns and doing crafts

| Version | Price Paid | Market Value |
|---|---|---|
| Original | | $________ |

## Pretty Patti™ 13

Bopper • #0205
Issued: July 3, 2001
Current - Moderate To Find

Birthdate: August 7
Hometown: Tysons Corner, Virginia
Favorites: Roller coasters, green nail polish, animals

| Version | Price Paid | Market Value |
|---|---|---|
| Original | | $________ |

## Rockin' Rosie™ 14

Bopper • #0200
Issued: July 3, 2001
Current - Moderate To Find

Birthdate: October 11
Hometown: Plano, Texas
Favorites: Horseback riding, sleep-overs, telling secrets

| Version | Price Paid | Market Value |
|---|---|---|
| Original | | $________ |

## Sassy Star™ 15

Bopper • #0201
Issued: July 3, 2001
Current - Moderate To Find

Birthdate: December 4
Hometown: Sarasota, Florida
Favorites: Going to the mall, gel pens, platform shoes

| Version | Price Paid | Market Value |
|---|---|---|
| Original | | $________ |

16

New!

## Sweet Sally™

Bopper • #0208
Issued: October 1, 2001
Current - Just Released

Birthdate: July 26
Hometown: Sandy Springs, Georgia
Favorites: Gymnastics, babysitting and anything pink

| Version | Price Paid | Market Value |
| --- | --- | --- |
| Original | | $ |

| Page Totals | Price Paid | Market Value |
| --- | --- | --- |
| | | |

# Beanie Kids™

Since Ty introduced the *Beanie Kids* in the summer of 2000, these charming guys and gals have pranced their way into many collectors' hearts. The collection's first holiday-oriented piece, "Noelle," was released in October 2001.

## Angel™ 1

Kid • #0001
Issued: January 8, 2000
Current - Moderate To Find

Birthdate: March 29, 1994

Be my best friend and then you will see, how very, very special you are to me!

| Version | Price Paid | Market Value |
|---|---|---|
| Original | | $________ |

## Blondie™ 2

Kid • #0017
Issued: January 1, 2001
Current - Moderate To Find

Birthdate: January 2, 1995

Please dress me up and take me out, making friends is what it's all about!

| Version | Price Paid | Market Value |
|---|---|---|
| Original | | $________ |

## Boomer™ 3

Kid • #0007
Issued: January 8, 2000
Current - Easy To Find

Birthdate: August 11, 1994

I like being noisy, it's lots of fun, then I get attention from everyone!

| Version | Price Paid | Market Value |
|---|---|---|
| Original | | $________ |

4

## Buzz™

Kid • #0010
Issued: June 24, 2000
Current - Easy To Find

Birthdate: November 24, 1997

My hair is short, so is my name
Please take me home, we'll play a game!

| Version | Price Paid | Market Value |
|---|---|---|
| Original | | $________ |

5

## Calypso™

Kid • #0011
Issued: June 24, 2000
Current - Easy To Find

Birthdate: June 28, 1997

Please be my friend, give me a chance
We'll sing all day and then we'll dance!

| Version | Price Paid | Market Value |
|---|---|---|
| Original | | $________ |

6

## Chipper™

Kid • #0008
Issued: January 8, 2000
Retired: August 11, 2000

Birthdate: July 20, 1997

Happy and cheerful, big hugs for all, smiling and laughing - life is a ball!

| Version | Price Paid | Market Value |
|---|---|---|
| Original | | $12 |

7

## Cookie™

Kid • #0013
Issued: June 24, 2000
Current - Moderate To Find

Birthdate: April 5, 1995

My name is Cookie and you'll agree
I'm as sweet as sweet can be!

| Version | Price Paid | Market Value |
|---|---|---|
| Original | | $________ |

| Page Totals | Price Paid | Market Value |
|---|---|---|

## Curly™

8

Kid · #0004
Issued: January 8, 2000
Retired: August 10, 2000

Birthdate: March 2, 1997

My curly hair is a sight to see,
a pretty bow makes me cute as can be!

| Version | Price Paid | Market Value |
|---|---|---|
| Original | | $12 |

## Cutie™

9

Kid · #0005
Issued: January 8, 2000
Current - Easy To Find

Birthdate: December 26, 1996

I can't help but give you a hug,
in your arms is where I feel snug!

| Version | Price Paid | Market Value |
|---|---|---|
| Original | | $________ |

## Ginger™

10

Kid · #0003
Issued: January 8, 2000
Current - Easy To Find

Birthdate: June 12, 1992

Everyone says I'm all sugar and spice,
so when we play, I'll always be nice!

| Version | Price Paid | Market Value |
|---|---|---|
| Original | | $________ |

## Jammer™

11

Kid · #0016
Issued: January 1, 2001
Current - Easy To Find

Birthdate: July 9, 1992

Take me home and you'll agree
I'm as cool as I can be!

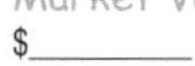

| Version | Price Paid | Market Value |
|---|---|---|
| Original | | $________ |

| Page Totals | Price Paid | Market Value |
|---|---|---|
| | | |

12

## Luvie™

Kid • #0014
Issued: January 1, 2001
Current – Easy To Find

Birthdate: February 14, 1994

All my love I give to you
I hope you love me that much too!

| Version | Price Paid | Market Value |
|---|---|---|
| Original | | $________ |

13

New!

## Noelle™

Kid • #0020
Issued: October 1, 2001
Current – Just Released

Birthdate: December 10, 1994

Family, friends and lots of cheer
This is my favorite time of year!

| Version | Price Paid | Market Value |
|---|---|---|
| Original | | $________ |

14

## Precious™

Kid • #0002
Issued: January 8, 2000
Current – Moderate To Find

Birthdate: May 15, 1993

Hey, look at me and give me a smile,
take me home and we'll play awhile!

| Version | Price Paid | Market Value |
|---|---|---|
| Original | | $________ |

15

## Princess™

Kid • #0012
Issued: June 24, 2000
Current – Moderate To Find

Birthdate: March 23, 1996

My hair is pretty, it's long and brown
Should we put it up or leave it down?

| Version | Price Paid | Market Value |
|---|---|---|
| Original | | $________ |

| Page Totals | Price Paid | Market Value |
|---|---|---|
| | | |

## Rascal™ 16

Kid • #0006
Issued: January 8, 2000
Current - Easy To Find

Birthdate: April 15, 1995

Hear me giggle and watch me dance,
I'll make you laugh, so give me a chance!

| Version | Price Paid | Market Value |
|---|---|---|
| Original | | $________ |

## Shenanigan™ 17

Kid • #0015
Issued: January 1, 2001
Current - Easy To Find

Birthdate: March 17, 1993

I'll bring you luck the whole year through
if you keep me close to you!

| Version | Price Paid | Market Value |
|---|---|---|
| Original | | $________ |

## Specs™ 18

Kid • #0018
Issued: January 1, 2001
Current - Easy To Find

Birthdate: September 25, 1991

Learning is so much fun to do
May I go to school with you?

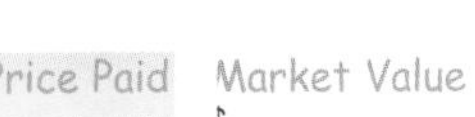

| Version | Price Paid | Market Value |
|---|---|---|
| Original | | $________ |

## Tumbles™ 19

Kid • #0009
Issued: January 8, 2000
Current - Easy To Find

Birthdate: September 3, 1996

A little bit naughty I'm known to be,
make sure you don't take your eyes off me!

| Version | Price Paid | Market Value |
|---|---|---|
| Original | | $________ |

| Page Totals | Price Paid | Market Value |
|---|---|---|
| | | |

# Ty Gear™

In the fall of 2000, Ty introduced *Ty Gear*, a line of clothes for the *Beanie Kids*. You can outfit the *Kids* in everything from silly costumes to everyday school clothes!

1

**Ballerina**
#0508
Issued: July 8, 2000
Current

Beanie Kids™ & Ty Gear™ are sold separately

| Version | Price Paid | Market Value |
|---|---|---|
| Original | | $_________ |

2

**Baseball**
#0511
Issued: July 8, 2000
Current

Beanie Kids™ & Ty Gear™ are sold separately

| Version | Price Paid | Market Value |
|---|---|---|
| Original | | $_________ |

3

**Beach Boy**
#0515
Issued: July 3, 2001
Retired

Beanie Kids™ & Ty Gear™ are sold separately

| Version | Price Paid | Market Value |
|---|---|---|
| Original | | $_________ |

4

**Beach Girl**
#0516
Issued: July 3, 2001
Current

Beanie Kids™ & Ty Gear™ are sold separately

| Version | Price Paid | Market Value |
|---|---|---|
| Original | | $_________ |

5

**Bride**
#0518
Issued: July 3, 2001
Current

Beanie Kids™ & Ty Gear™ are sold separately

| Version | Price Paid | Market Value |
|---|---|---|
| Original | | $_________ |

6

**Bunny**
#0512
Issued: January 1, 2001
Retired

Beanie Kids™ & Ty Gear™ are sold separately

| Version | Price Paid | Market Value |
|---|---|---|
| Original | | $_________ |

7

**Cheerleader**
#0500
Issued: July 8, 2000
Current

Beanie Kids™ & Ty Gear™ are sold separately

| Version | Price Paid | Market Value |
|---|---|---|
| Original | | $_________ |

8

**Doctor**
#0509
Issued: July 8, 2000
Current

Beanie Kids™ & Ty Gear™ are sold separately

| Version | Price Paid | Market Value |
|---|---|---|
| Original | | $_________ |

| Page Totals | Price Paid | Market Value |
|---|---|---|
| | | |

**9**

### Dress Up/ Sunday Best

#0513
Issued: January 1, 2001
Current

Beanie Kids™ & Ty Gear™ are sold separately

| Version | Price Paid | Market Value |
|---|---|---|
| Original | | $________ |

**10**

### Firefighter

#0506
Issued: July 8, 2000
Current

Beanie Kids™ & Ty Gear™ are sold separately

| Version | Price Paid | Market Value |
|---|---|---|
| Original | | $________ |

**11**

### Groom

#0519
Issued: July 3, 2001
Retired

Beanie Kids™ & Ty Gear™ are sold separately

| Version | Price Paid | Market Value |
|---|---|---|
| Original | | $________ |

**12**

### In-Line Skater

#0517
Issued: July 3, 2001
Current

Beanie Kids™ & Ty Gear™ are sold separately

| Version | Price Paid | Market Value |
|---|---|---|
| Original | | $________ |

**13**

### Pajamas

#0503
Issued: July 8, 2000
Current

Beanie Kids™ & Ty Gear™ are sold separately

| Version | Price Paid | Market Value |
|---|---|---|
| Original | | $________ |

**14**

### Party Tyme

#0510
Issued: July 8, 2000
Current

Beanie Kids™ & Ty Gear™ are sold separately

| Version | Price Paid | Market Value |
|---|---|---|
| Original | | $________ |

**15**

### Princess

#0501
Issued: July 8, 2000
Current

Beanie Kids™ & Ty Gear™ are sold separately

| Version | Price Paid | Market Value |
|---|---|---|
| Original | | $________ |

**16**

### School Days

#0505
Issued: July 8, 2000

Beanie Kids™ & Ty Gear™ are sold separately

| Version | Price Paid | Market Value |
|---|---|---|
| Original | | $________ |

**17**

New!

### Skeleton

#0522
Issued: Sept. 3, 2001
Current

Beanie Kids™ & Ty Gear™ are sold separately

| Version | Price Paid | Market Value |
|---|---|---|
| Original | | $________ |

**18**

### Snowboarder

#0514
Issued: January 1, 2001
Retired

Beanie Kids™ & Ty Gear™ are sold separately

| Version | Price Paid | Market Value |
|---|---|---|
| Original | | $________ |

19

### Soccer

#0502
Issued: July 8, 2000
Current

Beanie Kids™ & Ty Gear™ are sold separately

| Version | Price Paid | Market Value |
|---|---|---|
| Original | | $________ |

20

### Summer Fun

#0504
Issued: July 8, 2000
Current

Beanie Kids™ & Ty Gear™ are sold separately

| Version | Price Paid | Market Value |
|---|---|---|
| Original | | $________ |

21

New!

### The Count

#0521
Issued: Sept. 3, 2001
Current

Beanie Kids™ & Ty Gear™ are sold separately

| Version | Price Paid | Market Value |
|---|---|---|
| Original | | $________ |

22

### Witch

#0507
Issued: July 8, 2000
Current

Beanie Kids™ & Ty Gear™ are sold separately

| Version | Price Paid | Market Value |
|---|---|---|
| Original | | $________ |

| Page Totals | Price Paid | Market Value |
|---|---|---|
| | | |

# Jingle Beanies™

They're here! Ty has introduced a new line of ornaments featuring some of your favorite *Beanie Babies* designs. In addition to the "original 9" ornaments, there's a special ornament set available to BBOC members!

## 1997 Holiday Teddy™

1 New!

Bear • #3506
Issued: September 17, 2001
Current - Just Released

| Version | Price Paid | Market Value |
|---|---|---|
| Original | | $________ |

## 1998 Holiday Teddy™

2 New!

Bear • #3507
Issued: September 17, 2001
Current - Just Released

| Version | Price Paid | Market Value |
|---|---|---|
| Original | | $________ |

## 1999 Holiday Teddy™

3 New!

Bear • #3508
Issued: September 17, 2001
Current - Just Released

| Version | Price Paid | Market Value |
|---|---|---|
| Original | | $________ |

| Page Totals | Price Paid | Market Value |
|---|---|---|
| | | |

4 New!

## Clubby Edition™

**(set/4, Club exclusive)**

Bears • #3599
Issued: September 24, 2001
Current – Just Released

| Version | Price Paid | Market Value |
|---|---|---|
| Original | | $________ |

5 New!

## Halo™

Bear • #3504
Issued: September 17, 2001
Current – Just Released

| Version | Price Paid | Market Value |
|---|---|---|
| Original | | $________ |

6 New!

## Loosy™

Goose • #3501
Issued: September 17, 2001
Current – Just Released

| Version | Price Paid | Market Value |
|---|---|---|
| Original | | $________ |

7 New!

## Peace™

Bear • #3505
Issued: September 17, 2001
Current – Just Released

| Version | Price Paid | Market Value |
|---|---|---|
| Original | | $________ |

| Page Totals | Price Paid | Market Value |
|---|---|---|
| | | |

## Quackers™ 8

New!

Duck · #3500
Issued: September 17, 2001
Current - Just Released

| Version | Price Paid | Market Value |
|---|---|---|
| Original | | $________ |

## Rover™ 9

New!

Dog · #3503
Issued: September 17, 2001
Current - Just Released

| Version | Price Paid | Market Value |
|---|---|---|
| Original | | $________ |

## Twigs™ 10

New!

Giraffe · #3502
Issued: September 17, 2001
Current - Just Released

| Version | Price Paid | Market Value |
|---|---|---|
| Original | | $________ |

# Teenie Beanie Babies™

There were no new Teenie Beanie Babies promotions at McDonald's restaurants in 2001, but through the years there have been many memorable releases.

1

**1997 Teenie Beanie Babies™ Complete Set (set/10)**

1st Promotion
Issued: April 11, 1997
Retired: May 15, 1997

| Version | Price Paid | Market Value |
|---|---|---|
| Original | | $90 |

2

**1998 Teenie Beanie Babies™ Complete Set (set/12)**

2nd Promotion
Issued: May 22, 1998
Retired: June 12, 1998

| Version | Price Paid | Market Value |
|---|---|---|
| Original | | $35 |

3

**1999 Teenie Beanie Babies™ Complete Set (set/12)**

3rd Promotion
Issued: May 21, 1999
Retired: June 3, 1999

| Version | Price Paid | Market Value |
|---|---|---|
| Original | | $25 |

4

**2000 Teenie Beanie Babies™ Complete Set (set/29)**

4th Promotion
Issued: June 13, 2000
Retired: July 13, 2000

| Version | Price Paid | Market Value |
|---|---|---|
| Original | | $38 |

| Page Totals | Price Paid | Market Value |
|---|---|---|
| | | |

## 5

### 1999 Teenie Beanie Babies™ International Bears (set/4)

Issued: June 4, 1999
Retired: June 17, 1999

| Version | Price Paid | Market Value |
|---|---|---|
| Original | | $19 |

## 6

### 2000 Teenie Beanie Babies™ International Bears II (set/3)

Issued: June 20, 2000
Retired: July 13, 2000

| Version | Price Paid | Market Value |
|---|---|---|
| Original | | $14 |

## 7

### 2000 Teenie Beanie Babies™ American Trio (set/3)

Issued: October 25, 2000
Retired: November 9, 2000

| Version | Price Paid | Market Value |
|---|---|---|
| Original | | $18 |

## 8

### Antsy™

Anteater
3rd Promotion
#2 of 12
Issued: May 21, 1999
Retired: June 3, 1999

| Version | Price Paid | Market Value |
|---|---|---|
| Original | | $3 |

## 9

### Blizz™

White Tiger
4th Promotion
#10 of 18
Issued: June 27, 2000
Retired: July 13, 2000

| Version | Price Paid | Market Value |
|---|---|---|
| Original | | $4 |

## 10

### Bones™

Dog
2nd Promotion
#9 of 12
Issued: May 22, 1998
Retired: June 12, 1998

| Version | Price Paid | Market Value |
|---|---|---|
| Original | | $4 |

## 11

### Bongo™

Monkey
2nd Promotion
#2 of 12
Issued: May 22, 1998
Retired: June 12, 1998

| Version | Price Paid | Market Value |
|---|---|---|
| Original | | $6 |

## 12

### Britannia™

Bear
3rd Promotion
International Bear
Issued: June 4, 1999
Retired: June 17, 1999

| Version | Price Paid | Market Value |
|---|---|---|
| Original | | $4 |

## 13

### Bronty™

Brontosaurus
4th Promotion
Week #1
Issued: June 13, 2000
Retired: July 13, 2000

| Version | Price Paid | Market Value |
|---|---|---|
| Original | | $5 |

## 14

### Bumble™

Bee
4th Promotion
#6 of 18
Issued: June 20, 2000
Retired: July 13, 2000

| Version | Price Paid | Market Value |
|---|---|---|
| Original | | $4 |



| Page Totals | Price Paid | Market Value |
|---|---|---|
| | | |

15 

**Bushy™**
Lion
4th Promotion
#18 of 18
Issued: June 29, 2000
Retired: July 13, 2000

| Version | Price Paid | Market Value |
|---|---|---|
| Original | | $4 |

16 

**Chilly™**
Polar Bear
4th Promotion
Week #3
Issued: June 27, 2000
Retired: July 13, 2000

| Version | Price Paid | Market Value |
|---|---|---|
| Original | | $5 |

17 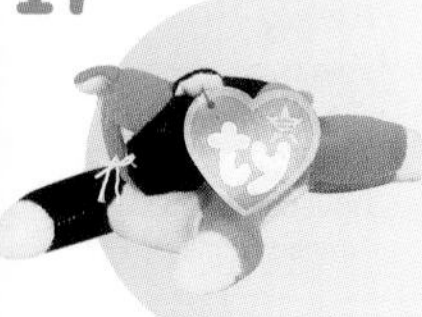

**Chip™**
Cat
3rd Promotion
#12 of 12
Issued: May 21, 1999
Retired: June 3, 1999

| Version | Price Paid | Market Value |
|---|---|---|
| Original | | $3 |

18 

**Chocolate™**
Moose
1st Promotion
#4 of 10
Issued: April 11, 1997
Retired: May 15, 1997

| Version | Price Paid | Market Value |
|---|---|---|
| Original | | $15 |

19 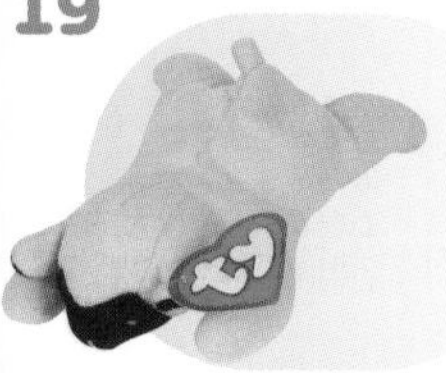

**Chops™**
Lamb
1st Promotion
#3 of 10
Issued: April 11, 1997
Retired: May 15, 1997

| Version | Price Paid | Market Value |
|---|---|---|
| Original | | $22 |

20 

**Claude™**
Crab
3rd Promotion
#9 of 12
Issued: May 21, 1999
Retired: June 3, 1999

| Version | Price Paid | Market Value |
|---|---|---|
| Original | | $3 |

21 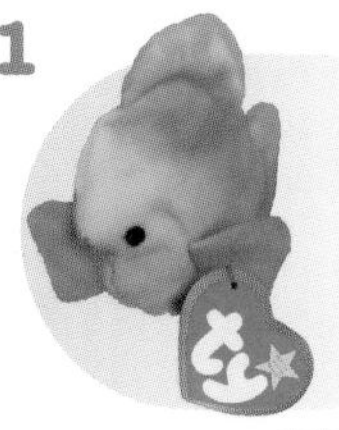

**Coral™**
Fish
4th Promotion
#14 of 18
Issued: July 4, 2000
Retired: July 13, 2000

| Version | Price Paid | Market Value |
|---|---|---|
| Original | | $4 |

22 

**Doby™**
Doberman
2nd Promotion
#1 of 12
Issued: May 22, 1998
Retired: June 12, 1998

| Version | Price Paid | Market Value |
|---|---|---|
| Original | | $6 |

23 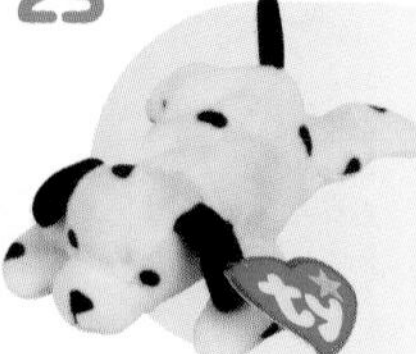

**Dotty™**
Dalmatian
4th Promotion
#4 of 18
Issued: June 13, 2000
Retired: July 13, 2000

| Version | Price Paid | Market Value |
|---|---|---|
| Original | | $4 |

24

**Erin™**
Bear
3rd Promotion
International Bear
Issued: June 4, 1999
Retired: June 17, 1999

| Version | Price Paid | Market Value |
|---|---|---|
| Original | | $4 |

| Page Totals | Price Paid | Market Value |
|---|---|---|
| | | |

## 25

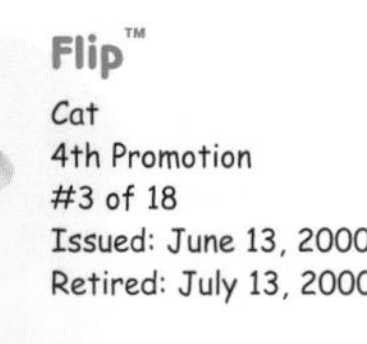

**Flip™**
Cat
4th Promotion
#3 of 18
Issued: June 13, 2000
Retired: July 13, 2000

| Version | Price Paid | Market Value |
|---|---|---|
| Original | | $4 |

## 26

**Flitter™**
Butterfly
4th Promotion
#8 of 18
Issued: June 20, 2000
Retired: July 13, 2000

| Version | Price Paid | Market Value |
|---|---|---|
| Original | | $4 |

## 27

**Freckles™**
Leopard
3rd Promotion
#1 of 12
Issued: May 21, 1999
Retired: June 3, 1999

| Version | Price Paid | Market Value |
|---|---|---|
| Original | | $4 |

## 28

**Germania™**
Bear
4th Promotion
International Bear
Issued: June 20, 2000
Retired: July 13, 2000

| Version | Price Paid | Market Value |
|---|---|---|
| Original | | $5 |

## 29

**Glory™**
Bear
3rd Promotion
International Bear
Issued: June 4, 1999
Retired: June 17, 1999

| Version | Price Paid | Market Value |
|---|---|---|
| A. Original | | $6 |
| B. Employee Bear | | $20 |

## 30

**Goldie®**
Goldfish
1st Promotion
#5 of 10
Issued: April 11, 1997
Retired: May 15, 1997

| Version | Price Paid | Market Value |
|---|---|---|
| Original | | $10 |

## 31

**Goochy™**
Jellyfish
4th Promotion
#16 of 18
Issued: July 4, 2000
Retired: July 13, 2000

| Version | Price Paid | Market Value |
|---|---|---|
| Original | | $4 |

## 32

**Happy™**
Hippo
2nd Promotion
#6 of 12
Issued: May 22, 1998
Retired: June 12, 1998

| Version | Price Paid | Market Value |
|---|---|---|
| Original | | $4 |

## 33

**Humphrey™**
Camel
4th Promotion
Week #3
Issued: June 27, 2000
Retired: July 13, 2000

| Version | Price Paid | Market Value |
|---|---|---|
| Original | | $5 |

## 34

**Iggy™**
Iguana
3rd Promotion
#6 of 12
Issued: May 21, 1999
Retired: June 3, 1999

| Version | Price Paid | Market Value |
|---|---|---|
| Original | | $3 |

| Page Totals | Price Paid | Market Value |
|---|---|---|
| | | |

35

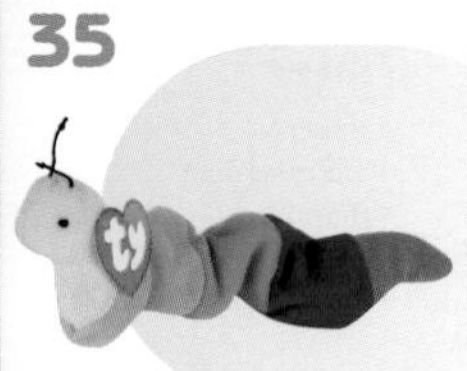

**Inch™**

Inchworm
2nd Promotion
#4 of 12
Issued: May 22, 1998
Retired: June 12, 1998

| Version | Price Paid | Market Value |
|---|---|---|
| Original | | $5 |

36

**Lefty™**

Donkey
American Trio
Issued: October 25, 2000
Retired: November 9, 2000

| Version | Price Paid | Market Value |
|---|---|---|
| Original | | $6 |

37

**Libearty™**

Bear
American Trio
Issued: October 25, 2000
Retired: November 9, 2000

| Version | Price Paid | Market Value |
|---|---|---|
| Original | | $6 |

38

**Lips™**

Fish
4th Promotion
#1 of 18
Issued: June 13, 2000
Retired: July 13, 2000

| Version | Price Paid | Market Value |
|---|---|---|
| Original | | $4 |

39

**Lizz™**

Lizard
1st Promotion
#10 of 10
Issued: April 11, 1997
Retired: May 15, 1997

| Version | Price Paid | Market Value |
|---|---|---|
| Original | | $9 |

40

**Lucky™**

Ladybug
4th Promotion
#5 of 18
Issued: June 20, 2000
Retired: July 13, 2000

| Version | Price Paid | Market Value |
|---|---|---|
| Original | | $4 |

41

**Maple™**

Bear
3rd Promotion
International Bear
Issued: June 4, 1999
Retired: June 17, 1999

| Version | Price Paid | Market Value |
|---|---|---|
| Original | | $4 |

42

**Mel™**

Koala
2nd Promotion
#7 of 12
Issued: May 22, 1998
Retired: June 12, 1998

| Version | Price Paid | Market Value |
|---|---|---|
| Original | | $4 |

43

**Millennium™**

Bear
4th Promotion
Issued: June 13, 2000
Retired: June 13, 2000

| Version | Price Paid | Market Value |
|---|---|---|
| Original | | $9 |

44

**Neon™**

Seahorse
4th Promotion
#13 of 18
Issued: July 4, 2000
Retired: July 13, 2000

| Version | Price Paid | Market Value |
|---|---|---|
| Original | | $4 |

| Page Totals | Price Paid | Market Value |
|---|---|---|
| | | |

## 45

### 'Nook™

Husky
3rd Promotion
#11 of 12
Issued: May 21, 1999
Retired: June 3, 1999

| Version | Price Paid | Market Value |
|---|---|---|
| Original | | $3 |

## 46

### Nuts™

Squirrel
3rd Promotion
#8 of 12
Issued: May 21, 1999
Retired: June 3, 1999

| Version | Price Paid | Market Value |
|---|---|---|
| Original | | $3 |

## 47

### Osito™

Bear
4th Promotion
International Bear
Issued: June 20, 2000
Retired: July 13, 2000

| Version | Price Paid | Market Value |
|---|---|---|
| Original | | $5 |

## 48

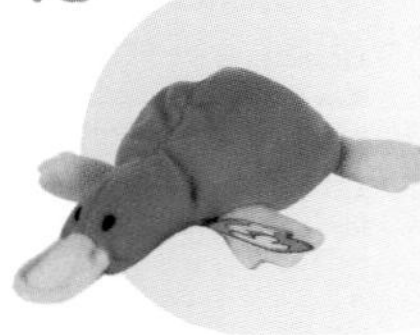

### Patti™

Platypus
1st Promotion
#1 of 10
Issued: April 11, 1997
Retired: May 15, 1997

| Version | Price Paid | Market Value |
|---|---|---|
| Original | | $21 |

## 49

### Peanut™

Elephant
2nd Promotion
#12 of 12
Issued: May 22, 1998
Retired: June 12, 1998

| Version | Price Paid | Market Value |
|---|---|---|
| Original | | $4 |

## 50

### Peanut™ (royal blue)

Elephant
4th Promotion
Week #3
Issued: June 27, 2000
Retired: July 13, 2000

| Version | Price Paid | Market Value |
|---|---|---|
| Original | | $5 |

## 51

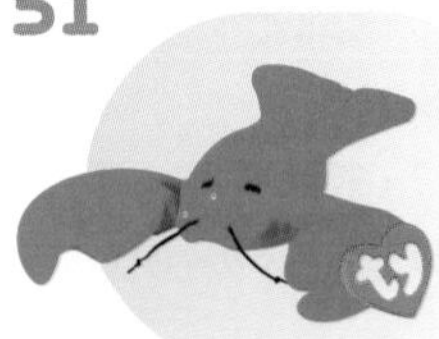

### Pinchers™

Lobster
2nd Promotion
#5 of 12
Issued: May 22, 1998
Retired: June 12, 1998

| Version | Price Paid | Market Value |
|---|---|---|
| Original | | $5 |

## 52

### Pinky™

Flamingo
1st Promotion
#2 of 10
Issued: April 11, 1997
Retired: May 15, 1997

| Version | Price Paid | Market Value |
|---|---|---|
| Original | | $30 |

## 53

### Quacks™

Duck
1st Promotion
#9 of 10
Issued: April 11, 1997
Retired: May 15, 1997

| Version | Price Paid | Market Value |
|---|---|---|
| Original | | $8 |

## 54

### Rex™

Tyrannosaurus
4th Promotion
Week #1
Issued: June 13, 2000
Retired: July 13, 2000

| Version | Price Paid | Market Value |
|---|---|---|
| Original | | $5 |

| Page Totals | Price Paid | Market Value |
|---|---|---|
| | | |

55

**Righty™**
Elephant
American Trio
Issued: October 25, 2000
Retired: November 9, 2000

| Version | Price Paid | Market Value |
|---|---|---|
| Original | | $6 |

56

**Rocket™**
Blue Jay
3rd Promotion
#5 of 12
Issued: May 21, 1999
Retired: June 3, 1999

| Version | Price Paid | Market Value |
|---|---|---|
| Original | | $3 |

57

**Schweetheart™**
Orangutan
4th Promotion
#12 of 18
Issued: June 27, 2000
Retired: July 13, 2000

| Version | Price Paid | Market Value |
|---|---|---|
| Original | | $4 |

58

**Scoop™**
Pelican
2nd Promotion
#8 of 12
Issued: May 22, 1998
Retired: June 12, 1998

| Version | Price Paid | Market Value |
|---|---|---|
| Original | | $4 |

59

**Seamore™**
Seal
1st Promotion
#7 of 10
Issued: April 11, 1997
Retired: May 15, 1997

| Version | Price Paid | Market Value |
|---|---|---|
| Original | | $14 |

60

**Slither™**
Snake
4th Promotion
#2 of 18
Issued: June 13, 2000
Retired: July 13, 2000

| Version | Price Paid | Market Value |
|---|---|---|
| Original | | $4 |

61

**Smoochy™**
Frog
3rd Promotion
#3 of 12
Issued: May 21, 1999
Retired: June 3, 1999

| Version | Price Paid | Market Value |
|---|---|---|
| Original | | $3 |

62

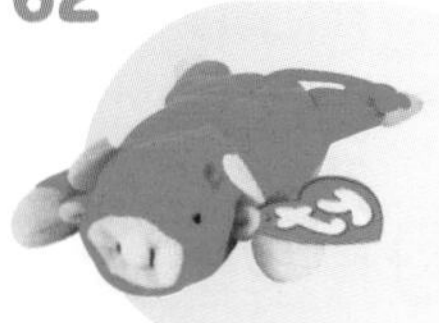

**Snort™**
Bull
1st Promotion
#8 of 10
Issued: April 11, 1997
Retired: May 15, 1997

| Version | Price Paid | Market Value |
|---|---|---|
| Original | | $7 |

63

**Spangle™**
Bear
4th Promotion
International Bear
Issued: June 20, 2000
Retired: July 13, 2000

| Version | Price Paid | Market Value |
|---|---|---|
| Original | | $5 |

64

**Speedy™**
Turtle
1st Promotion
#6 of 10
Issued: April 11, 1997
Retired: May 15, 1997

| Version | Price Paid | Market Value |
|---|---|---|
| Original | | $14 |

| Page Totals | Price Paid | Market Value |
|---|---|---|
| | | |

## 65

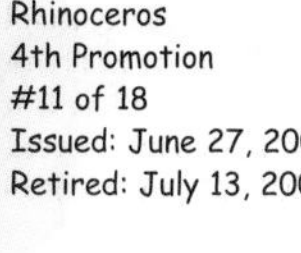

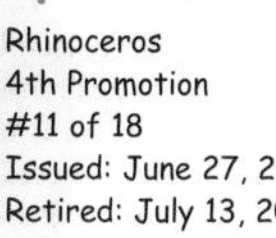

### Spike™

Rhinoceros
4th Promotion
#11 of 18
Issued: June 27, 2000
Retired: July 13, 2000

| Version | Price Paid | Market Value |
|---|---|---|
| Original | | $4 |

## 66

### Spinner™

Spider
4th Promotion
#7 of 18
Issued: June 20, 2000
Retired: July 13, 2000

| Version | Price Paid | Market Value |
|---|---|---|
| Original | | $4 |

## 67

### Springy™

Bunny
4th Promotion
#17 of 18
Issued: June 29, 2000
Retired: July 13, 2000

| Version | Price Paid | Market Value |
|---|---|---|
| Original | | $4 |

## 68

### Spunky™

Cocker Spaniel
3rd Promotion
#4 of 12
Issued: May 21, 1999
Retired: June 3, 1999

| Version | Price Paid | Market Value |
|---|---|---|
| Original | | $3 |

## 69

### Steg™

Stegosaurus
4th Promotion
Week #1
Issued: June 13, 2000
Retired: July 13, 2000

| Version | Price Paid | Market Value |
|---|---|---|
| Original | | $5 |

## 70

### Sting™

Ray
4th Promotion
#15 of 18
Issued: July 4, 2000
Retired: July 13, 2000

| Version | Price Paid | Market Value |
|---|---|---|
| Original | | $4 |

## 71

### Stretchy™

Ostrich
3rd Promotion
#10 of 12
Issued: May 21, 1999
Retired: June 3, 1999

| Version | Price Paid | Market Value |
|---|---|---|
| Original | | $3 |

## 72

### Strut™

Rooster
3rd Promotion
#7 of 12
Issued: May 21, 1999
Retired: June 3, 1999

| Version | Price Paid | Market Value |
|---|---|---|
| Original | | $3 |

## 73

### The End™

Bear
4th Promotion
Issued: June 30, 2000
Retired: July 13, 2000

| Version | Price Paid | Market Value |
|---|---|---|
| Original | | $8 |

## 74

### Tusk™

Walrus
4th Promotion
#9 of 18
Issued: June 27, 2000
Retired: July 13, 2000

| Version | Price Paid | Market Value |
|---|---|---|
| Original | | $4 |

| Page Totals | Price Paid | Market Value |
|---|---|---|
| | | |

**75**

### Twigs™

Giraffe
2nd Promotion
#3 of 12
Issued: May 22, 1998
Retired: June 12, 1998

| Version | Price Paid | Market Value |
|---|---|---|
| Original | | $6 |

**76**

### Waddle™

Penguin
2nd Promotion
#11 of 12
Issued: May 22, 1998
Retired: June 12, 1998

| Version | Price Paid | Market Value |
|---|---|---|
| Original | | $4 |

**77**

### Zip™

Cat
2nd Promotion
#10 of 12
Issued: May 22, 1998
Retired: June 12, 1998

| Version | Price Paid | Market Value |
|---|---|---|
| Original | | $5 |

| Page Totals | Price Paid | Market Value |
|---|---|---|
| | | |

# Sports Promotion Beanie Babies®

*Beanie Babies* giveaways at sporting events have been a big hit ever since "Cubbie" was introduced at a Chicago Cubs game in 1997.

## Canadian Special Olympics

❑ **Maple™** Market Value: $220
Canadian Special Olympics 8/97 & 12/97 · N/A

❑ **Valentino™** Market Value: $100
Canadian Special Olympics 6/98, 9/98 & 10/98 · N/A

## Major League Baseball

❑ **1999 Signature Bear™** Market Value: $50
New York Yankees 5/9/99 · N/A

❑ **Addison™** Market Value: $90
Chicago Cubs 5/20/01 · LE-10,000

❑ **Aurora™** Market Value: $30
Chicago Cubs 9/10/00 · LE-12,000

❑ **Batty™** Market Value: $30
Milwaukee Brewers 5/31/98 · LE-12,000

❑ **Batty™** Market Value: $28
New York Mets 7/12/98 · LE-30,000

❑ **Batty™** Market Value: $35
Seattle Mariners 5/29/99 · LE-15,000

❑ **Blizzard™** Market Value: $35
Chicago White Sox 7/12/98 · LE-20,000

❑ **Bones™** Market Value: $75
New York Yankees 3/10/98 · N/A

❑ **Chip™** Market Value: $34
Atlanta Braves 8/19/98 · LE-12,000

❑ **Chocolate™** Market Value: $30
Seattle Mariners 9/5/98 · LE-10,000

❑ **Cubbie™** Market Value: $90
Chicago Cubs 5/18/97 · LE-10,000

❑ **Cubbie™** Market Value: $70
Chicago Cubs 9/6/97 · LE-10,000

❑ **Cubbie™** Market Value: $250
Chicago Cubs 1/16-1/18/98 · LE-100

❑ **Cubbie™** Market Value: $200
Chicago Cubs 1/15-1/17/99 · N/A

❑ **Curly™** Market Value: $40
New York Mets 8/22/98 · LE-30,000

❑ **Daisy™** Market Value: $180
Chicago Cubs 5/3/98 · LE-10,000

❑ **Derby™** Market Value: $35
Houston Astros 8/16/98 · LE-15,000

## Major League Baseball, cont.

❑ **Early™** Market Value: $35
Milwaukee Brewers 6/12/99 · LE-12,000

❑ **Ears™** Market Value: $60
Oakland A's 3/15/98 · LE-1,500

❑ **Erin™** Market Value: $38
Chicago Cubs 8/5/99 · LE-12,000

❑ **Fortune™** Market Value: $35
Kansas City Royals 6/6/99 · LE-10,000

❑ **Glory™** Market Value: $100
All-Star Game 7/7/98 · LE-52,000 approx.

❑ **Goatee™** Market Value: $32
Arizona Diamondbacks 7/8/99 · LE-10,000

❑ **Goochy™** Market Value: $30
Tampa Bay Devil Rays 4/10/99 · LE-10,000

❑ **Gracie™** Market Value: $50
Chicago Cubs 9/13/98 · LE-10,000

❑ **Hippie™** Market Value: $40
Minnesota Twins 6/18/99 · LE-10,000

❑ **Hissy™** Market Value: $40
Arizona Diamondbacks 6/14/98 · LE-6,500

❑ **KuKu™** Market Value: $30
Detroit Tigers 7/11/99 · LE-10,000

❑ **Lucky™** Market Value: $42
Minnesota Twins 7/31/98 · LE-10,000

❑ **Luke™** Market Value: $35
Texas Rangers 9/5/99 · LE-15,000

❑ **Mac™** Market Value: $45
St. Louis Cardinals 6/14/99 · LE-20,000

❑ **Mel™** Market Value: $40
Anaheim Angels 9/6/98 · LE-10,000

❑ **Millennium™** Market Value: $40
Chicago Cubs 9/26/99 · LE-40,000

❑ **Millennium™** Market Value: $40
New York Yankees 8/15/99 · N/A

❑ **Peace™** Market Value: $40
Oakland A's 5/1/99 · LE-10,000

❑ **Peanut™** Market Value: $40
Oakland A's 8/1/98 · LE-15,000

❑ **Peanut™** Market Value: $35
Oakland A's 9/6/98 · LE-15,000

❑ **Pinky™** Market Value: $30
Tampa Bay Devil Rays 8/23/98 · LE-10,000

# Sports Promotion Beanie Babies®



### Major League Baseball, cont.

- ❑ **Pugsly™** Market Value: $35
  Atlanta Braves 9/2/98 • LE-12,000
- ❑ **Pugsly™** Market Value: $35
  Texas Rangers 8/4/98 • LE-10,000
- ❑ **Roary™** Market Value: $30
  Kansas City Royals 5/31/98 • LE-13,000
- ❑ **Rocket™** Market Value: $45
  Toronto Blue Jays 9/6/98 • LE-12,000
- ❑ **Rover™** Market Value: $38
  Cincinnati Reds 8/16/98 • LE-15,000
- ❑ **Sammy™** Market Value: $325
  Chicago Cubs 1/15-1/17/99 • N/A
- ❑ **Sammy™** Market Value: $40
  Chicago Cubs 4/25/99 • LE-12,000
- ❑ **Scorch™** Market Value: $30
  Cincinnati Reds 6/19/99 • LE-10,000
- ❑ **Slippery™** Market Value: $30
  San Francisco Giants 4/11/99 • LE-15,000
- ❑ **Sly™** Market Value: $40
  Arizona Diamondbacks 8/27/98 • LE-10,000
- ❑ **Smoochy™** Market Value: $38
  St. Louis Cardinals 8/14/98 • LE-20,000
- ❑ **Stretch™** Market Value: $40
  New York Yankees 8/9/98 • N/A
- ❑ **Stretch™** Market Value: $42
  St. Louis Cardinals 5/22/98 • LE-20,000
- ❑ **Stripes™** Market Value: $35
  Detroit Tigers 5/31/98 • LE-10,000
- ❑ **Stripes™** Market Value: $30
  Detroit Tigers 8/8/98 • LE-10,000
- ❑ **Tiny™** Market Value: $30
  Houston Astros 7/18/99 • LE-20,000
- ❑ **Tuffy™** Market Value: $32
  San Francisco Giants 8/30/98 • LE-10,000
- ❑ **Valentina™** Market Value: $60
  New York Mets 5/30/99 • LE-18,000
- ❑ **Valentino™** Market Value: $90
  New York Yankees 5/17/98 • LE-10,000
- ❑ **Waves™** Market Value: $35
  San Diego Padres 8/14/98 • LE-10,000
- ❑ **Weenie™** Market Value: $45
  Tampa Bay Devil Rays 7/26/98 • LE-15,000

### National Basketball Association

- ❑ **Baldy™** Market Value: $60
  Philadelphia 76ers 1/17/98 • LE-5,000
- ❑ **Bongo™** Market Value: $50
  Cleveland Cavaliers 4/5/98 • LE-5,000
- ❑ **Chocolate™** Market Value: $48
  Denver Nuggets 4/17/98 • LE-5,000
- ❑ **Claude™** Market Value: $80
  Sacramento Kings 3/14/99 • LE-5,000
- ❑ **Curly™** Market Value: $50
  San Antonio Spurs 4/27/98 • LE-2,500
- ❑ **Pinky™** Market Value: $48
  San Antonio Spurs 4/29/98 • LE-2,500
- ❑ **Snort™** Market Value: $38
  Chicago Bulls 4/10/99 • LE-5,000
- ❑ **Strut™** Market Value: $40
  Indiana Pacers 4/2/98 • LE-5,000
- ❑ **Whisper™** Market Value: $30
  Milwaukee Bucks 2/28/99 • LE-5,000

### National Football League

- ❑ **Blackie™** Market Value: $45
  Chicago Bears • In Club Kits • LE-20,000
- ❑ **Blackie™** Market Value: $45
  Chicago Bears 11/8/98 • LE-8,000
- ❑ **Chocolate™** Market Value: $65
  Dallas Cowboys 9/6/98 • LE-10,000
- ❑ **Chocolate™** Market Value: $38
  Tennessee Oilers 10/18/98 • LE-7,500
- ❑ **Curly™** Market Value: $36
  Chicago Bears 12/20/98 • LE-10,000
- ❑ **Derby™** Market Value: $44
  Indianapolis Colts 10/14/98 • LE-10,000

### National Hockey League

- ❑ **Baldy™** Market Value: $45
  Washington Capitals 2/20/99 • LE-5,000
- ❑ **Blackie™** Market Value: $45
  Boston Bruins 10/12/98 • LE-5,000
- ❑ **Bones™** Market Value: $40
  Chicago Blackhawks 10/24/98 • LE-5,000
- ❑ **Chocolate™** Market Value: $50
  Toronto Maple Leafs 1/2/99 • LE-3,000
- ❑ **Gobbles™** Market Value: $42
  Phoenix Coyotes 11/26/98 • LE-5,000

| Page Totals | Price Paid | Market Value |
| --- | --- | --- |
| | | |

# Sports Promotion Beanie Babies®

*National Hockey League, cont.*

❑ **Gobbles™** Market Value: $40
St. Louis Blues 11/24/98 · LE-7,500

❑ **Hippie™** Market Value: $48
St. Louis Blues 3/22/99 · LE-7,500

❑ **Roam™** Market Value: $40
Buffalo Sabres 2/19/99 · LE-5,000

❑ **Spunky™** Market Value: $35
Buffalo Sabres 10/23/98 · LE-5,000

❑ **Tuffy™** Market Value: $40
New Jersey Devils 10/24/98 · LE-5,000

❑ **Waddle™** Market Value: $40
Pittsburgh Penguins 10/24/98 · LE-7,000

❑ **Waddle™** Market Value: $38
Pittsburgh Penguins 11/21/98 · LE-7,000

*Women's National Basketball Association*

❑ **Bongo™** Market Value: $55
Charlotte Sting 7/17/98 · LE-3,000

❑ **Curly™** Market Value: $55
Charlotte Sting 6/15/98 · LE-5,000

❑ **Curly™** Market Value: $50
Cleveland Rockers 8/15/98 · LE-3,200

❑ **Dotty™** Market Value: $55
Los Angeles Sparks 7/31/98 · LE-3,000

❑ **Mel™** Market Value: $40
Detroit Shock 7/25/98 · LE-5,000

❑ **Mystic™** Market Value: $40
Los Angeles Sparks 8/3/98 · LE-5,000

❑ **Mystic™** Market Value: $55
Washington Mystics 7/11/98 · LE-5,000

❑ **Scoop™** Market Value: $50
Houston Comets 8/6/98 · LE-5,000

# Sports Promotion Beanie Buddies®

*Major League Baseball*

❑ **Peace™** Market Value: $45
Chicago Cubs 4/30/00 · LE-12,000

*Major League Baseball, cont.*

❑ **Spangle™** Market Value: $55
New York Yankees 5/29/00 · LE-12,000

# Sports Promotion Beanie Boppers™

*Major League Baseball*

❑ **Bronx Bomber™** Market Value: $125
New York Yankees 8/5/01 · LE-18,000

*Major League Baseball, cont.*

❑ **Ivy Leaguer™** Market Value: $80
Chicago Cubs 9/30/01 · LE-10,000

# Total Value Of My Collection

| BEANIE BABIES® | | | BEANIE BABIES® | | | BEANIE BABIES® | | |
|---|---|---|---|---|---|---|---|---|
| Page # | Price Paid | Market Value | Page # | Price Paid | Market Value | Page # | Price Paid | Market Value |
| Page 27 | | | Page 49 | | | Page 71 | | |
| Page 28 | | | Page 50 | | | Page 72 | | |
| Page 29 | | | Page 51 | | | Page 73 | | |
| Page 30 | | | Page 52 | | | Page 74 | | |
| Page 31 | | | Page 53 | | | Page 75 | | |
| Page 32 | | | Page 54 | | | Page 76 | | |
| Page 33 | | | Page 55 | | | Page 77 | | |
| Page 34 | | | Page 56 | | | Page 78 | | |
| Page 35 | | | Page 57 | | | Page 79 | | |
| Page 36 | | | Page 58 | | | Page 80 | | |
| Page 37 | | | Page 59 | | | Page 81 | | |
| Page 38 | | | Page 60 | | | Page 82 | | |
| Page 39 | | | Page 61 | | | Page 83 | | |
| Page 40 | | | Page 62 | | | Page 84 | | |
| Page 41 | | | Page 63 | | | Page 85 | | |
| Page 42 | | | Page 64 | | | Page 86 | | |
| Page 43 | | | Page 65 | | | Page 87 | | |
| Page 44 | | | Page 66 | | | Page 88 | | |
| Page 45 | | | Page 67 | | | Page 89 | | |
| Page 46 | | | Page 68 | | | Page 90 | | |
| Page 47 | | | Page 69 | | | Page 91 | | |
| Page 48 | | | Page 70 | | | Page 92 | | |
| Subtotals | | | Subtotals | | | Subtotals | | |

| Grand Total: | Price Paid | Market Value |
|---|---|---|
| | | |

# Total Value Of My Collection

| BEANIE BABIES® | | | BEANIE BABIES® | | | BEANIE BABIES® | | |
|---|---|---|---|---|---|---|---|---|
| Page # | Price Paid | Market Value | Page # | Price Paid | Market Value | Page # | Price Paid | Market Value |
| Page 93 | | | Page 115 | | | Page 137 | | |
| Page 94 | | | Page 116 | | | Page 138 | | |
| Page 95 | | | Page 117 | | | Page 139 | | |
| Page 96 | | | Page 118 | | | Page 140 | | |
| Page 97 | | | Page 119 | | | Page 141 | | |
| Page 98 | | | Page 120 | | | Page 142 | | |
| Page 99 | | | Page 121 | | | Page 143 | | |
| Page 100 | | | Page 122 | | | Page 144 | | |
| Page 101 | | | Page 123 | | | Page 145 | | |
| Page 102 | | | Page 124 | | | BEANIE BUDDIES® | | |
| Page 103 | | | Page 125 | | | Page 146 | | |
| Page 104 | | | Page 126 | | | Page 147 | | |
| Page 105 | | | Page 127 | | | Page 148 | | |
| Page 106 | | | Page 128 | | | Page 149 | | |
| Page 107 | | | Page 129 | | | Page 150 | | |
| Page 108 | | | Page 130 | | | Page 151 | | |
| Page 109 | | | Page 131 | | | Page 152 | | |
| Page 110 | | | Page 132 | | | Page 153 | | |
| Page 111 | | | Page 133 | | | Page 154 | | |
| Page 112 | | | Page 134 | | | Page 155 | | |
| Page 113 | | | Page 135 | | | Page 156 | | |
| Page 114 | | | Page 136 | | | Page 157 | | |
| Subtotals | | | Subtotals | | | Subtotals | | |

| Page Totals: | Price Paid | Market Value |
|---|---|---|
| | | |

# Total Value Of My Collection

| BEANIE BUDDIES® | | |
|---|---|---|
| Page # | Price Paid | Market Value |
| Page 158 | | |
| Page 159 | | |
| Page 160 | | |
| Page 161 | | |
| Page 162 | | |
| Page 163 | | |
| Page 164 | | |
| Page 165 | | |
| Page 166 | | |
| Page 167 | | |
| Page 168 | | |
| Page 169 | | |
| Page 170 | | |
| Page 171 | | |
| Page 172 | | |
| Page 173 | | |
| Page 174 | | |
| Page 175 | | |
| Page 176 | | |
| Page 177 | | |
| Page 178 | | |
| Page 179 | | |
| Subtotals | | |

| BEANIE BUDDIES® | | |
|---|---|---|
| Page # | Price Paid | Market Value |
| Page 180 | | |
| Page 181 | | |
| Page 182 | | |
| Page 183 | | |
| Page 184 | | |
| Page 185 | | |
| **BEANIE BOPPERS™** | | |
| Page 186 | | |
| Page 187 | | |
| Page 188 | | |
| Page 189 | | |
| Page 190 | | |
| **BEANIE KIDS™** | | |
| Page 191 | | |
| Page 192 | | |
| Page 193 | | |
| Page 194 | | |
| Page 195 | | |
| **TY GEAR™** | | |
| Page 196 | | |
| Page 197 | | |
| Page 198 | | |
| Subtotals | | |

| JINGLE BEANIES™ | | |
|---|---|---|
| Page # | Price Paid | Market Value |
| Page 199 | | |
| Page 200 | | |
| Page 201 | | |
| **TEENIE BEANIES™** | | |
| Page 202 | | |
| Page 203 | | |
| Page 204 | | |
| Page 205 | | |
| Page 206 | | |
| Page 207 | | |
| Page 208 | | |
| Page 209 | | |
| Page 210 | | |
| **SPORTS PROMOS** | | |
| Page 211 | | |
| Page 212 | | |
| Page 213 | | |
| Subtotals | | |

| Grand Total: | Price Paid | Market Value |
|---|---|---|
| | | |

# Swing Tags & Tush Tags

Every Ty product has a heart-shaped paper tag on the ear and a tag sewn into the seam of its body. The following chart will illustrate the different "generations."

## Swing Tags

### Zodiac Collection™

2000-Current

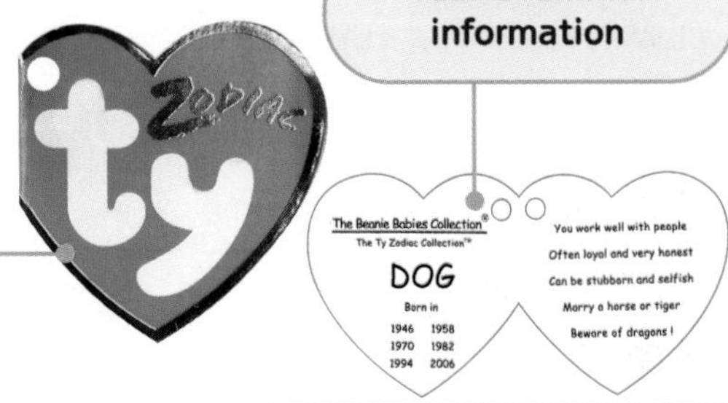


Year & animal information

"ZODIAC" in gold lettering

### Beanie Babies®

Generation 1

Early 1994-Mid 1994

Animal name and style number

Single-sheet swing tag; skinny "ty" logo with gold outline

Generation 2

Mid 1994-Early 1995

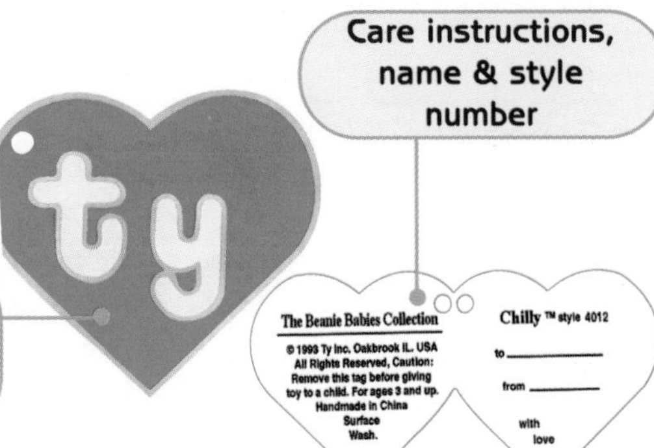


Care instructions, name & style number

Tag opens like a book

## Generation 3
Mid 1995-Early 1996

"Beanie Babies™";
corporate addresses

Puffier "ty" logo

The Beanie Babies ™ Collection
© Ty Inc.
Oakbrook IL. U.S.A.
© Ty UK Ltd.
Waterlooville, Hants
PO8 8HH
© Ty Deutschland
90008 Nürnberg
Handmade in China

Garcia ™ style 4051
to
from
with
love

## Generation 4
Early 1996-Mid 1997

Birthdate, poem &
"Visit our web page!!!"

Yellow star; "ty" logo
without gold outline

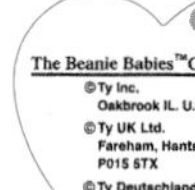

The Beanie Babies™ Collection
© Ty Inc.
Oakbrook IL. U.S.A.
© Ty UK Ltd.
Fareham, Hants
PO15 5TX
© Ty Deutschland
90008 Nürnberg
Handmade in China

Doodle™ style 4171
DATE OF BIRTH : 3 - 8 - 96
Listen closely to "cock-a-doodle-doo"
What's the rooster saying to you?
Hurry, wake up sleepy head
We have lots to do, get out of bed!
Visit our web page!!!
http://www.ty.com

## Generation 5
Early 1997-Late 1999

Birthdate written out;
web address shorter

New typeface
in early 1997

The Beanie Babies Collection®
© Ty Inc.
Oakbrook, IL. U.S.A.
© Ty Europe Ltd.
Fareham, Hants
PO15 5TX, U.K.
© Ty Canada
Aurora, Ontario
Handmade in China

Pinky™
DATE OF BIRTH: February 13, 1995
Pinky loves the everglades
From the hottest pink she's made
With floppy legs and big orange beak
She's the Beanie that you seek!
www.ty.com

New typeface
in mid-1998

"Gasport" changed to
"Gosport" in mid-1998

The Beanie Babies Collection®
© Ty Inc.
Oakbrook, IL. U.S.A.
© Ty Europe
Gosport, Hampshire, U.K.
© Ty Canada
Aurora, Ontario
Handmade in China

## Generation 6
Early 2000-Current

Corporate addresses
include "Ty Japan"

Iridescent silver star
with yellow "2000"

The Beanie Babies Collection®
© Ty Inc.
© Ty Canada
© Ty Europe
© Ty Japan
Handmade in China

The Beginning™
DATE OF BIRTH: January 1, 2000
Beanie Babies can never end
They'll always be our special friends
Start the fun because we're here
To bring you hope, love and cheer!
www.ty.com

## Generation 7
Early 2001-Current

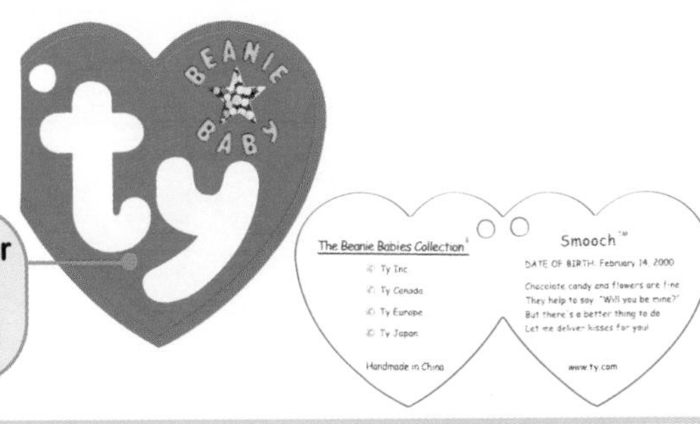


Small iridescent silver star with "BEANIE BABY" in yellow type

# Beanie Buddies®

## Generation 1
1998-Late 1999

Ty Europe changed from "Fareham" to "Gasport" to "Gosport"

Yellow Star

## Generation 2
Early 2000-Current

Corporate addresses include "Ty Japan"

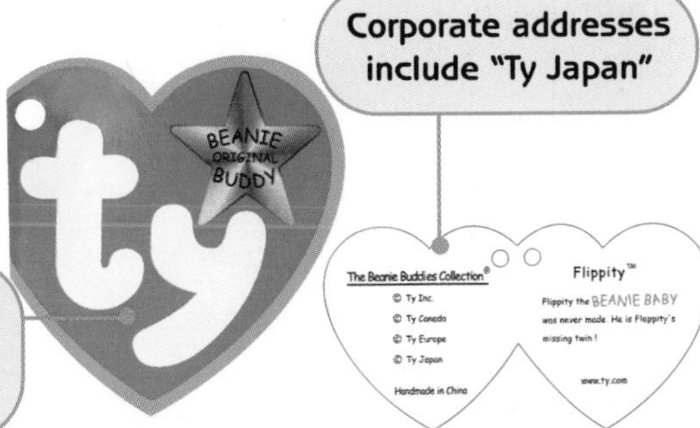


"BEANIE BUDDIES" in pastel star

# Teenie Beanie Babies™

## Version 1
1997

Trademark "TM/MC"

Teenie Beanie Babies™/MC
Patti™/MC
©Ty Inc.
Oakbrook, IL
Printed in China
Imprimé en Chine

"ty" logo outlined in gold

## Version 2
1998

Web address; trademark "TM/MC/MR"

Teenie Beanie Babies TM/MC/MR
Bongo TM/MC/MR ©Ty Inc. Oakbrook, IL
www.ty.com
Printed in China
Imprimé en Chine

## Version 3
1999

Trademark "TM"

Larger swing tags; yellow star; "ty" logo without gold outline

TEENIE ORIGINAL BEANIE

Teenie Beanie Babies TM
©Ty Inc. Oakbrook, IL.
Stretchy the Ostrich™
www.ty.com
Printed in China
Imprimé en Chine

## Version 4
2000

"Imprimè en Chine" deleted

TEENIE ORIGINAL BEANIE

Teenie Beanie Babies TM
©Ty Inc. Oakbrook, IL
Dotty™ the Dalmatian
www.ty.com
Printed in China

## Beanie Kids™
2000

Birthdate, poem & web address

"BEANIE KIDS" in pastel lettering

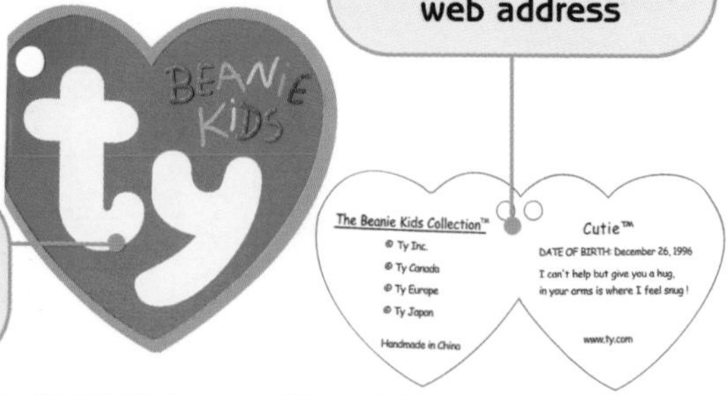

BEANIE KIDS

The Beanie Kids Collection™
© Ty Inc.
© Ty Canada
© Ty Europe
© Ty Japan
Handmade in China

Cutie™
DATE OF BIRTH: December 26, 1996
I can't help but give you a hug,
in your arms is where I feel snug!
www.ty.com

# Tush Tags

## Beanie Babies®

### Version 1

© 1993 TY INC.,
OAKBROOK IL, U.S.A.
ALL RIGHTS RESERVED
HAND MADE IN CHINA
SURFACE WASHABLE

ALL NEW MATERIAL
POLYESTER FIBER
& P.V.C. PELLETS
PA. REG #1965
FOR AGES 3 AND UP

Looped tag; horizontal layout

Production & company information in black ink

### Version 2

HAND MADE IN CHINA
© 1993 TY INC.,
OAKBROOK IL, U.S.A.
SURFACE WASHABLE
ALL NEW MATERIAL
POLYESTER FIBER &
P.V.C. PELLETS
REG. NO PA - 1965(KR)
FOR AGES 3 AND UP
CE

Folded tag; vertical layout; "ty" logo inside a red heart

Production & company information in red ink

### Version 3

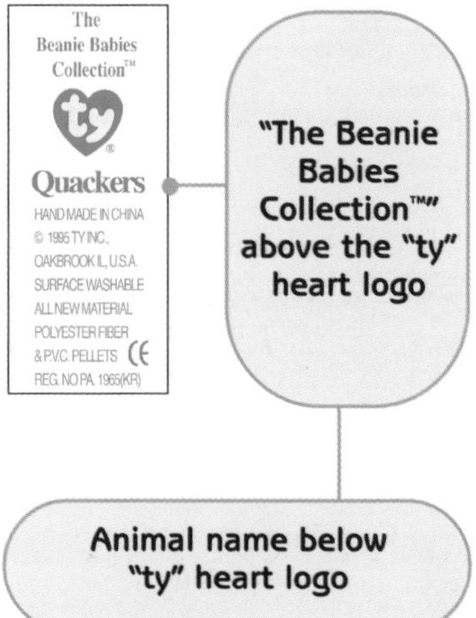


Animal name below "ty" heart logo

### Version 4

Red star on upper left side of "ty" heart logo

A clear sticker with red star appears next to logo in some earlier versions

## Version 5

The Beanie Babies® Collection™
Hissy™
HAND MADE IN CHINA
© 1997 TY INC.,
OAKBROOK IL, U.S.A.
SURFACE WASHABLE
ALL NEW MATERIAL
POLYESTER FIBER
& P.V.C. PELLETS
REG. NO PA. 1965(KR)

Registration mark after "Beanie Babies" in collection name in late 1997

Trademark symbol after the animal's name

## Version 6

The Beanie Babies Collection®
Fetch™
HAND MADE IN CHINA
© 1998 TY INC.,
OAKBROOK IL, U.S.A.
SURFACE WASHABLE
ALL NEW MATERIAL
POLYESTER FIBER
& P.E. PELLETS
REG. NO PA. 1965(KR)

Registration mark after the word "Collection"; some tags note change from "P.V.C." to "P.E." pellets

Oval red stamp with numbers & Chinese characters in some tush tags in mid-1998

## Version 7

Millenium™
HANDMADE IN CHINA
© 1999 TY INC.,
OAKBROOK, IL. U.S.A.
SURFACE WASHABLE
ALL NEW MATERIAL
POLYESTER FIBER
& P.E. PELLETS
REG. NO PA. 1965(KR)

Hologram with two designs and collection name

Red heart on tag in disappearing ink

## Version 8

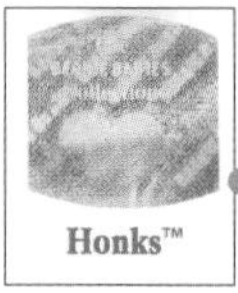

Honks™

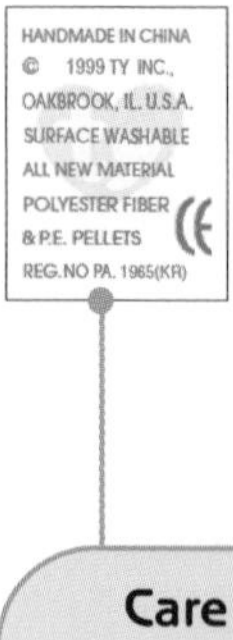

HANDMADE IN CHINA
© 1999 TY INC.,
OAKBROOK, IL. U.S.A.
SURFACE WASHABLE
ALL NEW MATERIAL
POLYESTER FIBER
& P.E. PELLETS
REG. NO PA. 1965(KR)

Unfolded tag in summer of 1999

Care instructions on reverse side

## Beanie Buddies®

### Version 1

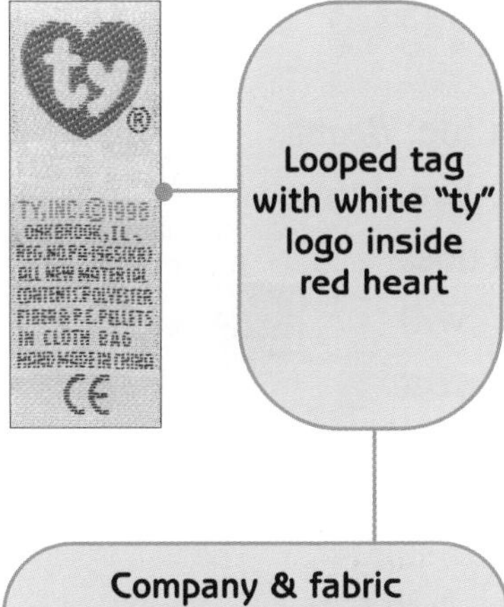


### Versions 2 & 3

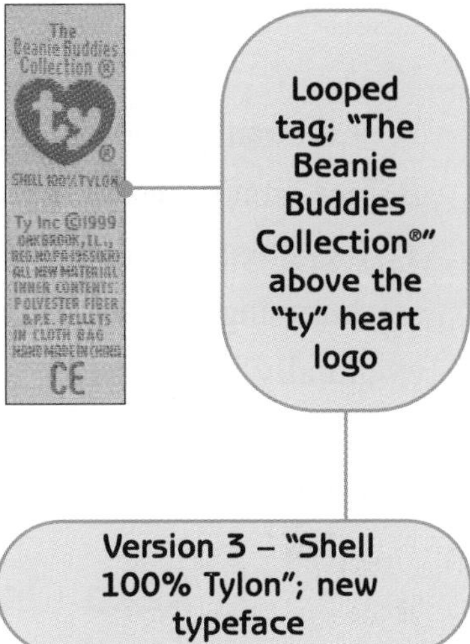


## Beanie Kids™

## Teenie Beanie Babies™

# Secondary Market Overview

Like many good things in life, *Beanie Babies* aren't around forever. Every time Ty Inc. creates a new piece, it does so knowing that the piece will eventually be retired to that great "toy box in the sky" and it will then become hard to find at your local store.

## Keep On Top Of It

Ty Inc. is particularly good at letting its valued customers know when a piece is retired. Every time a piece retires, the company's official web site (***www.ty.com***) makes an official announcement, and many other websites report news on Ty retirements. By keeping track of retirements, you can begin checking your favorite collectibles stores to try and find retired pieces before Ty stops shipping them to stores. Even if the retailer doesn't have what you want, he or she may be able to connect you with other collectors who do have it, and are willing to sell or trade for it.

## The Paper Chase

If your trip to the store proves fruitless, there are many other ways to find a retired piece. Many newspapers have a "Collectibles"category in the classified section. Browsing through this section is a great way to search for your piece, or meet other people who might know where to find it. It's also possible for you to post an ad of your own in this section, stating what you're looking for.

## Let's Go Surfing!

As useful as your favorite store or local newspaper may be, the area they reach is limited. If you want to search beyond your town or state, the best place to start looking is on the Internet. Logging on can bring you to an entire world of chat rooms, fan sites, on-line auctions and even message boards where you can find collectors who share your fondness for *Beanies*. The Ty website even features the Beanie Board of Trade, where you can find plenty of *Beanies* available for sale or trade.

## Rules Of The Trade

The intrepid search for those rare and retired *Beanies* can always be lots of fun. But it's not uncommon to end up paying too much for a special *Beanie*, or getting the wrong one entirely. This doesn't have to happen – just a few precautions can help you accomplish your goal. All Ty products are produced for a limited amount of time. Many of the holiday pieces are available for a few months and tend to be more valuable. If your piece was only produced for a short time, it should be more valuable than others, so expect to pay a little more for it.

By looking at your piece's swing tags and tush tags, you can determine its approximate age: the older generations tend to be considerably more valuable than the more recent ones. By knowing your piece's generation, you can prepare for how much you can expect to pay.

Finally, it helps to know with whom you're dealing with in a Beanie sale. Check into the dealer's reputation with other collectors and find out what they have to say. Several of the Internet's best auction sites let you investigate the seller before you buy something.

## Happy Hunting!

Above all, finding that ultra-rare, retired Beanie is a joy in itself. The hunt can be every bit as fun as finding your quarry, so don't hesitate to stop and make some friends along the way. In your search, you'll be sure to come across plenty of folks who love Beanies as much as you do. The great secondary market hunt awaits!

# Beanie™ Variations

As you check the *Beanies* in your collection or on the shelf of your favorite retailer, you may come across one that seems to be a little bit different. Depending on the piece, these variations can mean the difference between an average piece and a valuable rare one.

## True Colors

Elephants may never forget – but they do like to have fun with colors! The *Beanie Baby* "Peanut" was a dark royal blue shade for the first four months of its three-year term. The later versions of "Peanut" are sky blue which are not as coveted on the secondary market.

But color changes don't always involve the entire animal. Versions of the holiday 2000 "Roxie" the reindeer have turned up with a black nose after it was first issued with a red nose. So don't be fooled into thinking your "Roxie" is a fake because of the different colors!

## Tag - You're It!

Without its tag, a *Beanie Baby* loses much of its value as a collectible. Since those tags are part of the item as a whole, it's important to look at them when dealing with variations. Some of the early versions of "Princess" have tush tags that read "P.V.C. Pellets" rather than the "P.E. Pellets."

When "Nana" was released in 1995, the adorable monkey was barely around for a month before being renamed "Bongo." Although it's still the same old monkey, the "Nana" version is worth substantially more than the piece with the tag that says "Bongo." It's a similar story with the Canadian exclusive "Maple," who was originally going to be called "Pride," and several pieces was produced with his tush tag reading the old name.

## Decisions, Decisions!

Plenty of Beanies go through design changes before Ty Inc. agrees on just how the critter should look. "Tank" the armadillo originally had seven plates along his back, but gained two more after a few months. The piece was on the market for a year before Ty eventually added a shell and kept the nine plates. It's interesting quirks like these that keep collectors looking closely!

# About Face

If you had to sit down and describe the face of a typical *Beanie Babies* bear, could you do it? It seems like an easy thing to do, but over the years, the *Beanie* bear has been a bear of many faces.

Nowhere is this more obvious than in those colorful chums aptly named "Teddy." The "old face" teddy, very much reminiscent of teddies of the Victorian era, had an elongated nose and widespread eyes. The "new face" bear seemed to have undergone a bit of a facial tuck in which his nose became shorter and rounder and his eyes were moved closer together.

From that point on, the bears seemed to be quite comfortable in their skins . . . uh . . . faces.

That is until 2001 when "Patriot," "Poopsie" and the *Birthday Beanies* brought about three whole new looks, barely resembling their *Beanie* bear counterparts – but in fact, looking more like those of the "old face" past.

# Beanie™ Birthdays

Do you share a birthday with a *Beanie Baby*, *Beanie Bopper* or *Beanie Kid*? (New releases are listed in color.)

## JANUARY

Jan. 1, 1999 - **Millennium™**
Jan. 1, 2000 - **Ty 2K™**
Jan. 1, 2000 - **The Beginning™**
Jan. 2, 1995 - **Blondie™ *(Kid)***
Jan. 2, 1998 - **Zero™**
Jan. 3, 1993 - **Spot™**
Jan. 4, 2000 - **Glow™**
Jan. 5, 1997 - **KuKu™**
Jan. 6, 1993 - **Patti™**
Jan. 8, 1999 - **Tiptoe™**
Jan. 9, 2001 - **Starlett™**
Jan. 10, 1999 - **Groovy™**
Jan. 13, 1996 - **Crunch™**
Jan. 14, 1997 - **Spunky™**
Jan. 14, 2000 - **Halo II™**
Jan. 15, 1996 - **Mel™**
Jan. 17, 1998 - **Slippery™**
Jan. 18, 1994 - **Bones™**
Jan. 18, 2000 - **Scurry™**
Jan. 21, 1996 - **Nuts™**
Jan. 23, 1999 - **Schweetheart™**
Jan. 23, 2000 - **Frigid™**
Jan. 24, 2000 - **Swampy™**
Jan. 25, 1995 - **Peanut™**
Jan. 25, 1999 - **Wallace™**
Jan. 25, 2000 - **Wiggly™**
Jan. 26, 1996 - **Chip™**
Jan. 26, 2000 - **Fleecie™**
Jan. 27, 2000 - **Bushy™**
Jan. 30 - **Jazzy Jessie™ *(Bopper)***

## FEBRUARY

Feb. 1, 1996 - **Peace™**
Feb. 1, 2000 - **Niles™**
Feb. 3, 1998 - **Beak™**
Feb. 3, 2000 - **Aurora™**
Feb. 3 - **Huggable Holly™ *(Bopper)***
Feb. 4, 1997 - **Fetch™**
Feb. 5, 1999 - **Osito™**
Feb. 8, 2000 - **Periwinkle™**
Feb. 9, 1999 - **Scaly™**
Feb. 10, 2000 - **Grace™**
Feb. 11, 1999 - **Silver™**
Feb. 11, 2000 - **Trumpet™**
Feb. 13, 1995 - **Pinky™**
Feb. 13, 1995 - **Stinky™**
Feb. 13, 2000 - **Sunny™**
Feb. 14, 1994 - **Luvie™ *(Kid)***
Feb. 14, 1994 - **Valentino™**
Feb. 14, 1998 - **Valentina™**
Feb. 14, 2000 - **Sarge™**
Feb. 14, 2000 - **Smooch™**
Feb. 17, 1996 - **Baldy™**
Feb. 17, 2000 - **Speckles™**
Feb. 19, 1998 - **Prickles™**
Feb. 20, 1996 - **Roary™**
Feb. 20, 2000 - **Morrie™**
Feb. 21, 1999 - **Amber™**
Feb. 22, 1995 - **Tank™**
Feb. 22, 2000 - **Sneaky™**
Feb. 23, 1999 - **Paul™**
Feb. 24, 2000 - **Swoop™**
Feb. 25, 1994 - **Happy™**
Feb. 27, 1996 - **Sparky™**
Feb. 28, 1995 - **Flip™**
Feb. 28, 2000 - **Rufus™**
Feb. 29, 2000 - **Springy™**

# March

March 1, 1998 - **Ewey™**
March 2, 1995 - **Coral™**
March 2, 1997 - **Curly™** ***(Kid)***
March 5, 2001 - **Frills™**
March 6, 1994 - **Nip™**
March 8, 1996 - **Doodle™**
March 8, 1996 - **Strut™**
March 9, 1999 - **Clubby II™**
March 10, 1999 - **Swirly™**
March 11, 1999 - **Honks™**
March 12, 1997 - **Rocket™**
March 13, 2001 - **Celebrate™**
March 14, 1994 - **Ally™**
March 15, 1999 - **Lips™**
March 17, 1993 - **Shenanigan™** ***(Kid)***
March 17, 1997 - **Erin™**
March 17, 2000 - **Shamrock™**
March 18, 2000 - **Purr™**
March 20, 1997 - **Early™**
March 19, 1996 - **Seaweed™**
March 21, 1996 - **Fleece™**
March 23, 1998 - **Hope™**
March 23, 1996 - **Princess™** ***(Kid)***
March 25, 1999 - **Knuckles™**
March 25, 2000 - **Sakura™**
March 28, 1994 - **Zip™**
March 29, 1994 - **Angel™** ***(Kid)***
March 29, 1998 - **Loosy™**
March 30 - **Jolly Janie™** ***(Bopper)***
March 31, 2001 - **Poopsie™**

# April

April 1, 1999 - **Neon™**
April 3, 1996 - **Hoppity™**
April 4, 1997 - **Hissy™**
April 5, 1997 - **Whisper™**
April 5, 1995 - **Cookie™** ***(Kid)***
April 6, 1998 - **Nibbler™**
April 7, 1997 - **GiGi™**
April 8, 2000 - **Aruba™**
April 10, 1998 - **Eggbert™**
April 11, 2000 - **Peekaboo™**
April 12, 1996 - **Curly™**
April 13, 2000 - **Squirmy™**
April 14, 1999 - **Almond™**
April 15, 1995 - **Rascal™** ***(Kid)***
April 15, 1999 - **Pecan™**
April 16, 1997 - **Jake™**
April 18, 1995 - **Ears™**
April 19, 1994 - **Quackers™**
April 20, 2000 - **Brigitte™**
April 21, 1999 - **Chipper™**
April 22, 2000 - **Cashew™**
April 23, 1993 - **Squealer™**
April 23, 2000 - **Eggs™**
April 25, 1993 - **Legs™**
April 27, 1993 - **Chocolate™**
April 27, 2000 - **Fetcher™**
April 28, 1999 - **Eucalyptus™**
April 30, 2000 - **Cinders™**
April 30, 2001 - **Classy™**

## May

May 1, 1995 - **Lucky™**
May 1, 1996 - **Wrinkles™**
May 2, 1996 - **Pugsly™**
May 3, 1996 - **Chops™**
May 4, 1998 - **Hippie™**
May 4, 2001 - **Pierre™**
May 5, 2001 - **Kirby™**
May 6, 2000 - **Sniffer™**
May 7, 1998 - **Nibbly™**
May 8, 2000 - **Dearest™**
May 9, 2000 - **Cheezer™**
May 10, 1994 - **Daisy™**
May 11, 1995 - **Lizzy™**
May 13, 1993 - **Flash™**
May 14, 2000 - **Tricks™**
May 15, 1993 - **Precious™** ***(Kid)***
May 15, 1995 - **Snort™**
May 15, 1995 - **Tabasco™**
May 18, 1999 - **Cheeks™**
May 19, 1995 - **Twigs™**
May 20 - **Kooky Kandy™** ***(Bopper)***
May 20, 2001 - **Addison™**
May 20, 1999 - **Slowpoke™**
May 21, 1994 - **Mystic™**
May 23, 2000 - **Howl™**
May 24, 2000 - **Chinook™**
May 25, 2000 - **Runner™**
May 26, 2000 - **India™**
May 27, 1998 - **Scat™**
May 28, 1996 - **Floppity™**
May 29 - **Bubbly Betty™** ***(Bopper)***
May 29 - **Cuddly Crystal™** ***(Bopper)***
May 29, 1998 - **Canyon™**
May 29, 2000 - **Patriot™**
May 30, 1996 - **Rover™**
May 31, 1997 - **Wise™**

## June

June 1, 1996 - **Hippity™**
June 2, 1999 - **Flitter™**
June 3, 1996 - **Freckles™**
June 3, 1996 - **Scottie™**
June 4, 1999 - **Wiser™**
June 5, 1997 - **Tracker™**
June 6, 2000 - **Wisest™**
June 7, 2000 - **Smart™**
June 8, 1995 - **Bucky™**
June 8, 1995 - **Manny™**
June 10, 1998 - **Mac™**
June 11, 1995 - **Stripes™**
June 12, 1992 - **Ginger™** ***(Kid)***
June 13, 2000 - **Lurkey™**
June 14, 1999 - **Spangle™**
June 15, 1996 - **Scottie™**
June 15, 1998 - **Luke™**
June 16, 1998 - **Stilts™**
June 17, 1996 - **Gracie™**
June 18, 2001 - **Hero™**
June 19, 1993 - **Pinchers™**
June 23, 1998 - **Sammy®**
June 24, 2000 - **Kaleidoscope™**
June 27, 1995 - **Bessie™**
June 28, 1997 - **Calypso™** ***(Kid)***
June 29, 2000 - **Tradee™**
June 30, 2000 - **Bananas™**
June 30, 2000 - **Clubby III™**

## July

July 1, 1996 - **Maple™**
July 1, 1996 - **Scoop™**
July 2, 1995 - **Bubbles™**
July 3, 2000 - **Prince™**
July 4, 1996 - **Lefty™**
July 4, 1996 - **Righty™**
July 4, 1997 - **Glory™**
July 4, 2000 - **Lefty 2000™**
July 4, 2000 - **Righty 2000™**
July 4, 2000 - **USA™**
July 5, 2000 - **Oats™**
July 6, 2000 - **Buzzy™**
July 7, 1998 - **Clubby®**
July 8, 1993 - **Splash™**
July 9, 1992 - **Jammer™** *(Kid)*
July 12, 2000 - **Cassie™**
July 14, 1995 - **Ringo™**
July 15, 1994 - **Blackie™**
July 17 - Loveable Lulu™ *(Bopper)*
July 19, 1995 - **Grunt™**
July 20, 1995 - **Weenie™**
July 20, 1997 - **Chipper™** ***(Kid)***
July 23, 1998 - **Fuzz™**
July 25, 2000 - **Diddley™**
July 26 - Sweet Sally™ *(Bopper)*
July 26, 2000 - **Beani™**
July 28, 1996 - **Freckles™**
July 29, 2000 - **Pellet™**
July 30, 2000 - **Nectar™**
July 31, 1998 - **Scorch™**

## August

Aug. 1, 1995 - **Garcia™**
Aug. 1, 1998 - **Mooch™**
Aug. 4, 2001 - **Clubby IV™**
Aug. 5 - Bronx Bomber™ *(Bopper)*
Aug. 6, 2000 - **Whiskers™**
Aug. 7 - Pretty Patti™ *(Bopper)*
Aug. 7, 2000 - **Hopper™**
Aug. 8, 2000 - **Propeller™**
Aug. 9, 1995 - **Hoot™**
Aug. 11, 1994 - **Boomer™** ***(Kid)***
Aug. 12, 1997 - **Iggy™**
Aug. 13, 1996 - **Spike™**
Aug. 14, 1994 - **Speedy™**
Aug. 16, 1998 - **Kicks™**
Aug. 17, 1995 - **Bongo™**
Aug. 18 - Footie™ *(Bopper)*
Aug. 18, 2001 - **Cheery™**
Aug. 20, 2000 - **Huggy™**
Aug. 22, 2001 - **Darling™**
Aug. 23 - Dazzlin' Destiny™ *(Bopper)*
Aug. 23, 1995 - **Digger™**
Aug. 24, 2000 - **Hornsly™**
Aug. 27, 1995 - **Sting™**
Aug. 28, 1997 - **Pounce™**
Aug. 31, 1998 - **Halo™**

## September

Sept. 2 - Holiday Heidi™ *(Bopper)*
Sept. 3, 1995 - **Inch™**
Sept. 3, 1996 - **Claude™**
Sept. 3, 1996 - **Tumbles™** ***(Kid)***
Sept. 4, 2000 - **China™**
Sept. 5, 1995 - **Magic™**
Sept. 8, 1998 - **Tiny™**
Sept. 9, 1997 - **Bruno™**
Sept. 12, 1996 - **Sly™**
Sept. 14, 2000 - **Poseidon™**
Sept. 15, 2000 - **Nipponia™**
Sept. 16, 1995 - **Derby™**
Sept. 16, 1995 - **Kiwi™**
Sept. 18, 1995 - **Tusk™**
Sept. 21, 1997 - **Stretch™**
Sept. 25, 1991 - **Specs™** ***(Kid)***
Sept. 25, 2000 - **Dinky™**
Sept. 26, 2000 - **Slayer™**
Sept. 27, 1998 - **Roam™**
Sept. 28, 2000 - **Unity™**
Sept. 29, 1997 - **Stinger™**
Sept. 30 - Ivy Leaguer™ *(Bopper)*
Sept. 30, 2001 - **Jester™**

## October

Oct. 1, 1997 - **Smoochy™**
Oct. 2, 1998 - **Butch™**
Oct. 3, 1990 - **Germania™**
Oct. 3, 1996 - **Bernie™**
Oct. 6, 2000 - **Hairy™**
Oct. 7, 2000 - **Dizzy™**
Oct. 9, 1996 - **Doby™**
Oct. 10, 1997 - **Jabber™**
Oct. 11 - Rockin' Rosie™ ***(Bopper)***
Oct. 12, 1996 - **Tuffy™**
Oct. 13, 2000 - **Fraidy™**
Oct. 14, 1997 - **Rainbow™**
Oct. 16, 1995 - **Bumble™**
Oct. 16, 2000 - **Buckingham™**
Oct. 17, 1996 - **Dotty™**
Oct. 18, 2000 - **Creepers™**
Oct. 19, 2000 - **Siam™**
Oct. 20, 2000 - **Buzzie™**
Oct. 22, 1996 - **Snip™**
Oct. 24, 2000 - **Kooky™**
Oct. 25, 2000 - **Scary™**
Oct. 27, 2000 - **Haunt™**
Oct. 28, 1996 - **Spinner™**
Oct. 29, 1996 - **Batty™**
Oct. 30, 1995 - **Radar™**
Oct. 31, 1995 - **Spooky™**
Oct. 31, 1998 - **Pumkin'™**
Oct. 31, 1999 - **Sheets™**

## November

Nov. 3, 1997 - **Puffer™**
Nov. 4, 1998 - **Goatee™**
Nov. 6, 1996 - **Pouch™**
Nov. 7, 1997 - **Ants™**
Nov. 9, 1996 - **Congo™**
Nov. 11, 2000 - **Regal™**
Nov. 12, 2001 - **Float™**
Nov. 14, 1993 - **Cubbie™**
Nov. 14, 1994 - **Goldie®**
Nov. 18, 1998 - **Goochy™**
Nov. 20, 1997 - **Prance™**
Nov. 21, 1996 - **Nanook™**
Nov. 22, 2000 - **Dart™**
Nov. 24, 1997 - **Buzz™** ***(Kid)***
Nov. 27, 1996 - **Gobbles™**
Nov. 28, 1995 - **Teddy™** (brown)
Nov. 29, 1994 - **Inky™**
Nov. 30, 2000 - **Snowgirl™**

## December

Dec. 1, 2000 - **Roxie™**
Dec. 2, 1996 - **Jolly™**
Dec. 3, 2000 - **Jinglepup™**
Dec. 4 - Sassy Star™ ***(Bopper)***
Dec. 6, 1997 - **Fortune™**
Dec. 6, 1998 - **Santa™**
Dec. 7, 2000 - **Mellow™**
Dec. 8, 1996 - **Waves™**
Dec. 10, 1994 - Noelle™ ***(Kid)***
Dec. 12, 1996 - **Blizzard™**
Dec. 14, 1996 - **Seamore™**
Dec. 15, 1997 - **Britannia™**
Dec. 16, 1995 - **Velvet™**
Dec. 17, 2000 - **Giganto™**
Dec. 18, 2000 - **Mistletoe™**
Dec. 19, 1995 - **Waddle™**
Dec. 21, 1996 - **Echo™**
Dec. 22, 1996 - **Snowball™**
Dec. 23, 2000 - **Midnight™**
Dec. 24, 1995 - **Ziggy™**
Dec. 24, 2000 - **2000 Holiday Teddy™**
Dec. 24, 2000 - **2001 Holiday Teddy™**
Dec. 25, 1996 - **1997 Teddy™**
Dec. 25, 1998 - **1998 Holiday Teddy™**
Dec. 25, 1999 - **1999 Holiday Teddy™**
Dec. 26, 1996 - **Cutie™** ***(Kid)***
Dec. 30, 2000 - **Flashy™**

# Alphabetical Index



Below is an alphabetical listing of all the *Beanie Babies*, *Beanie Buddies*, *Beanie Boppers*, *Beanie Kids*, *Ty Gear*, *Jingle Beanies* and *Teenie Beanie Babies* and their pages in the Value Guide.

## Beanie Babies®

## Beanie Buddies®

## Beanie Boppers™



## Beanie Kids™

## Ty Gear™



## Jingle Beanies™



## Teenie Beanie Babies™